Life, Death, Rebirth

How do Pagans deal with death and dying? Where ~~do you turn for support~~? What do you do to honor the passing of a friend, a teacher, or a familiar? *Entering the Summerland* provides a framework from which to create your own unique funeral rites. Even though you may be physically isolated from other Pagans, you are no longer alone when it comes to handling this most trying of life's challenges.

Comfort, guidance, and direction—*Entering the Summerland* is solely devoted to dealing with death, grieving, and afterlife concepts from a Pagan point of view. Not only does this book fill a void, but it also discusses the topic from a wide range of perspectives and provides you with practical advice on funeral planning, talking with Pagan children about death, and sources you can contact for support groups and Pagan clergy/counselors.

Explore Pagan festivals and customs from all over the world that celebrate and honor death, the dead, and the eternal hope of rebirth. Learn new ways to deal with a wide range of situations, from the death of a loved one, to the loss of a pet, or the passing of an Elder, regardless of tradition. Here are practical suggestions for honoring the ancestors, dealing with grief, and creating meaningful memorials and rituals to remember departed loved ones.

About the Author

Edain McCoy became a self-initiated Witch in 1981, and has been an active part of the Pagan community since her formal initiation into a large San Antonio coven in 1983. She has been researching alternative spiritualities since her teens, when she was first introduced to Kaballah (Jewish mysticism). Today, she is part of the Wittan Irish Pagan tradition and is a Priestess of Brighid within that tradition. An alumnus of the University of Texas (BA in history), she currently pursues part-time graduate and undergraduate studies at Indiana University. Edain has taught classes in guided meditation and automatic writing, and occasionally works with students who wish to study Wiccan and Celtic Witchcraft. She is an ordained minister of the Universal Life Church, and is a member of the Indiana Historical Society, the Author's Guild, the Wiccan/Pagan Press Alliance, and is a former woodwind player for the Lynchburg, Virginia, symphony. A descendant of the infamous feuding McCoy family of Kentucky, Edain also proudly claims as a forefather Sir Roger Williams, the seventeenth-century religious dissenter.

To Write to the Author

If you wish to contact the author or would like more information about this book, please write to the author in care of Llewellyn Worldwide and we will forward your request. Both the author and publisher appreciate hearing from you and learning of your enjoyment of this book and how it has helped you. Llewellyn Worldwide cannot guarantee that every letter written to the author can be answered, but all will be forwarded. Please write to:

Edain McCoy
% Llewellyn Worldwide
P.O. Box 64383, Dept. K665-3
St. Paul, MN 55164-0383, U.S.A.

Please enclose a self-addressed stamped envelope for reply, or $1.00 to cover costs.
If outside U.S.A., enclose international postal reply coupon.

Free Catalog from Llewellyn Worldwide

For more than ninety years, Llewellyn has brought its readers knowledge in the fields of metaphysics and human potential. Learn about the newest books in spiritual guidance, natural healing, astrology, occult philosophy, and more. Enjoy book reviews, New Age articles, a calendar of events, plus currently advertised products and services. To get your free copy of *Llewellyn's New Worlds of Mind and Spirit*, send your name and address to:

Llewellyn's New Worlds of Mind and Spirit
P.O. Box 64383, Dept. K665-3
St. Paul, MN 55164-0383, U.S.A.

Llewellyn's World Religion & Magick Series

Entering the
SUMMER
LAND

*Customs and Rituals of Transition
into the Afterlife*

Edain McCoy

1996
Llewellyn Publications
St. Paul, Minnesota 55164-0383, U.S.A.

FIRST EDITION
First Printing, 1996

Cover art by Liz Phillips
Cover design by Anne Marie Garrison
Editing and book design by Rebecca Zins

Illustrations in Chapters 1 and 2 from *Devils, Demons, Death and Damnation* by Ernst and Johanna Lehner (1971) are used by kind permission of Dover Publications, Inc., New York.

Library of Congress Cataloging-in-Publication Data

McCoy, Edain, 1957-
    Entering the Summerland: customs and rituals of transition into the afterlife / Edain McCoy. —1st ed.
        p.   cm. —(Llewellyn's world religion & magick series)
    Includes bibliographical references and index.
    ISBN 1-56718-665-3 (trade pbk.)
    1. Death—Religious aspects. 2. Future life. 3. Reincarnation. 4. Paganism—Rituals. 1. Title. 11. Series: Llewellyn's world religion & magick series.
BL504.M43 1996
291.3'8—dc20

96-9052
CIP

Llewellyn Publications
A Division of Llewellyn Worldwide, Ltd.
P.O. Box 64383, Dept. K665-3
St. Paul, MN 55164-0383, U.S.A.

Llewellyn's World Religion & Magick Series

At the core of every religion, at the foundation of every culture, there is magick.

Magick sees the world as alive, as the home humanity shares with beings and powers both visible and invisible with whom and which we can interface to either our advantage or disadvantage—depending upon our awareness and intention.

Religious worship and communion is one kind of magick, and just as there are many religions in the world, so are there many magickal systems.

Religion and magick are ways of seeing and relating to the creative powers, the living energies, the all-pervading spirit, the underlying intelligence that is the universe within which we and all else exist.

Neither religion nor magick conflict with science. All share the same goals and the same limitations: always seeking truth and forever haunted by human limitations in perceiving that truth. Magick is technology based upon experience and extrasensory insight, providing its practitioners with methods of greater influence and control over the world of the invisible before it impinges on the world of the visible.

The study of world magick not only enhances your understanding of the world in which you live, and hence your ability to better live, but brings you into touch with the inner essence of your long evolutionary heritage and most particularly—as in the case of the magickal system identified most closely with your genetic inheritance—with the archetypal images and forces most alive in your whole consciousness.

Other Books by the Author

Witta: An Irish Pagan Tradition

A Witch's Guide to Faery Folk

How to Do Automatic Writing

Celtic Myth & Magick

The Sabbats: A New Approach to Living the Old Ways

In a Graveyard at Midnight

Lady of the Night: A Handbook of Moon Magick & Rituals

Forthcoming Books

Inside a Witches' Coven

Making Magick

A Very Special Dedication
In Memory of Donald Byron Taylor

Dad, thanks for all the encouragement. This one is for you.
Remember I love you always and miss you very, very much.

Merry meet,
Merry part,
And merry meet again!

Contents

Introduction

NOTHING IN LIFE IS INEVITABLE EXCEPT TAXES AND death! How many times a week do we hear this tired axiom stated and restated either by friends, coworkers, or the press? And how many times do we nod our agreement, thinking more about the shortcomings of our paychecks than the termination of our earthly life spans?

In truth, the only inevitable universal fact is that all living things must die. Taxes, as we all know, can be eliminated, or at least greatly reduced, by the intervention of a good accountant or a shrewd tax attorney. Death, on the other hand, cannot be put off by a fast-talking lawyer. Death comes when he chooses and takes whom he wants whether rich or poor, ready or not. Death is the one single facet of the life experience that we will all endure and in which we all are equal.

The subjects of death, dying, and the afterlife make a great many persons uncomfortable. To dwell upon or discuss these topics forces us to face our own mortality, to probe into the great unknown—well, it can be a very scary prospect indeed. Even Pagans and Wiccans,[1] who, in general, appear to have a healthier view of death than mainstream persons, will sometimes veer away from these issues because they can arouse unpleasant feelings.

Modern Pagans have had other difficulties when they face the death of a loved one—the dearth of resources for help in creating private or public funeral rituals, for locating appropriate support groups, for finding qualified Pagan clergy/counselors to speak with, and even for looking into the many ways in which life, death and rebirth are viewed in the many traditions of their faith.

It is probably safe to say that for the majority of people, it is their chosen religion to which they look for fulfillment of these needs. Other major religions, those in what we often refer to as the "mainstream," have long had books, counselors and support organizations readily available to them. With a 1992 survey done by the Institute for the Study of American Religion at the University of California, Santa Barbara, proclaiming Paganism to be the fastest growing religious movement in the United States—one clearly making gains all around the world today—the need for Pagan resources in these areas will be growing at alarming rates. Organizations are just now being formed to deal with professional counseling, ordination of professional clergy, and the establishment of burial grounds. But that covers only part of the need. Sources for understanding on a deep inner level the nature of the soul and its progression through life, death, and the afterlife as viewed in Pagan spirituality are often wholly or partly lacking.

Without assuming vast prior knowledge of Pagan tenets and ritual methods, *Entering the Summerland* attempts to begin filling that void for the Pagan world by exploring those facets of life and death from a variety of traditions and approaches. Views of the afterlife vary not only by spiritual tradition, but also within the individual consciousness. Discussing afterlife beliefs, even among one's coreligionists, will inevitably yield a vast array of hypotheses, ones those espousing are ready to vociferously defend. These beliefs, so carefully thought out by each of us, represent our personal cosmology and our tenuous hold on our personal sense of identity and mortality.

While no single book could ever hope to present every subtle nuance of death and afterlife beliefs among Pagans, *Entering the Summerland* takes many of the most accepted concepts and ideas about death and crafts them into a framework for open discussion, ritual structure, funeral planning, and bereavement support. It also attempts to legitimize griefs that are not yet acceptable to the larger society in which we live. Mourning the loss of a pet or a familiar (a Witch/Pagan's working animal partner) is one such example.

Again, be aware that no two Pagans experience or view death, dying, and grief in the exact same way. Nor do any two share precisely the same ideas about what awaits us in the afterlife and how it should be honored here on earth any more than two Christians, Jews, et cetera, share the same reactions and beliefs. All we and our coreligionists can do is start with our common ground and then share our ideas openly, taking the best and discarding the worst from each, and hopefully by doing so create more meaningful rituals and greater access to bereavement support for our entire community. For those who do not share an acceptance of all the ideas presented here, I can only offer consolation in that I also do not accept all the concepts about death and the afterlife that many of my fellow Pagans do. What I share is common ground in the basic tenets of western Pagan thought and a desire to expand my horizons. No matter what we choose to believe as individuals or as Pagans, all of our ideas are valid, and our needs and expressions of them are deserving of respect.

The title of this book comes from the popular Wiccan name for the Land of the Dead. Though it is certainly not the only appellation by which this realm is known in Paganism, it is one whose persistent imagery cannot be easily ignored. Summerland is not a mere euphemism to cover up discomfort with afterlife topics, but is a sincere vision of an otherworldly resting place where the snows never fall and the fields are never bare. It is an expression of our collective assertion that a pleasant way station does indeed exist between this life and whatever experiences—in this world or others—await us with new challenges, new loves, and new triumphs. As Pagans facing a new era of growth and trials, we should be as steadfastly prepared to meet these challenges as our ancestors were when meeting theirs. One of the first steps in meeting this challenge is preparing ourselves for death and the afterlife by reconciling ourselves to the fact that it is merely another of the many rites of passage in our existence.

One

Pagan Concepts of Death and the Afterlife

IN THE LATE TWENTIETH CENTURY PHYSICAL DEATH has been clinically defined as the point at which the last visible sign of brain activity ceases. This usually occurs some five to six minutes after all other vital signs, such as heart rate and respiration, have failed. By contrast, the basic spiritual definition of death is when some vital life force (the soul, spirit, et cetera) packs up and leaves the physical body for good. This might be due to an accident, trauma, illness, or even the will of the self to die. Many Pagans believe this spiritual death can occur long before the cessation of a heartbeat, or before the falling off of brain waves can be noted by modern machines.

Like birth, death was one of the first great mysteries of humankind. Without EEG (brain wave) machines, heart monitors, and respirators, early humans had to rely on their own instincts and powers of observation to decide just what constituted the state of death. Hunting for food and clothing had taught them that death was necessary for life to continue, but it hadn't provided an answer to the mystery of the missing animating force. What was it? Where did it go? Would it return?

Some scholars estimate that the first stirrings of humanity's religious feeling can be traced to protohumans who looked to the moon for divine inspiration nearly 100,000 years ago. A more realistic date for the implementation of religion as we would think of it today can be dated back about 40,000 years ago, a period from which we can see archaeological evidence of belief in an afterlife. Retrieved from burial mounds, barrows, and long-forgotten graves are the remains of humans lovingly cradled into fetal positions and interred along with personal possessions. Included among these grave offerings were coins, food, and weapons—items the community clearly thought the deceased might need wherever he or she was going.

The question naturally arising from these actions is: Where does the spirit go after death? In an effort to create a framework for these answers, explanatory stories—the first myths—were passed around the evening fires. These eventually were passed on to the next generation of questioners, and soon a cultural consensus was formed about the nature of the spirit and the afterlife.

All religions are based on mythology, Paganism included. Even though many of the ancient myths have been rewritten or tampered with in other ways, they are still the primary basis for our group cosmology (concepts concerning the origin and nature/structure of the universe) and eschatology (concepts about the end of universe), including our beliefs surrounding death and the afterlife. Refinements in those concepts are naturally to be found within each separate Pagan tradition and within each individual. Of all world mythology, none is so widely disseminated or intrigues humanity so much as the promise of an otherworldly realm inhabited by spirits of the dead. Even mainstream religions, who have largely viewed mythology as the cosmologic explanations of the ignorant, have their afterlife worlds: Christians have "heaven," Muslims have "paradise," and Jews have "the world to come." Unfortunately, the function of these worlds is often one of coercion to a lifetime obedience rather than a complex realm that we would want to visit through meditations and astral travel, as Pagans sometimes do.

For cultures and religions outside the mainstream, the understanding of the afterlife world can be a more complex matter, with the realm of the dead sometimes having many levels of existence and meaning. Most often these are conceptualized as an upperworld, middleworld, and underworld, distinctions which have less to do with location than with the characteristics of the realm and its inhabitants. Collectively these realms make up what we often refer to as the Otherworld, or the Summerland.

From cultures all over the world the sentiments and perceptions about the Land of the Dead share many similarities. Perhaps these can be explained through archetypes, mental symbols that operate on a universal level. Or perhaps the original myths merely traveled to other lands as the first tribes of early humans migrated, and only changed superficially to conform to the needs of the new culture that was developing.

Likewise, literally thousands of names exist throughout the world that are synonymous with Summerland, most of them taken directly from ancient mythology. Again, it must be understood that these are not merely euphemisms intended to cover discomfort, but titles meant to accurately convey the character and scope of the one particular part of the Otherworld under discussion. This can be seen clearly in the Irish myth of the Voyage of Maelduin, who ventures with his ship and crew for seventeen years visiting thirty-two different islands in the Otherworld, each with its own distinct character and laws.

The following list is meant to convey only a very broad, general idea of the many names by which the Summerland has been known in Paganism. Nowhere near all of these can be listed as some cultures have hundreds of names all their own.

Annwfn/Avalon (Welsh-Cornish)
Castle of Riches (Welsh)
Castle of Glass (Welsh)
The Dark Plain (Celtic)
Dark Star (Central African)
Elysian Fields (Greek)
Gresholm Island (Anglo-Saxon)
Gwlad Yr Haf (Welsh)
Hades (Greco-Roman)
Hel (Teutonic)
I-Breasil (Welsh)
Isle of the Blessed (Irish)
Land of the Great Cauldron (Celtic)
Land of the Alive (Irish)
Land of the Ever-Young (Irish)
Land of the Setting Sun (Cherokee)
Land Under the Waves (Manx)
The Low Road (Scottish)
Lyonesse (Breton)

Continued on next page

Meslam (Babylonian)

Realm of Illusion (Gnostic)

Somerset (English)

Uffern (Celtic-Saxon)

Valhalla (Norse)

Vela (Slavic)

World to Come (Hebrew-Canaanite)

Ys (Breton-Cornish)

Sometimes the names for the Summerland have been used to denigrate the beliefs of another religion. Two cases in point are Hel, the Teutonic underworld which became the torturous Christian Hell, and the Happy Hunting Ground of the Great Plains tribes of North America. In the first example, Hel was distorted in order to link Paganism with the Christian Satan and bring in converts through fear. The second example shows European ignorance of the ancient beliefs of their own people, for in virtually all European myths the Summerland is portrayed as a place where food is always in abundance and no one goes hungry. For example, the Celtic God Manannan is said to hold a nightly Otherworld feast of pigs that magickally regenerated themselves by dawn, the Greeks have their tranquil Elysian Fields, and the Norse have their Valhalla whose inhabitants have a similar eternal feast. For the Native Americans, the Happy Hunting Ground is such a place, one where want is never known, though it was referred to derisively by Euro-Americans on their extermination campaigns.

Because the element of water was associated with death and birth long before recorded history, most of these lands are said to be across lakes, rivers, or oceans. In Greek mythology it is a river, and in Celtic lore it is a sea. In the Pacific Northwest region of the United States, the native people used to place their dead in a canoe and set them adrift down the river toward the sea, where they would find the afterworld waiting for them. Sometimes caves, symbols of the birth canal of the Great Mother, are similarly employed. For example, the Greek underworld is accessed through a cave which, incidentally, ends at a river that must be crossed to reach the final destination.

✽ Messengers of Death from the Otherworld

Death omens are known throughout every culture in the world, the majority of these involving inanimate objects, animals, incidents of clairaudience, or unusual weather phenomena, rather than by warnings from Otherworld inhabitants. But a fascinating few, gleaned from the annals of mythology and folklore, provide the foundation of our Pagan beliefs in messengers from the Summerland who come to let us—and sometimes others around us—know that our time on earth is nearly over.

Probably the most well-known of these is the Irish *beansidhe*, or banshee, a faery spirit who is attached to a particular Celtic family and who can be heard keening her mourning song the night before a death in the family. The banshee is notorious throughout the Celtic world. She is called the *cointeach* in Scotland, the *cyhiraeth* in Cornwall, *gwrach y rhibyn* in Wales, and *eur-cunnere noe* in Celtic Brittany.

Another popular death messenger is the Germanic *Erlkonig*, or Elf King, who will appear only to one who is about to die and can be neither seen nor heard by anyone else.

In west central Africa the warning spirits are the *epgunugan,* who appear at festivals dressed in burial shrouds and dance with the celebrants. The tribe then considers itself fairly warned that one of their members will not be with them when the next festival time rolls around.

The *fylgiar* faery of Iceland is a personal spirit attached to any person who has been born with a caul, or thin membrane, over his or her head. The fylgiar comes to his familiar human to warn him or her of impending death, the condition in which he appears telling that person something about the sort of death he or she will face. The fylgiar is believed to accompany his person to Valhalla, the Nordic Land of the Dead, where he remains until the human soul is comfortable and accepting of its new state of being.

From Scotland comes the intriguing myth of the otherworldly dog known as Black Angus (or *cu sith* in Scot's Gaelic, meaning "faery dog") who has been reportedly seen by both the low- and highborn. He is a large black dog with yellow eyes and sharp fangs who roams the northern English and Scottish countryside, showing himself with a growl to those who will die within a fortnight.

From western Europe and Russia come the legend of the fetch, or *doppelgänger.* Folklore tells us that each of us has a spirit who is a mirror image of ourselves, a shadow self who lives in the Summerland and who is seen by us just days before our death. Most often the image will appear standing just behind us as we gaze into a mirror or other reflective surface. In England, a variation of the fetch is seen in the "fetch light," a luminous golden ball that occasionally appears near the home of a loved one who is soon to die.

Perhaps more numerous and well-known than death omens are the apparitions and other phenomena announcing to us that a death has just occurred. Pick up any book on ghost hunting or parapsychology and you are likely to come across at least one account where the spirit of someone recently deceased appears to his or her family to say farewell. Other common phenomena include rapping noises, particularly at doors or hearths; indoor winds; unusual animal activity or noise, especially from dogs; hearing the disembodied voice of the deceased, sometimes even in the form of a phone call; loud booming noises outdoors; sudden drops in indoor temperature; the sound of shattering glass; a clock which suddenly stops; the appearance of the ghost of the deceased at the precise moment of death; or reports of the deceased appearing very much alive at a remote location at the time of death.

I was once forewarned that a death had occurred when I was a passenger in a car on a relaxed Sunday afternoon. While riding along chatting aimlessly, I was

These symbols of death/Death date to a seventeenth-century booklet produced by the Order of the Rose Cross (the Rosicrucians).

suddenly overcome with the feeling that I had lost something. The sensation was similar to that felt when you are out shopping and realize that you are not carrying something you should be, such as a purse or a package. My arms felt unusually light, my hands tingled, my heart raced, and I was overpowered with a sense of privation. Knowing that someone I loved was near death at that time, I did wonder briefly if this was an omen, but the sensation soon passed and I went about my plans for the day thinking it was all my imagination. By the time I arrived home that evening, I had managed to forget about the incident until I saw the flashing red light on my

answering machine indicating that someone had been trying repeatedly to reach me. Sure enough, the person to whom my thoughts had turned during that odd experience had indeed died at the very moment I was feeling his loss.

If you think you would prefer having a death omen rather than being taken by surprise, pay close attention to your dreams if you know someone who is terminally ill. On one occasion I was warned three days ahead of time that someone I knew was going to die. I had a clear dream vision of this man sitting all alone in a small boat that was gliding along on a still, wide river through a ubiquitous fog-shrouded night, heading for a distant shore. The image was very brief, but quite clear, and the symbolism so unmistakable that it woke me up immediately.

❧ The Entity Death

Many Pagans—but certainly not all—believe in the legends of death as a sentient entity, capitalized in this case as a proper noun: Death. This is one of the most controversial areas of Pagan death concepts, probably because beliefs about the entity Death have little basis in myth. They come to use through much-repeated folktales and oral legends, and as such have become an accepted part of some Pagan traditions. Acceptance and consideration of these legends have even invaded the popular culture. Death as an entity, presented as a complex character with his own problems and feelings, has occasionally been portrayed on stage or in film. The comic play *On Borrowed Time* and the dark 1930s film *Death Takes a Holiday* are probably the best-known of these.

As an entity, Death has been thought of by Pagans in a variety of guises: as a minor deity, a faery, an angel, a demon, or an Otherworld inhabitant of unknown species, and he is usually, but not universally, depicted as male. His appearance—be it factual or archetypal in origin— varies little from culture to culture. To most, he looks a bit like Charles Dickens' Ghost of Christmas Future with his brooding countenance and hooded cape obscuring his features. Often he carries with him a scythe, a symbol of cutting down the life of humankind. Or he might have with him a sword, an hourglass, or a single rose. In some cultures he drives a coach or cart on his nightly rounds, invariably drawn by otherworldly black horses.

Perhaps the most widely-known personification of Death is Azrael, an entity with pre-patriar-

A 1489 depiction of Death with his scythe.

chal Hebrew roots (i.e. before the codification of modern Judaism by the priests) who has come into Gnostic (Christian mystic) and Kaballistic (Jewish mystical) teachings and into the angelic pantheon of Ceremonial Magick as the "Angel of Death." Though Azrael, whose name translates as "helper of the God," is nearly always viewed as a male entity, he has occasionally been depicted as female. In

Islamic folklore Azrael has many faces, all kept veiled so that one is not accidentally struck by his androgynous beauty and lured from the body prematurely.

An entire Pagan-style cult has grown up around Azrael, with Westgate Press of New Orleans (see Appendix B for address) publishing a fair portion of the rites and beliefs of Azrael's followers. Not everyone is interested in these highly controversial rituals that require the ritualist to take some personal risks. Some Pagans dismiss this area of study as being outside of Paganism, and therefore of little value to their spiritual lives. Others are drawn in fascination to explore this dark side of existence, which they claim helps them learn to understand and overcome the fear of death/Death. Regardless of how you view the Death entity or how you feel about necromantic rituals, reading through the Westgate material is an excellent way to come to know Azrael on intimate terms.[1]

The English-speaking world best knows Death as the Grim Reaper, the skeleton-faced, scythe-wielding spirit who comes to us and cuts the cord of our lives when our time is over. The Gaulish Celts knew this image as Sucellos, nicknamed the "harvester of the spirit," an entity who may have had roots in the Roman God Saturn, who is associated with time and self-undoing.

Another Celtic personification of Death is Ankou, recognized in Brittany and rural Ireland by the sound of his creaking cart going up the road to pick up his latest victim. He needs only to open the door to his cart, or to touch the person he has come for, and life will flee. Some legends tell of persons who have bargained with Ankou at the last moment and been given more earthly time in return for some task or gift. But those who succeed must do their talking well ahead of time, for Irish folklore says that once the death cart has left the Otherworld for earth it may not return empty.

Feelings about the death cart legend vary from person to person. In *The Fairy Faith in Celtic Countries*, author and researcher W.Y. Evans-Wentz tells of a Roscommon County family who heard the death cart rolling by their cottage almost nightly, yet when they looked outside they could see nothing that could produce this fearsome sound. In the Walt Disney film *Darby O'Gill and the Little People*, the cart is portrayed as a black Victorian hearse complete with a headless driver who, without preamble, tells the one he has come for to step inside. Darby does, and the door slams shut behind him, leaving him alone and afraid as the coach roars off for the Otherworld. On the other hand, nineteenth century American poet Emily Dickinson saw intriguing possibilities in the death coach legends and wrote:

> *Because I could not stop for death,*
> *He kindly stopped for me.*
> *The carriage held but just ourselves*
> *And immortality.*[2]

For the Aztecs of pre-Columbian Mexico, Death was called Miquiztli, an inter-cessory between the Gods or Goddesses of death and the people. Blood sacrifices were a recognized part of Aztec life, many of them aimed at appeasing Miquiztli so that he would not take their souls to the death deities at the deities' command.

Most cultures merely refer to the entity Death by whatever word their language uses for death, capitalizing it as appropriate when referring to a specific being. It is in these cultures where the line of demarcation separating the entity of Death from deities of death and the Otherworld are most often blurred. A case in point is Thanatos, the Greek God of death who, over the past millennium, has been given the job of the Grim Reaper—to go out and gather the souls whose time has come rather than merely holding court in the Otherworld as many death deities do. He has been depicted to appear the way the western mind commonly views the Grim Reaper, with a hooded cloak and a skeletal face. Thanatos is also the twin brother of Hypnos, God of sleep. The connection between the two says a lot for the way both sleep and death were viewed by the ancients, since in most mythologies twins were often supposed to be one single being, their duality being merely symbolic of the two primary manifestations of their sphere of influence.

Another example of this merging of Death/death deities is Abraxas, once an Assyrian death God whose name has come to personify Death. His name means "the enemy," and he has been given the traditional role of Death in his culture.

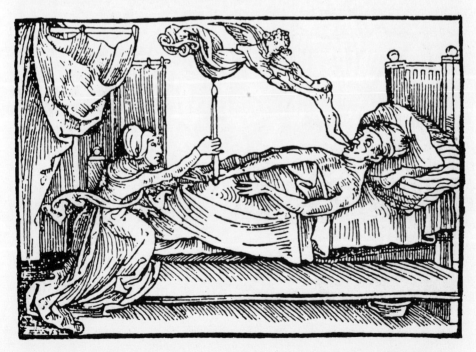

A 1508 German engraving showing the Angel of Death taking the soul from a dying man.

A 1463 German engraving showing Death as a hunter and a reaper.

In China, the God Yen-Wang's job is to decide when a life span has ended. At this point he severs the cord of life, which has been spun for each individual by the Goddess of creation.

Without a doubt the most sophisticated personification of Death on record is the naughtily suave Baron Samedi of Haitian/Voodun/Santeria origin. All three of these traditions have their roots in the Paganism of Africa and were only overlaid with a thin veneer of Catholicism in order to protect them in the New World. The Baron dresses formally, wearing a top hat and tails, and is well spoken and courtly, though his humor is said to be quite risqué. When called upon by his followers he flaps the tails of his jacket to let it be known he is present.

One of the feminine personifications of Death is Oya from west central Africa, often seen as a deity (*Orisha* in Yoruban) in her own Yoruban-Santerian pantheon. In variance to the cloaked male figure, Oya, whose name means "she who cries," is perceived as a mighty cyclonic wind who sucks out the souls of humanity and blows an opening in the veil between the world of the living and the realm of the dead so her victims may pass through.

Another feminine personification can be found in the art of the ancient Etruscans. Their Death was Tuchlcha, a beak-faced woman with serpents for hair who sported a perpetually menacing stare that could kill.

Occasionally we come across myths about deities who actually do Death's job, themselves making the nightly rounds searching out souls to take back to the Summerland. One of these is the Welsh deity Gwyn Ap Nuad, who rides through the night on his white horse with his ferocious hounds on what has been called the "Great Hunt," the hunt being a

One of the earliest extent depictions of Death, this dates to the late fifteenth century. This engraving was used to mark vials of poison in the same way the skull and crossbones is used today.

metaphor for gathering lost souls. Some rural Welsh folks claim they can hear the ghostly hoofbeats of his wild chase by night. Another example is found in Shinto, the native Pagan faith of Japan, where it is the Goddess Yuki-Onne who steps in just after Death has done his job and escorts the soul safely to the Summerland.

Extant myths can tell us much about death deities and can reveal to us the ways various peoples in the past viewed the death experience and what they expected to find in the afterlife (a listing and brief description of death and afterlife deities appears in Appendix C).

❧ Discovering How We Feel About Death

As previously stated, the Summerland is merely another of the many names for the Otherworld, the place to which all life returns upon death. It is fair to say that on this concept most Pagans agree, but just what happens after this is a matter of debate, one that is moot since none of us can say for certain just what lies beyond that last breath we take.

It is also fair to say that Pagans tend to have a healthier attitude toward death than non-Pagans. This assumption is based largely on two threads that wind through our collective life cycles: one, our constant interactions with the cycles of the seasons and the use of nature's ebb and flow as a pattern for our own existence; and two, the widespread acceptance of the doctrine of rebirth (in some form or another) rather than a belief in eternal punishment and reward based on the actions of a single lifetime. Test your own attitude toward death by taking the following mental tests:

Experiment 1

Imagine you are walking through the city streets, happy and confident, heading somewhere specific in a great hurry. You are walking along, focused upon the task at hand. Then, all of a sudden, you fall into a deep abyss. After you land and have a chance to look around, you realize this to be a place from which you cannot emerge. As you realize that the path you were on is forever lost to you, you begin to assess your surroundings. What does the place look like and how do you feel about it?

Experiment 2

You are on the top floor of a tall building enjoying the view when, suddenly, you fall. Down, down you fall. You see the ground rising quickly to meet you and you brace for impact. But, miraculously, you pass right through the pavement and keep on falling until you come to a gentle rest in a single small room from which you quickly realize you cannot emerge. What does the place look like and how do you feel about it?

Experiment 3

You are passing down a long hallway waving at friends and family in the side rooms. You are having a pleasant time when you reach a bend in the corridor. You turn the corner expecting to continue on, but instead you come face to face with a wall. As you turn to go back, you realize that you are blocked in and will not be able to leave this place. You are stuck and cannot go backward or forward. What does the place look like and how do you feel about it?

Experiment 4

You are walking in the woods when you find yourself at the base of a huge old oak tree that draws your attention. As you circle the tree for a closer look you suddenly find yourself sucked into a great hole in the trunk. Down, down you fall until you come to a gentle rest in an enclosure beneath the root system. One look around tells you that you can never get out. What does the place look like and how do you feel about it?

Similar tests have been credited to numerous preeminent psychologists, including Carl Jung, who mapped out much of the archetypal language we use in metaphysics. In each experiment the visualization of movement and progress in the beginning of the exercises represents your life. The sudden cessation of movement and the enclosure/blockage represents your physical death. The sensations you have and the way you visualize the place in which you find yourself should tell you much about your own attitude toward death. For example, if the places you find yourself in make you feel desperately forlorn or if they appear to you bleak and foreboding, then it may be that your attitude toward death is one of bleakness. On the other hand, if you feel fairly secure in your new space and see the empty rooms/ground as blank canvases on which you can create new things, then your attitude is exceptionally well-adjusted.

Don't be confused into thinking that you have to find every feeling you experience during these experiments just hunky-dory. All new situations—like dying—make us somewhat ill at ease. And certainly no one should want to die, but the fact remains that we all will sooner or later, and to live in fear of one's end makes both life and death miserable.

Experiment 5

Another experiment you might try (one which may be a lot more entertaining) is writing your own epitaph. What you choose to leave behind as your final words says a lot about how you view your life, your death, and your afterlife hopes.

The Epitaph Experiment

An epitaph (from the Greek *epitaphios,* meaning "at the tomb") is a mini-eulogy or written inscription on a gravestone or mausoleum that is commemorative in nature. The oldest known examples have been found on Egyptian sarcophagi dating to 4000 B.C.E. which honor the family or personal deity of the deceased. The Romans used epitaphs on cremation urns, and the Greeks are credited with being the first to use them to record the name of the deceased along with a birth and death date as we are accustomed to seeing on modern gravestones. The practice of using epitaphs was believed to have been introduced to western Europe by the Romans, and by the fourteenth century it was a very popular custom in England and France.

Throughout Britain, Ireland, and France, and in older graveyards in the United States and Canada, one often stumbles on humorous or macabre epitaphs. When the grave-rubbing craze hit its peak in the mid-1970s, the rush was on to collect rubbings with unusual epitaphs, and several books were published containing some of the more entertaining or sobering ones. An epitaph can be composed by the family or friends of the deceased, but the most memorable are crafted prior to death by the deceased themselves. Most of us have heard of the cry from beyond that reads: I TOLD YOU I WAS SICK, or are familiar with screen actor Clark Gable's witty epitaph: BACK TO SILENTS. I saw a sobering one once in an old Virginia graveyard which read: TARRY NOT LONG WITH ME THIS DAY/SOON ENOUGH YOU WILL BE HERE TO STAY.

Within the framework of our religion, one which teaches that death is no barrier to learning and growing, reviving the custom of epitaphs can be a way in which we share our legacy and beliefs with those who come to visit the place where our bodies lie. Grab a piece of paper and experiment with a few lines. Who knows? You may come up with one the grave rubbers will be scrambling for. You might want to encourage a loved one to create an epitaph for him- or herself. This can be good therapy for someone heading toward the end of a terminal illness because it gives the dying person a sense of being able to express personal feelings and ideas even after death. Or, if you want to leave an epitaph behind on the headstone of a loved one and the rest of your family feels it is appropriate, by all means do it.

I was once at a Samhain party where writing our epitaphs was part of the entertainment. We divided into small groups and wrote not only our own final words, but suggested some for our friends. We all had a good laugh, and so, I'm sure, did the spirits with us that night.

❧ Diversity in Pagan Afterlife Concepts

Over three-quarters of the population, whether religious or not, say they believe in some type of afterlife (source: 1993 Gallup Poll). Certainly all religions have their afterlife promises—ours included—many of them based on mythology. Some religious traditions have even felt moved to provide detailed descriptions of the afterworld. The Koran details both paradise and hell, and both the Egyptian and Tibetan *Book of the Dead* describe the afterlife journey for their followers.

Like the population as a whole, Pagans show a diverse belief in afterlife concepts. A few have even expressed their belief in no afterlife at all, though they clearly remain small in number. Others accept the idea of a great cosmic mix into which we are all taken after death where we become one again with the universal consciousness from which all things spring. This concept is also based on mythology, and is especially prominent among those following Celtic ways.

Though there have been no hard-core statistics taken from the Pagan community to show us exactly what we each believe, it is clear that Pagans as a whole embrace the idea of regeneration/rebirth as part of their afterlife concept. This assumption is based on Pagan writings found in magazines, forums, books, and in the personal expressions one commonly hears when Pagans gather to talk. Our many mythologies support these beliefs with stories of other-life transformations such as those of Blodeweudd's and Edain's, and cyclic return-from-the-Summerland heroes/heroines such as Ishtar, Persephone, Kore, and Maelduin.

Within this framework there are numerous ideas about just how, why, and where rebirth occurs. We can break the transformation concepts down into three broad categories:

1. Transmutation/transmigration
2. Genetic memory
3. Earthly reincarnation

Transmutation/transmigration is the transfer of the spirit into another concrete form without first traveling to the Summerland. For example, a spirit which recently left an earthly body might wander for a while, eventually finding a home in a tree, stone, or even another recently abandoned body. The Celtic Druids appeared to accept this premise and may have designed rites around attempting to direct the course of the soul into a desired object or body.

Transmutation can also refer to the temporary transformation into a host being for the express purpose of transporting the soul to the Summerland. Celtic mythology tells of many deaths where the person becomes a bird, and African mythology uses a serpent for this same function.

Genetic memory puts forth the theory that rather than actually living separate—or perhaps sequential—lives in other bodies, the soul merely remembers the past through gene imprinting. Any past life memories that are received, either in deliberately altered states of consciousness, randomly, or in sleep, are the result of flashes of information being passed from the genetic imprint to the conscious mind. Persons who espouse this theory insist that aside from fictional psycho-dramas dreamed up by the imaginative subconscious, genetic memory is the most likely cause of these innerworld fantasies. Because your progenitors expand exponentially as you travel backward in time (i.e. you have four grandparents, eight great-grandparents, sixteen great-great grandparents, et cetera) virtually all cultures and eras can be accessed. Genetic memory is also in line with Kaballistic teachings, which have long taught that your children are your *kaddish*, or "those who will remember."

Belief in earthly reincarnation has taken a not-so-gentle beating in the popular press over the past several decades, egged on by mainstream clergy who have forgotten that both Judaism and Christianity once espoused this afterlife tenet that is one of the very oldest beliefs known to humankind. Past life memories, whether spontaneous or induced, have been decried by them at worst as fantasies of Satan and at best as mere delusions.

Reincarnation has also been criticized as being the most comforting of all afterlife beliefs because it deals with a known quantity—our earthly life. While reincarnation is arguably more comforting than thoughts of eternal damnation, the idea of having to start life all over again and face once more its trials and uncertainties is not what most of us would call especially comforting. Analogize this dubious sense of comfort to that of a small child nervously awaiting the first day of school. The child may know where he will be going, who his teacher will be, and have even been told ad infinitum what will be expected of him, but that doesn't make facing it any less spooky.

Pagans base their beliefs in reincarnation on the same evidence our ancestors did: the cycles of nature. Every spring we see the rebirth of the earth, and every winter we watch her die, knowing with certainty that she will be reborn the following spring. The Wheel of the Year turns, all things come and go and come again, everything to its season. When we apply this to the life cycle of humanity it is easy to see from where this ancient idea sprang.

The way in which souls reincarnate has been a matter for much controversy, and, if you have ever engaged in one of these debates, you know it is one that is fascinating and filled with twists and paradoxes. Discussions on this topic have kept me, and several friends, wide awake into the proverbial wee hours of the morning haggling over all the possibilities and theories.

Among the many views on the inner-workings of reincarnation espoused in the Pagan community are:

- The omnipresent all-life of the universal spirit
- Movement into a variety of concurrent lives separate from the universal spirit
- A variety of lives experienced through an oversoul
- A succession of individual lives based on personal karma
- Repetition of same/similar life to learn a lesson
- Supportive kin groups with or without group karma

The all-life concept is firmly rooted in the belief in omnipresent time. Some Pagan cultures, most notably those whose myths involve numerous shapeshifting creatures/beings, believe in omnipresent time wherein all time—past, present and future—exists in one great here and now. In recent years modern theoretical physics has backed up this belief with studies of its own, yet one more example of how science is proving the validity of more and more of the ancient ways every year. This theory of rebirth asserts that we all live in the constant here and now, and the only way we experience "other" lives is through our universal connection. Those who accept this thinking believe that we are really not individuals, but part of a universal whole, and that after death we return to a state of oneness where all experiences become known to all aspects of this self. This theory can explain why hundreds of different persons claim to have been regressed (a term for viewing past lives through a deliberately induced altered state of consciousness) believing themselves to have been Napoleon or Cleopatra. It also makes a good case for why contact with the spirits of the dead is possible: we are all part of each other and all existing at any given moment as part of a universal consciousness, which can be accessed somewhat like the collective unconscious as hypothesized by psychiatrist Carl Jung.

Many of those who accept the all-life concept reject the idea that the purpose of earthly existence is to balance out negative and positive acts or to learn profound lessons. They believe the purpose of living is simply to enjoy being alive, to live happily, to experience new things, and—as your kindergarten report card was worded—"to work and play well with others."

Similar to the all-life concept is that of experiencing a variety of concurrent lives, either in linear or omnipresent time, where a soul splits into many parts and has many simultaneous and/or sequential experiences. This theory explains why some individuals suddenly experience a profound emotional/mental link with another person whom they have never met, or why they regress to only specific lifetimes over and over. Persons who espouse this belief also claim that souls can switch host bodies in mid-life to increase the variety of their life experiences. This, they say, not only explains amnesia (a mental disorder characterized by large blocks of forgetfulness), but also why some people believe themselves to be "walk-ins," beings from other worlds who take possession of a physical body upon its death before that death has been noticed.

A similar concept is that of the oversoul. This theory states that we are all siblings in a soul group headed by a parent oversoul. This oversoul makes the decision about where and when to incarnate, then splits itself into as many parts as is needed to fulfill these lives. It maintains subconscious contact with all its undersouls and, when each life is over, the undersouls return once more to become part of the oversoul and to share experiences and knowledge.

A succession of lives based on karma (including human incarnations into other species) is the idea most people first think of whenever reincarnation is mentioned, even though many magickal folks and lots of New Agers have rejected this idea as being too simplistic. Karma is the belief that what we do in one life, all the good and all the bad, must be accounted for in the next life, usually focusing on the bad and being magnified in proportion to the original deed. The drawback to this theory is that it leaves very little room for the exercise of free will, and many who espouse it tend to fall into a "blame the victim" mentality, forgetting that if *everything* must be the result of karma, then nothing requiring the balancing of karma would ever have occurred in the first place. Persons who accept this concept of the afterlife often believe that the spirit of the deceased can only be contacted until it reincarnates, after which communication with it becomes impossible. They also believe that eventually the soul "perfects" itself by balancing out all its negative karma and thus can get off the cycle of reincarnation and progress into a perfected Otherworld.

Kin groups and soul groups reincarnating together to fulfill some type of group karma is another theory of reincarnation, and one decidedly less popular, particularly among Pagans. This theory hypothesizes that we return to the earthly plane repeatedly with the same souls as our friends and family, both to work out our karma with them and as a form of mutual support through life. Those who accept this idea believe that, in some cases, group karma may be at work where a family or group was involved in an event of great importance. During each incarnation, some members of the group remain in spirit and function as spirit guides to assist their loved ones in making wise decisions, avoiding disasters, or fulfilling their karmic destiny.

This group karma concept may possibly have roots in a very old karmic concept—that of universal karma, or collective responsibility for any wrongdoings.

An ancient Hebrew teaching echoes this belief. It says that to save a single life is as if one saved the whole world, but to take a life is as if to kill the whole world.

Another theory of reincarnation is that the same life, or similar ones, is repeated over and over until the soul is either happy with the final outcome or has learned a particular lesson from them. These folk view time as being cyclical, a never-ending circle that we can hop on and off of at various points so that the soul can move backward or forward in time depending on what is most beneficial to its growth. They also feel that contact with the person's spirit can only be maintained until reincarnation, after which it is unable to be contacted.

A variety of books are available which discuss spirit contact, spirit guides, and reincarnation from every conceivable viewpoint. There are also a number of excellent books and tapes (both audio and video) available for teaching you how to do past life regression or assisting you in making contact with the dead. If either of these topics interests you, please check Appendix B and the Bibliography for more information.

⚘ A Meditation for Understanding the Polarity in Death and Life

One of those rare, almost universally accepted tenets of Paganism is that of polarity. Though there are some variations on this theme among individuals and traditions, in essence this doctrine asserts things that appear to be complete opposites, with no overlap of energies, are really two halves of a whole, each a part of a balanced oneness. The best example is that of the Goddess and the God. Each is separate, but at the same time they are part of the oneness that is the creative power of the universe. In magick and in ritual, these polarities are often balanced inside the circle so that they can both lend their energies to the effort of making oneness "complete." Polarity is often conceptualized as a wheel where each thing/item/idea is simply an integral part of the ever-turning cycle of existence.

This doctrine is in opposition to the concept of duality, the belief that all opposites are wholly separate, warring entities with no sharing of energies or essence. Dualism is conceptualized as being linear with each thing/item/idea placed on a finite continuum between an "evil" universe and a "good" universe. The best, and probably the most often cited, example of this thinking is the relationship between the Christian God and his Satan.[3]

Other popular polarities often used in Pagan magick/ritual are light and dark, day and night, old and new, yin and yang, upperworld and underworld, male and female, water and air, and fire and earth.

Life and death are also polarities that are very much a part of each other. The thinking of Pagans and non-Pagans alike vacillates wildly between these poles whenever one or the other of these states suddenly becomes too scary for us to deal with. The thing to remember is that being corporeal is not a wholly bad thing anymore than being in spirit is a picnic. Being in spirit does not make you a sage any more than being human makes you stupid. How many of you cringe, as I do, when you hear someone refer to the deceased as being "in a better place now," as if the earth was at the "evil universe" end of the duality continuum? The state of being alive and that of being dead both have their distinct sets of advantages and disadvantages; both are ending and beginning points in our journey of existence, and value judgments cannot be placed on them.

The best way to understand the polarities of life and death is to meditate on them. My personal visualizations of this conception presented here are not intended to convey the idea that they are universally accepted among Pagans, but they are a way for you to begin exploring these ideas. The following guided meditation (see Chapter 2, p. 44 for a discussion of guided meditation) uses these images to help you and your deep subconscious mind fully grasp this idea.

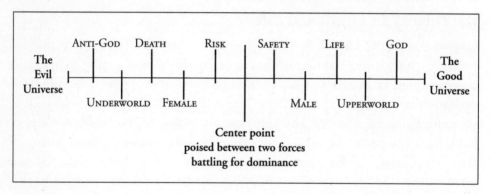

The dualistic model of existence.

Allow yourself to fully relax your body and quiet your mind. This is best done in a place where the lighting is subdued and where you will likely be undisturbed for at least thirty minutes. When you feel fully relaxed, begin to visualize your inner self rising out of your body and flying up higher and higher into the sky. See yourself moving through a series of planes, one characterized by darkness, followed by one of light, then darkness again, and so on. As you rise, sense the atmosphere around you becoming thinner as it is more and more removed from the earthly plane.

As you rise to the final plane on this journey, see yourself coming to a plane where, stretched out before you in the void, is a large circle with an infinite number of spokes reaching out from its center point and connecting to the edge of the slowly turning wheel. Each spoke represents the entire continuum of different aspects of existence: love, the seasons, death, wealth, et cetera. Each spoke is linked back to the great wheel where it merges into the endless cycle of beginnings, endings, and new beginnings.

Allow your inner self to fly down and stand on the center point. You are now poised at the center of the universe, and surrounding you is all that ever was, is, or will be. Pick any spoke at random and begin to walk out its radius. Go as far out as you like, and as you go, sense and feel what is there. After a few moments, return to the center and begin walking out the opposite spoke (in the other direction) and do the same. For example, if you are on the spoke of summer, feel the heat of the noonday sun and sense the essence that is summer. Then walk out the winter spoke and sense and see what it has to teach you. Most of all, focus on the oneness that links them, and feel how much a part of each other they truly are: how one could not exist without the other. Keep in mind that, even if you reach the far end of the spoke, you will only find yourself on the rim of the wheel, and if you follow the wheel around to the opposite end, you will only find yourself at the end of the polarity spoke.

You may explore as many of these polarities as you like before asking to be shown the spoke of death. When it makes itself known to you, walk out as far as you are comfortable and sense and see what it has to teach you. When you are finished, return to the center point and walk out on the opposite spoke of life. Go as far as you like, allowing the spoke to teach you about itself. Learn that life and death are each a part of the other, one being unable to exist without its polar opposite.

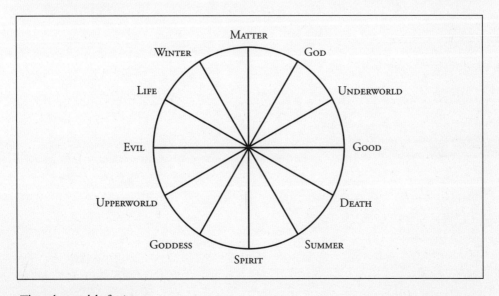

The polar model of existence.

When you are finished with the exercise, allow your inner self to fly back down to your physical body using the same visualization you took to get out. Rejoin yourself when you are ready. You may awaken yourself as soon as you like to record your discoveries in your magickal diary or Book of Shadows.

Two

Pagan Funeral Customs, Old and New

EVIDENCE FROM ARCHAEOLOGICAL DISCOVERIES establishes that interment practices reflecting after-life beliefs are at least 40,000 years old, perhaps even 60,000.[1] In the excavated graves from this period are found the fossilized remains of flowers, tools, jewelry, and totem animals. Many of the bodies have been discovered in a fetal position, another strong hint that our ancestors believed in some form of rebirth.

Food is without a doubt the most often-made burial offering. Neanderthal gravesites, Native American burial mounds, and Egyptian pyramids have all had in them the remains of game animals and other foods. Bowls and urns which likely held water or wine are also readily found. Providing sustenance for the deceased is still practiced in Paganism today. Feasts or libations are set out for the spirits on special holidays, and year-round in homes with ancestor altars. The reasons for this are likely twofold: while the Summerland is thought to be a land of never-ending plenty, the worlds which lie in between apparently are not, and offerings of food help sustain the soul until it reaches its destination or when it is traveling back and forth to visit living loved ones. Also, most ancient cultures had strict rules of hospitality which, if breached, could bring down the wrath of the deities. Therefore all souls in need of refreshment and sanctuary, both incarnate and discarnate, are offered whatever food and drink is within the means of the head of the household.

Tools, weapons, and jewelry are the next most often-seen items in a burial site. All over the world excavations have unearthed a treasure trove of these items thought needed by the spirit travelers on the road to the Summerland, either to make other needed items, to fight specters who attempt to block progress, or to pay those who may offer assistance. For example, the Lakota Indians, who were interred above ground, were always laid to rest with personal weapons and talismans.

Weaponry was also included in burial within cultures whose myths tell us that its slain heroes and warriors will rise to fight again when their country needs them. The most durable example of this is in England's semi-divine King Arthur, dubbed the "once and future king," who "sleeps" with his warrior legions in a secret location awaiting the call of his nation.

Items crafted in colors associated with death or the afterlife have also been found. In Egypt and in eastern North America, red ochre was used to anoint bodies before burial. Powdered iron ore (or *ochre*), a substance that has the color of blood—blood being symbolic of life, not death—was clearly a way of wishing the deceased a speedy return to the living. Black (the color of mourning and death in most of the west) and white (the color of mourning and death in most of the east) are also found, usually as clothing or shrouding to cover the body.

Items are also seen that suggest a soul might need some help on its afterlife journey. Lamps, flints, and other items that can be used to shed light have been placed with bodies, and, in South American burial sites, numerous figurines of guide dogs have been unearthed.

Eggs, those ancient symbols of life and regeneration, have been found in graves the world over. This again suggests that rebirth in some form or another was an accepted part of the spiritual beliefs of our ancestors.

The petrified remains of wooden death masks have been found in graves, particularly in Polynesia, Africa, and the Americas. Sometimes these were intended to preserve the likeness of the deceased, other times they were items of protection to scare away discarnate predators. Others may have been sacred masks, symbols of deities or totem animals that had been used by the deceased in rituals, possessions which those who buried him thought might be useful in the next world. Masks made of crafted metal or even gold, as found in the Egyptian pyramids, have been discovered all over western Europe, Central America, eastern Asia, and North Africa. Death masks have also been made that were kept in the homes of loved ones rather than buried. Sometimes these masks were casts of the face made with a clay compound just after death and were kept as mementos by family members (see Chapter 8, p. 146 for instructions on making death masks for personal rituals).

In Greece, a coin was placed into the mouth of the deceased so that he or she could pay Charon, the ferryman charged with rowing spirits across the river Styx into the Underworld—for a price.

The opposing ideas of either preserving the body eternally or allowing it to decay as quickly as possible have also had their adherents. In Egypt, mummification, a form of preservation using chemicals taken from plant life, was both a skill and an art form. Many of the mummified corpses are still remarkably well-preserved after 3,000 years. In contrast to Egypt, other cultures believed that if one were to be allowed to reincarnate, the old body must be completely decayed in order to free the soul from its attachment to its former home. The earliest inhabitants of England and some Native American tribes practiced this type of body disposal. The ancient Hebrews also followed this custom, and this is the reason the most orthodox of modern Jews shun the use of any metal on the body or casket and avoid embalming (a modern technique which further preserves the body) wherever laws mandating this practice can be circumvented.

Many cultures preferred to set the bodies of the loved ones adrift so that they would sail to the Summerland (see Chapter 1, page 8), while others left the bodies exposed to the elements, wrapped them up and placed them above ground, or burned them. Unfortunately few of these survive since the elements, predators, and (alas) thieves and souvenir hunters have destroyed these remains. This practice is linked to the mythologies of many lands that tell us a great river, or other body of water, must be traversed to arrive at the Summerland.

❧ Ancient Custom Meets Modern Funeral

Depending on how accepting your loved ones are about your religion, there are things you can do to allow yourself to feel more a part of a funeral whose structure and focus lies outside of your spiritual orientation.

Perhaps the easiest thing for you to do is ask that a certain item of meaning to you be placed in the casket for burial with your loved one. When my father's doctors told us he had only weeks left to live, I gave my mother a pink and black stone I purchased many years ago in a southern Utah rock shop that was carved into the shape of an egg. I had extensively used the stone in rituals honoring the Goddess, in Bealtaine rites, and in personal fertility spells. In other words, I had used this ancient symbol of rebirth whenever issues of life were a concern. I felt the stone was very much linked to me and I wanted to make sure it was placed in the casket and buried with my father. Search through your own magickal cabinet and see what is there that might function in this way for you. Such a small thing can be an amazingly comforting anchor for your mind to latch on to when the minister, priest, rabbi, et cetera, goes off on a tangent that is meaningless to you.

Placing a half-burned candle into the casket is another idea that uses similar symbolism. The half-burned candle represents that life is not really over, it is only extinguished for the moment, and there is still more to burn when the candle of life is relit. You can further link the candle to the deceased by enacting a ritual in which it is extinguished at, or close to, the time of death.[2]

In both of my grandfathers' caskets garlands of blood-red carnations were left, each individual one in the chain purchased for this purpose by a different grandchild. Other flowers with mystical, magickal, or personal meanings can be also left behind (see Chapter 8, p. 142 for a list of flower symbolism).

Before her death, my maternal grandmother was careful to give away nearly all items of importance to her. She wanted to assure herself that certain items went to a specific child or grandchild, and she enjoyed seeing her treasures cherished by another generation of her family. The one thing she kept, and even asked to be buried with, was her thin, gold wedding ring. During her entire twelve years as a widow she never stopped talking about the day she and my grandfather would be together again in the afterlife. The wedding ring was her talisman, the magickal catalyst that would guide her to him again. Other talismans serving to protect the spirit on its journeys or that help reunite loved ones in the Summerland might also be left in the casket.

Be creative in terms of how the body is prepared whether or not burial or cremation was chosen as a method for disposing of the earthly shell. Both anointing the body with perfumes or oils or ritually washing it have long and noble histories. Both practices are still used in various modern religious sects.

Dressing the deceased Pagan in ritual robes or other ritual dress is another viable option for bringing your ancient spiritual beliefs into the modern funeral. With the revived popularity of using burial shrouds as opposed to street dress, the robed option might not appear unusual even to the critical eyes of your most conservative relative.

Ritual jewelry may also be placed upon the corpse. As previously mentioned, jewelry has been found in excavated buried sites nearly 40,000 years old. Of course, if you will be having an open-casket funeral and fear someone might take offense at the large silver pentacle lying on their relative's chest, you may want to tuck it under the collar of the robe or place it down inside the coffin out of the sight of probing eyes.

Some Pagans have made provisions about what is to be done with their working tools—such as athames, wands, et cetera—after their passing. Sometimes these are left to favored students or to children. Other times the Pagan wishes to have the tools destroyed. I first came across reference to this practice through the writings of High Priestess Lady Sheba,[3] who instructed her daughter to destroy her tools upon her passing. For years afterwards I wondered why anyone would want to do this to items so carefully collected and cultivated. It wasn't until I realized just how much of the Pagan's/Witch's own energies are invested in the working tools that I could understand why someone would wish them gone forever, their intense energies grounded permanently. Perhaps, I thought, the spirit would rest easier knowing any personal energy that might tie it to the earthly plane was freed.

Placing ritual tools inside the casket to be burned or buried can serve this function very well. Cremation would destroy them along with the body and would have the added symbolism of uniting forever the energies of tool and master. Burial would ground the energy of the tools in the most literal way possible, and would also put them out of reach of anyone else who might want to use them.

A final note about items you wish to bury or burn with your loved ones: funeral directors are open to leaving just about whatever you wish inside the casket as long as nothing illegal is going on. You will, however, have to inform them which items are there for display (such as a wedding ring that is to be passed on to a grandchild) and which will be left behind (such as the aforementioned pentacle).

If you cannot have a full-blown Pagan requiem service, you might be able instead to add a single sentence to the funeral rites, such as this one that has been bandied about in Pagan circles for a long time: *Sleep gently in the arms of the Mother.* This sentence expresses our belief in the Goddess as the beginning, end, and re-beginning point of life. For those who ask about it later—is not the act of burial placing a body directly into the arms of the Earth Mother? Rest in Peace!

❧ Today's Pagans in Mourning

Pain and tears are natural when you are faced with the death of someone you love, no matter what afterlife beliefs you hold or how you choose to honor a life no longer coinciding with your own. Even if you firmly accept the doctrine of reincarnation and the inevitability of togetherness again in another life, you can be sure that it will never be exactly the same as it was in this life. Your spirits may reunite, but so many things that made each of you unique in this incarnation—your family, your culture, your physical appearance, your intellect—will never all come together in exactly the same configuration again.

While we Pagans don't enjoy facing the death of a loved one any more than anyone else, our spiritual system tries to teach acceptance of this natural part of life, and our funerals reflect this ideal. The one common thread running through Pagan final rites is the theme of transition or continuance rather than of an ending. When I first began my formal journey in Paganism in 1980, it was my belief that we all shared many other beliefs about how bodies were handled. My early Craft experiences, my reading, and my conversations with other Pagans led me to believe there was an almost universal, concerted effort made not to indulge in what might be called the "death denial" practices of the mainstream religions—dressing up bodies as if they are ready to go to church, insisting the deceased look only as if sleeping, or rushing the newly dead into a cryogenic tank to be frozen for posterity. While researching this book over the past year, I have discovered these are not practices universally shunned by Pagans, though they still seem to be the practices of a minority, and perhaps even of a growing minority.

Personal needs and tastes come into play in how we deal with a corpse, as do the teachings of our individual traditions. Certainly the ancient Egyptians carried out elaborate body preservation rituals, and Egyptian Pagan traditions are still popular today. With the proliferation of computers, the information superhighway has also had its impact on Pagan funeral practices. The growing number of Techno-Pagans, folks who meet via the Internet for exchange of information, coven meetings, and other rituals, have made practices once relegated to the pages of science fiction novels—such as cryogenics, the freezing of bodies for possible revival at a later date—more acceptable and more commonplace.

The decision to have a body present and/or visible at a memorial service and how it is or is not adorned is usually left up to the deceased's family, and more often than not will reflect the religious practices of that family. For instance, open caskets are forbidden in Judaism, while some Christian sects encourage the practice to make the death seem "real." The sight of a dead body makes the vast majority of people uneasy, a fact that can probably be traced to worries about our own mortality. In some Pagan cultures the dead were actively feared and were disposed of as soon as possible. For example, the Lodagaba of west central Africa disguised the youngest family members to keep their souls from being stolen away by the recently deceased. In other cultures the ancestor spirits were called upon for guidance and protection as soon as they had been given a sufficient rest period.

In my experience, Pagans rarely fight the feeling of grief and will allow themselves to mourn in any way they feel is appropriate for as long as needed—something I feel is healthy. The formal memorial rites set the tone for mourners, and can either help the survivors overcome their grief or prolong it. Meaningful rites in which mourners feel they have made their peace with the loved one and said their final good-byes undoubtedly work best. This requires that those closest to the deceased be given lots of input into the structure and atmosphere of the ritual.

Whether you choose a solemn ritual, a spirited one, or a combination of the two is up to you, and any can be meaningful. You can play lots of New Orleans-style jazz music, some of which was written expressly for funerals, and host a raucous wake to party one last time with your loved one, or you can play stolid Gregorian chants and keep the event low-intensity. Do what feels right to you, and what you think your loved one would most have wanted for him- or herself.

As a whole, modern Pagans tend to avoid the word *funeral* when discussing memorial services, though the only apparent reason for doing so seems to be to separate our own rituals from those of the mainstream. If you like this word you should feel free to use it, since it has no inherently non-Pagan hidden meaning. Mainstream religions also tell us that funerals are for the living but, as often as not, Pagans believe final rites are also held for the spirit of the dead whom they presume to be nearby. Making this distinction may be the reason for the general shunning of the familiar term.

The terms *passing-over ritual* and *final rites of passage* are the two most often heard in Pagan/Wiccan circles in reference to a funeral, though in truth they, and other less frequently used terms, have their own meanings and functions.

Funeral

Funeral is a Middle English word for the formal religious service given as the body of the deceased is disposed of in whatever way the family deems appropriate. The term itself comes from the Latin word *funeris*, a term once used to refer exclusively to a procession to the burial site. Processions are part of both ancient and modern Pagan celebrations, and are still used in many death observances which take place in cemeteries.

Passing-Over Ritual

The term *passing over* comes from the concept of making a passage—of leaving one plane of existence for another—and this is probably the most commonly used name for a Pagan funeral service. These rituals can occur anytime after physical death, and may even occur more than once. They are rarely done with the body present, partly because Pagans see no connection between the earthly shell and the spirit that has been released from it, and partly because many of our loved ones are non-Pagan and our rites are unwelcome in mainstream services. Passing over is also an appropriate term to use when referring to rites that assist the spirit in making the transition to death.

Final Rite of Passage

This phrase is often used interchangeably with "passing-over ritual," but is more correctly used when a rite is specifically performed to assist the spirit of the deceased to the Summerland. The term reflects the Pagan belief in death as being merely another stage of life, a rite of passage—the last in this lifetime—that, like the others, is ritually observed and commemorated.

Memorial Rite

Memorial rite is the term usually applied to rituals held on the anniversary of the birth or death of a loved one, times at which their lives are remembered and commemorated by those left behind. The word *memorial* literally means "in memory." The mainstream often uses this term to refer to a funeral service where the body of the deceased is not present.

Requiem

The word *requiem* is another term often shunned in Paganism because of its close association with Catholicism. In the Catholic funeral mass this is the first word spoken in the traditional Latin service, which is how it came to be known as a generic term for a funeral. In spite of its origins, the word is not so far removed from Pagan ideology as it might seem at first. It comes from the Latin *re*, meaning "again," and *quies*, meaning "still" or "quiet." Interesting wording for a religion that dropped reincarnation from its official doctrine in the fifth century, isn't it? By using the term requiem to refer to any sort of memorial ritual, we are summing up in one ancient word our own beliefs and hopes in the eternal cycle of life, death, and rebirth.

Transition Rite

This is another term for "passing-over ritual" that simply acknowledges physical death is not a final ending, but merely a segue into another existence. Because of this, any rite of passage in the Pagan life cycle (i.e. handfasting, birth, initiation, et cetera) could be properly referred to as a transition rite.

❧ On Cemeteries

In general, Pagan folk approach a cemetery with the same respect they give all sacred sites, regardless of personal viewpoints on just who or what is there. Among Pagans *coimetrophobia*, or fear of cemeteries, is almost unknown. Few of us find them repugnant or scary, and even fewer give in to popular superstitions such as holding our breath as we walk past a graveyard so as not to make the dead people jealous. But even given these views, we do not traipse boldly about in them without regard to the feelings of those spirits who may be attached to the place. It is a sacred spot, and how we choose to make our approach often depends on which culture we draw our personal Pagan tradition from.

The Egyptians built the famous pyramids to house their honored dead, making sure to include all the accoutrements the deceased might need in the afterlife. As followers of nature religions, Pagans have lain their folks to rest in the shelters nature offers, such as caves, bogs, under trees or in trees, or exposed them to the elements.[4] Celtic burial cairns, stone mounds dating back as many as four thousand years, appear both to be sacred sites—such as Newgrange Cairn—as well as places where evil spirits or faeries lurk. The Anglo-Saxons dug long barrows, or ditches, for communal burials. Native American burial sites—both above and below ground—were held sacred, viewed as a gathering place not only for ancestor spirits but for deities as well. These places had their own guardian spirits and, even today, those who trespass on these lands sometimes find the old legends coming out to haunt them (no pun intended).

From evidence found in the annals of medieval European church law, it is reasonable to assume that burial grounds were once the sites of lavish rituals to honor the dead, ones which included singing, dancing, and probably the invocation of deities. As such, these sites took the place of the sacred circle wherein modern Pagans hold rites and rituals.[5] In the sixteenth century the church issued an ekase (an ecclesiastic law or papal bull) banning dancing and eating in burial grounds in an effort to suppress Pagan afterlife views among the peasantry.

The Santeria and Voodun traditions, which mix mainstream religion with African Paganism, still reflect this old belief through their assertion that cemeteries make powerful sites for ritual, spellcraft, or for opening communication with the dead. Often their spells require some accoutrement from a cemetery, such as a piece of headstone, to make the spell work.

Pagan cemeteries in the modern sense have been unknown until recently, most of us having to be content either to be buried in conventional graveyards, many of which are operated by religious organizations who do not share our spiritual views, or to be cremated and have our ashes scattered to nature. As of this writing, a group in Washington State has set aside some land with the intention of developing a Pagan cemetery, and a group in England has formed a hospice, created a cemetery, and set up a trust to assist other Pagan groups in doing the same (addresses for both organizations can be found in Appendix B). Several other organizations are following suit, including Circle Sanctuary, which is probably the best-known nature spirituality center in North America.[6] Hopefully, as we continue to grow in numbers so will our burial sites, so that we can feel free to honor our dead in ways meaningful to us without censure by the community or by other religions.

Talk of Pagan burial grounds nearly always leads to the controversial issue of graveyard magick, another area where Pagans differ sharply in their approach. Some of this is due to differences in tradition, others to general beliefs about the

A German engraving (circa 1600) shows Pagans gamboling in the cemetery in defiance of church law.

nature of the cemetery and the spirits who dwell there.[7] The source of graveyard magickal energy can be viewed in one of four ways: one, as merely another manifestation of the power that flows naturally from any sacred space since, much like any magickal circle, a graveyard is a space that has been consecrated and set aside as sacred. Two, as a manifestation of power coming from those places "in between," a Celtic concept prevalent in modern Witchcraft teaching that places and times not clearly of one dimension or another possess a special magick all their own. Cemeteries fall into this category because, though they are part of our physical world of the living, they are also part of the spirit world of the dead. Three, as power coming from the discarnate spirits of those who are interred there, particularly from benevolent ancestor spirits. Or four, as power originating in otherworldly guardian spirits or deities of the graveyard who must be approached as divine and appeased as any deity would need to be before his or her power is appropriated.

Whenever we use a catalyst for our magick, be it a stone from our own backyard or an herb picked in a cemetery, we are in essence borrowing the energies of that item/place and asking it to work on our behalf. In any magickal operation it is wise to consider first just what these energies are, from where or whom they emanate, and what—if anything—they might ask from us in return. While most practitioners of nature religions are accustomed to asking for permission to take things from nature, some Pagans feel that a graveyard is another matter altogether, and that serious problems can ensue even when permission is clearly given to borrow graveyard energies. Of course, there are other Pagans, just as skilled and experienced, who regard these concerns as ridiculous.

Another view holds that the souls of the dead are to be found nowhere near the graveyard, hence there is no need for deities and guardian spirits to be there either. Why, they reason, would the dead want to be at the cemetery? Nothing is there but the remains of their earthly shells and perhaps a monument bearing the name they wore in life—all meaningless now. Pagans with this viewpoint feel that the souls of the dead are either in the Summerland, have reincarnated, or are lingering around the places and people they hold dear—and that is certainly **not** in the graveyard!

🌹 Making Friends with the Cemetery

For those Pagans who are uneasy around cemeteries, here are some ways to overcome this problem that, never forget, is purely a result of acculturation by a society that fears its own mortality.

- Try taking long walks in a cemetery on a warm, sunny day. Read the headstones as you stroll past and try to imagine what the people memorialized there might have been like in life. What made them happy or sad? What were they passionate about? How were they like or unlike you? How did they face death? And who loved them enough to lay them to rest in this spot? Try to see the cemetery as a keeper of memories rather than a repository of sorrows.

- Take a picnic to a graveyard alone or with others. Feasting in burial grounds is an ancient Pagan tradition in many cultures, one which is still followed by some sects of mainstream religions (see Chapter 5). If you are nervous about going alone, either because you suffer from coimetrophobia or because the cemetery is too isolated for personal safety, ask a trusted friend to accompany you.

- Try talking to the headstone of a relative, friend, or to one which draws your attention. Many people indulge in this practice even though we know intellectually that the spirit of the deceased is likely not present, only the decaying remains. Yet there are few of us—Pagan or not—who have not spoken aloud to a loved one in a cemetery. Have yourself an amicable little chat so that you can start to think of the cemetery as a friendly place.

- Seek out the guardian or deity of the cemetery to assist you. Many Pagan traditions and cultures believe that each burial ground has its own deity and/or guardian spirit that protects it from harm and watches over the souls whose bodies rest there. In Roman traditions it is the Manes who watch over burial grounds, in Santeria it is the Goddess Oya, in Celtic traditions it is usually faeries such as the Scottish Red Cap, and in Appalachia it is the spirit of the last person to be buried there. Upon entering the cemetery, call out a greeting and blessing to the guardian. You may even wish to bring a small offering as a token of your good will. Explain to him/her why you have come, ask assistance in learning to love this sacred place, and allow him or her to guide you through the cemetery, relying on your intuition to keep the contact. You may be pleasantly surprised by what you are taught.

• Allow yourself to focus on the life to come rather than on death by making random gravesite offerings of apples, flowers, eggs, wreaths, or other items symbolizing rebirth (see Chapter 8 for more on grave offerings, rituals, and the cemetery guardian).

❦ An Alternative to Cemeteries

A few ecologically-minded Pagans have made public their agreement with some environmental groups who feel too much land has been tied up in cemeteries and that, with the world population currently doubling itself every twenty years, we cannot afford to tie up any more. Some Pagans have expressed the desire for memorial parks in which the ashes of a cremated body can be buried or scattered. Plaques and natural monuments could be a part of this, with a permanent listing recorded somewhere—perhaps even in stone—of the persons whose ashes have been left behind. The park could serve as a Pagan gathering site, sacred land on which all may worship or honor their dead. Truly there can be fewer tributes as appropriate for someone in a nature religion than to have a sapling planted over their ashes that will grow into a fine shade tree all can enjoy.

Certainly in the near future a number of Pagan cemeteries and memorial parks will be functioning, and we will each have to make these choices for ourselves as well as for our loved ones. Whatever decisions we make should reflect our personal likes and dislikes as well as a concern for the planet as a whole. There is no reason why with care and planning both options cannot fulfill both needs.

❦ On Grief Counseling and Terminal Illness

Though Pagan clergy and mental health professionals have been counseling the grieving for years, it has only been recently that we Pagans have realized our shortage of qualified help. Seeking assistance during the grief period is not the only part of the death process for which counseling may be needed. Paganism is above all else a life-affirming faith, hence our attempts to reconcile ourselves with death as merely another rite of passage through life. This does not mean we are any better equipped to deal with grief than our non-Pagan brothers and sisters, only that our beliefs about the afterlife are different.

There is probably no greater shock than finding that you, or a loved one, are terminally ill. As I write this book, my own father suffers from a terminal illness and, as his family, we have been called upon to make some difficult decisions since he is no longer able to make these for himself. You may find the advice of a dispassionate outsider who shares your spiritual point of view very welcome, especially when you are asked if you want a suffering loved one resuscitated when death occurs or if you want to have life support equipment hooked up or removed.

As the "weeks to live" prognosis first given in my father's case turned into agonizing months with no end in sight, I found it necessary to my sanity to have someone to talk with about the situation. I have frequently bounced some of my ideas and concerns off a friend of mine (and a recent initiate into the Craft), a biofeedback and occupational therapist who has worked with illness support programs at one of the largest hospitals here in Indiana. She not only shares my spiritual point of view, but I know that she cares about me and my family without being so involved that her emotions cloud her better judgment.

One of the most difficult aspects of death to deal with is the fact the grieving process does not necessarily start with death. Certainly part of the difficulty with my father's situation is that we, the family, know the end is coming swiftly, and yet we cannot say our good-byes properly because he simply does not know who we are most of the time. The grieving process has begun, though death is still some time away. If you find yourself in this type of situation, you may wish to embark on some type of formal grief counseling, or at least find someone you can talk with who shares your spiritual outlook on life and death.

Unless you come from a Pagan family, family counseling is not a good idea. For instance, members of my father's family cover the complete spectrum of spiritual viewpoints: there are Jews and Christians, fundamentalists and liberals, Pagans and atheists. No one spiritual counselor could ever hope to reconcile such diversity.

Assisted suicide for the terminally ill, or what we once termed "euthanasia," has been in the forefront of the news for several years. As with any other topic of public controversy, this is one on which Pagans do not agree. Assisted suicide is when someone who is hopelessly, terminally ill wishes to end his or her life either to spare their estate the burden of further, pointless medical bills, or to spare themselves the physical pain that their illness will cause in the end. While we give this courtesy of a dignified death to our pets, we find humans still largely resistant to the idea, though its popularity is gaining.

The arguments against assisted suicide are predictable, and at least the first one has merit: miracles of recovery do happen. Remissions happen. The person in question could live relatively pain-free for several more years. Second, orthodox, mainstream religious leaders feel assisted suicide violates their deity's right to take the life he has given. They call it an abomination, a sin. Third, they feel to assist in ending a life is murder and should be—and has been—prosecuted as such.

Arguably, only the person who has to face immediate death should be the one to make these decisions, which is why an increasing number are taking their own lives before they reach a point where they would have to ask for help to do so and thus implicate a loved one in murder.

❧ The Death Watch

Our Pagan ancestors generally followed one of two systems when dealing with the death of a member of their clan: one, they stood watch together over the body, gathering the clan together in the last days of the life. If the dying person was a leader of the clan, then a new chieftain would be chosen by the clan, or named by the dying person if it were possible. And two, other tribes followed a custom where the dying person went off on his or her own, to a locale either known or unknown to the family, and died alone. The purpose of this was to align one's self with the deities and spirit guides before death. Either of these scenarios is probably more palatable to today's Pagans than dying in the sterile and impersonal atmosphere of a hospital, and should be considered where feasible.

If you are ever called upon to be part of a death watch—events increasingly common with in-home hospice care becoming more and more popular—there are things you can do to Paganize the experience that should bring comfort to both you and other friends and family who are present, whether or not they are Pagan. Certainly discussing the joy that the dying person brought to your life can ease the tension of the waiting as well as make the transition easier on all of you. This practice has Celtic origins and is still a popular part of Irish funeral customs today.[8]

You may also want to consider another old practice of unknown origin—that of placing a single, lighted candle at the feet and the head of the dying person. These are usually left in place until the body is removed for burial. The candle at the feet is to illuminate the pathway for the spirit, and the one at the head is for protection. This gentle custom is rarely offensive to anyone as it is still used in many rural communities by Christians, among the Irish, and among smaller religious sects elsewhere.

You might also want to take yourself into a lightly altered state of consciousness through meditation and watch the demise with the power of your second sight. Pagans naturally see their surroundings in this way much of the time (if we didn't we would likely be following another religion), and you may find this relatively easy to do. In this state you may actually see the spirit of the dying person leave the physical body, or you may find that it is already wandering about the room unable to move on until Death (the entity) comes for it.

Even if you are unable to see Death come for your loved one with your physical eyes, you can learn to sense the deathly presence so that his next appearance will be easily recognizable to you. In one of the climactic scenes of the movie *Something Wicked This Way Comes*, Jonathan Price's character (interestingly named "Mr. Dark") has been taunting Jason Robards' character about his advanced age and all the lost opportunities of his life, and orders his handmaiden to give Robards' character the experience of death so that he will know it when it returns for him. While the film's scene is intended to stir up feelings of dread on the presumption that no one could possibly want to know what dying feels like, it does not speak for everyone. There can actually be a lot of comfort in knowing what death feels like and what the presence of Death entails. Though the movie does not emphasize this aspect, it is the experience of Death coupled with the recognition of the power of love that ultimately frees Robards' character from his inner tortures.

Trying to experience death (the state of being) itself is definitely not a recommended practice. Still, the lure of the unknown pulls at us, making some of us take risks, exhibiting the behavior that psychologists refer to as the "death wish." Remember the film *Flatliners*, about a group of medical students who took turns stopping each other's heartbeats and respiration for several minutes? The film was intensely provocative, though few of us would want to have taken our turn on the table.

The best way to understand what happens in the interim between lives is to explore the experience through past life regression (discussed in Chapter 1) or through books that discuss the subject in-depth. Some metaphysical teachers and researchers have tried to take good, deep-level hypnosis subjects through a past life's death and into the interim. Two disparate events usually occur: one, the subjects all find they initially experience whatever events and manifestations the culture and religion of that lifetime had taught them to expect, or two, they find themselves in nearly identical circumstances that are nothing like they expected to find. To look further into this aspect of death, check out any of the books on the market which cover near-death experiences (called NDEs), or pick up Dr. Michael Newton's *Journey of Souls* (St. Paul: Llewellyn, 1994), which chronicles his fascinating research into life-between-life experiences.

❧ Getting the Final Rites You Want

Very few families have not had to go through the misery of trying to second guess what a loved one would want at his or her own funeral. Because the vast majority of us do not like thinking about our own demise, only a small percentage of us ever pre-plan our funerals in any detail. For Pagans, this pre-planning is especially important if we have family who do not share our religious views or, worse yet, are hostile toward them.

Virtually all funeral homes have **pre-plan/pre-pay packages** available to those who are interested in pursuing this course. One of the greatest advantages of this type of pre-planning is that, once a contract is signed and paid for, the price can never be raised. With the average cost of an American funeral currently running between $8,000 and $10,000, and with no end in sight to rising costs, this can be a big hedge against inflation for younger people. Another advantage is that the funeral home will give you a planning booklet that can be returned to them to keep on file for you. These booklets ask every conceivable question about your final ritual wishes: open or closed casket, cremation or burial, the music you like, the readings you prefer, the religious ideology you espouse, et cetera. Having written instructions like these to follow will make it very difficult for anti-Pagan family members to make drastic changes in the format you have chosen.

Living wills, drawn up by an attorney, are another way to go and can be of assistance should you ever reach a point in your health where you are unable to speak for yourself. In this document you can make your wishes for your passing-over service known and you can let your family and physicians know just how much you want done if you are clearly terminal, or to what stage of deterioration you want to reach, before they "pull the plug" on you. You can also specify your choice to be kept in a hospital, a nursing home, hospice care, or to be allowed to die at home, as most of our ancestors did until recent times. If you feel inclined to donate any of your organs, this too can be specified. Living wills can also empower an attorney to act on your behalf with regard to your finances. In the case of an incapacitating terminal illness, this allows your lawyer to release some of the money in your estate to health care providers before your death, taking the immediate financial burden off your family. Any family who has had to make even one of these heart-wrenching decisions for an incapacitated loved one can appreciate having written instructions to follow, whether or not they agree with everything in them.

For residents of the United States, free information and low-cost assistance for creating living wills can be obtained through Choices In Dying, Inc., the largest provider of specialized assistance and death/dying educational materials in the country. Choices In Dying, Inc. gears its informational packet to the specific laws of your own state. They provide forms and instructions for you to instruct others about your last wishes, and show you how to appoint a legal representative to see that these are carried out. The informational packet is free, and other educational materials are available at a reasonable cost (see Appendix B for more information and a toll-free number).

Living trusts are another way to go when looking at your last wishes. They function similarly to the living will, but they do not require an attorney's assistance and will save your heirs the need to hire a lawyer to probate the will after your death. Living trusts are completely revocable by you at any time in your life, and are currently recognized as legal in all fifty states (persons residing outside the United States will need to check national and/or provincial laws pertaining to this type of will). Most office supply stores carry blank copies of living trusts, or carry living trust kits that come with complete instructions.

You can also keep **your own list of written funeral instructions**, provided that a trusted friend or family member is made aware of its existence and location. They will do you no good if they are squirreled away in a dresser where they might not be found until several months after the fact. Such things do happen—we found my grandfather's wish list about four weeks after his funeral. The advantage to this type of home-kept list is that it can be updated anytime at your discretion with no cost to you. In it you can write your own obituary, list whom you want and do not want notified upon your death, as well as make requests about your requiem services. The big drawback to this type of document is that it is not binding upon anyone to carry it out, and any family member who does not like your requests can change them with few—if any—other members of the family ever being aware that your wishes are not being followed.

If you know already that a Pagan funeral, or even a funeral with a few Pagan allusions, will upset your entire family, you may want to request two services: one to please your family, and another for your coven and other members of the Pagan community. Whatever you decide, keep in mind that pre-planning in some form or another will help you get what you want.

ꗢ Guided Meditations for Exploring the Summerland

The following guided meditations are designed to help you personally experience the Summerland, or at least those reaches of it humans have been able to explore and return to tell about. They are no more risky to perform than any other guided meditation.

Where meditation is usually defined as a single focused thought/contemplation or the absence of thought, guided meditation involves dynamic thinking. Guided meditations take you on an inner/astral world journey to achieve a specific aim (in this case, exploring the Summerland), and can be very dramatic in nature. This is accomplished by heavily employing archetypal symbolism and fantasy images in the text that you follow with your mind. Usually this type of meditation takes you from the point of normal wakefulness down through the semi-sleeping states of consciousness (similar to those you reach while daydreaming), and then on down into a light sleep state in which your mind is fully alert to what is happening in the meditation text. The meditation brings you back to your waking self when the adventure is finished. Taking you full circle like this is why this type of exercise is called "guided" in the first place. Other names for this process are pathworking, awakened dreaming, lucid dreaming, and guided astral projection.

You can read these three guided meditations aloud for yourself with some measure of success, but they will work much better if you tape-record them for yourself or allow another person to read them to you. This will free you to fully concentrate on focusing your thoughts inward and outward, a process necessary to any successful innerworld journey. Reading through the meditations before actually doing them and familiarizing yourself with them is also beneficial.

Whenever guided meditation is discussed, there are always some who question whether the experiences are "real" or not. While it is true we often use the term "innerworld journey" to refer to these explorations, we are not saying that these are not real or valid experiences, only that they are taking place in the mind. These experiences occur on another plane of existence, one accessed *through* your mind. Never underestimate your mind as the most powerful tool you have for doing and achieving anything you want. After all, it is within your mind where all magick ultimately takes place.

Because of the great diversity in afterlife beliefs, both within different Pagan traditions and within each individual, these meditations cannot hope to address them all, nor do they try. They only attempt to cover the most common elements of entry into the underworld, middleworld, and upperworld, and try to provide a jumping-off point for your future personal explorations. Because some astral travelers become nervous at the thought of being left in the inner-realms without a guide, meditations of this type provide a voice to lead you back home after your adventures are complete.

Once you become comfortable with written ventures into the Summerland, try adding to, subtracting from, or modifying the meditations into a form suited to your personal vision of the Summerland. Feel free to deviate from the written path, call on stronger guides or deities to assist you further, and explore little-seen places in the afterlife. You may write out these new meditations and follow them with a tape recorder or a reader, or you may just wish to fly off and explore on your own. As long as you feel firmly in control and are unafraid, go for it!

If you find you are still having trouble letting go, or are put off by the idea of exploring the Summerland due to negative programming about the afterworld, try reading Annie Pigeon's delightful little book *A Visitor's Guide to the Afterlife* (New York: Kensington Press, 1995). Written like your basic travel guide, it contains a lot of humorous insights that not only help put you at ease, but also may stimulate your astral imagination in lively and unexpected directions.

The first part of the meditation is an induction designed to slow and focus brain activity. It has many cousins among Pagans and occultists and none are more right or better than any other. The best one is the one that works for you, and you should not feel stuck with having to use the one presented here. If you already have a method of inducing an altered, or receptive, state of consciousness that you are fond of, feel free to substitute yours for mine. In this case your own will work better for you because your subconscious is already cued to working with it. Most of this induction first appeared in my earlier book *A Witch's Guide to Faery Folk* (St. Paul: Llewellyn, 1994), the primary difference being that where the former used a rainbow bridge image to reach the Otherworld, this meditation utilizes the imagery of a cave. Caves are archetypically linked to the womb of the Great Mother, and figure heavily in shamanic and inner-journey imagery from many cultures.

The other imagery used to access each of the three realms also utilizes common concepts. We naturally conceptualize the underworld as being beneath us, which is why the first meditation uses downward imagery to get us there. Likewise, we view the middleworld as an unseen part of our own world, and the upperworld as somewhere "up there," even though we know these designations to be only metaphors that help us to comprehend a world we cannot fully remember in this life. While using these images is not the only way in which you can access the Summerland, they are ones that your conscious mind can most easily accept. If your conscious mind fights your inner journey, constantly questioning the validity of something making no sense to it, you are unlikely to do yourself much good.

If at any time during the meditation you feel uncomfortable, nervous, or frightened, you should increase the protection around your physical body with a strong white-gold light energy. After you do this, try to work through these fear blockages by realizing that your quest for knowledge is more important than any anxieties conjured up by a resistant human mind. If you are still uncomfortable, it is probably best that you return to full waking consciousness, or what some would term "returning to your body." You should then attempt to analyze just what it was that disturbed you so much, and try again later.

You will be in complete control throughout the entire exercise, fully able to regain your normal waking consciousness at any time. Trigger words for accomplishing this will be given to you during the relaxation part of the meditation.

Before you begin, you will need to find a place where you will not be disturbed for at least an hour. You may choose to either lie down or remain sitting. If you choose to recline, do make sure you are able to stay awake during the entire exercise. Falling asleep will cause you no harm and your subconscious will continue until the end of the meditation, but your conscious mind will lose all the benefits of the excursion.

If you wish, you may burn incense or play some music softly in the background (see Appendix A). These aid concentration for many, and they can certainly help to drown out the sounds and smells of the mundane world. Good incenses for Summerland exploration are those with associations with death and rebirth, such as lotus, jasmine, or apple blossom.

You may also wish to have on your physical person some type of protective symbol. This can be in the form of a talisman, such as a piece of pentagram-styled jewelry (the five-pointed star, which has come to symbolize western Paganism, particularly the branches of it known as Wicca or Witchcraft), protective herbs (such as cinnamon, basil, bay, myrrh, or clove) tied together in a colorful pouch, or a magickal tool lying across your lap. Choose whatever signals protection to you, regardless of what someone else recommends. Only that which triggers a protective response in your own mind will be effective for you. Other protective visualizations will be given during the course of the meditation.

Conclude each exercise by making a loud noise to alert your subconscious that you have returned to your normal consciousness. Bells, whistles, and alarms are all good, but so is a loud shout or a hooting laugh. This very physical sound helps prevent any bleed-over between the two worlds and may frighten away any astral entities who may have followed you home. It is both wise and traditional to make whatever statement you or your tradition normally uses to end rituals, such as "It is done" or "The rite is closed," to further get the message across that you are back in your own world.

Lastly, keep in mind the teaching of myths from around the globe that show us those who venture into the Otherworld rarely come out unchanged or unmoved in some way. After all, the purpose of the exercise is to learn, grow, and stretch the limits of our human potential.

Note: The phrases and sections marked off within parentheses ( ) are directions to the reader only, and should not be read aloud during the meditation.

❧ Relaxation Induction for All Three Meditations

Close your eyes and begin breathing rhythmically and deeply. Slow your thoughts. Quiet your mind. Center your spirit and feel your body begin to relax. Relax and let go. Focus inward, shutting out the physical world. You are slowing your mind, relaxing your body, and going inward.

With each breath you draw in, your mind slows itself more and more, falling inward. Falling, falling, going inward, reaching outward. Slower and slower. Deeper and deeper, into itself. Slower and deeper. And you continue to relax.

Now inhale deeply—as much air as you can take in (pause). Hold it (pause). Now exhale, very slowly, and as you do so, feel your body relax and all your tensions drain away. You relax even more. Your mind is quiet and your spirit is calm.

Inhale again, very deeply this time. Hold it for a few seconds (pause). Now exhale very, very slowly. All the tensions of your physical body have fallen away. You are relaxed and growing less and less aware of your physical shell.

One more time—inhale as deeply as you can and hold it (pause). Now exhale, slowly, allowing the last hold on your physical consciousness to slip away with it. Your mind is quiet and reflective, your body still and relaxed. Release it all. Relax, go deeper.

As the last gasp of breath leaves your body, you notice a tingling of energy deep within you. It is not a remnant of tension from your physical life beginning to stir within you, but an energy that is new and exciting, as if ignited by a divine source. Suddenly you feel yourself surrounded by this energy. It is the protective energy of your Goddesses and Gods that now surround your body in an egg of golden light, throbbing and sparkling about you as if kissed by the sun and blessed by the full moon. This egg of protective energy is born of the divinity that has always been within you and will never desert you. In times of stress or fear it will only glow brighter, its defenses stronger. It is all-knowing and far-reaching. It will protect your inert body as you travel to the astral realms, and it will also go with that part of you that is now ready to journey forth. It will guard and defend you.

You have no fear because you know that you are always in control. You know that if for any reason you wish to return to your body and to your normal waking consciousness, you can do so by saying to yourself the words "I am home." The words "I am home" will trigger both your subconscious and conscious minds that you wish to return immediately to your normal consciousness—and it will immediately happen. You can then open your eyes and go about your daily life unharmed. The words "I am home" will absolutely always bring you home.

You are very relaxed, and you have no fears, no worries, no concerns outside of your journey's goal. So feel yourself relax and go deeper . . . deeper . . . deeper into a meditative state. Feel yourself sinking—sinking so deep into yourself that you feel you can fly, so deep that you know you will not much longer be attached to the physical world. You have never felt so relaxed or so peaceful.

Now let go of your physical shell. For one last moment know it is a part of you and then let it go. Release it—it is not needed now. Become unaware of your legs (pause). Become unaware of your arms (pause). Become unaware of your back and stomach (pause). Relax your neck and shoulders and then become unaware of them. Feel them fall away from you like old clothes, and relax even more (pause).

As you feel yourself sinking deeper and deeper, you are ready to call upon your deities for the extra protection you need as you traverse the Summerland. With your mind, call out to your Goddess and ask her blessing upon your venture as you seek entrance to the Summerland (pause). Feel her approval. Accept her blessing. Feel her protective energy come to you, as sure and as safe as the arms of a loving mother. As if in answer to your plea, you notice above you a large pentagram. It blazes strongly with a blue-white flame. It is impenetrable to any but yourself, and with that knowledge you are able to relax even more.

Already the veil separating your everyday world from the Otherworld is blurred and you can feel the astral plane coming closer and closer. You sense its subtle energies. You know you will be there soon and you relax even more.

With your mind, call out to your God and ask his blessing upon your venture as you seek entrance to the Summerland (pause). Feel his strength and his assurance that you are safe and well, and that your journey is blessed. As if in answer to your plea you notice that a bright, golden shield has been raised over you, glowing golden like the sun. On the shield are carved intricate knots and pentagrams, and animals of strength and courage, the same that protected seekers of old. Ancient energies of protection and power are now with you.

With the glowing shield of the God, the pentagram of the Goddess, and your own protective energy pulsating around you, you feel warm and very sleepy, and yet incredibly energized. You know you are safe and protected, and you know that soon you will step from inside yourself and approach the gates of the Summerland.

You realize now that your physical body is completely numb. You are now so deep in trance that you can no longer feel any sensations of your physical body; it has no connection with you whatsoever. That mortal shell is now completely forgotten, and your separation from it nearly complete. You are so deep into yourself that your mind is reaching outward, stretching toward new worlds and new experiences. And you feel yourself begin to sway. That part of you able to go forth and travel unhindered by your physical being is anxious to begin the journey. It wants to leave. As you sway, you feel a sense of lightness and buoyancy drawing you closer to the Summerland.

As you continue to sway, you feel a weightless sensation in the pit of your stomach and suddenly you find you are no longer part of that heavy shell. You feel light and free and you move slowly upward—upward, out of, and away from your physical self.

You travel out a few yards and find that you are above your body, looking down at it. You see that it is safe and protected and will remain that way until you decide to return. You are now ready to go. You turn from your resting body and walk away, right through the wall and into the outdoors.

Moving swiftly above the ground you travel far and fast, drawn to a dense forest in the distance. As you get closer, you can see that the trees are bare and the woods are shrouded in winter. A surreal hush emanates from deep within the forest, a feeling enhanced by the blanket of undisturbed snow. Your feet touch the ground just outside the forest. You stop and look about you, somehow drawn into the winter woods.

You begin walking through the forest. All is quiet in this winterland. There have been no footprints before yours to mar the landscape; not even a bird twitters in the treetops. All about you is shrouded in an unearthly silence and you feel very alone. Not even the tread of your feet in the snow produces an audible sound.

Deeper and deeper into the forest you wander, and you realize that while you have been walking along night has fallen, but the bright waning moon above reflects off the white snow and illuminates your way.

Soon you come to a small clearing. At the far side of the clearing you see the dark mouth of a cave. The opening looks like the great yawning mouth of some sleeping earth giant. Above the opening, markings are carved into the stone face of the cave front. You move closer to get a better look. You see that they are magickal symbols, ancient sigils of eternity and rebirth. You gently run your fingers over them, wondering who carved these beloved signs and how long they have been here. The presence of these signs warms and comforts you.

Suddenly, the silence of the forest night is broken by faint whisperings coming from deep within the cave, murmurs that seem to be calling out to you with loving voices. Quickly your mind races over all that they could be and, though curious to press on, you wonder at the wisdom of entering uninvited into what is obviously a sacred place.

Deciding to take the symbols as a sign of good intent, you step into the mouth of the cave. The whisperings seem now to come straight out from the depths of the ground below you. Along the wall of the cave are several torch lights. You take one and begin pushing deeper into the cave. As you do, you notice at your feet three distinct pathways, each leading off into its own fissure in the wall—one to the left, one in the center, and one to the right. . . . .

(These fissures represent the paths to the underworld, middleworld, and upperworld respectively. Each time you visit the Summerland you may explore a different one. Suggestions follow for reworking this meditation to fit the images of these Summerland realms.)

Meditation for Exploring the Underworld

. . . You decide to take the path leading into the left fissure and, holding the torch ahead of you, boldly step into it.

The passage is narrow, but not overly close, and you keep moving onward. Along the walls are markings which at first look very much like graffiti. Aside from symbols, some names and dates have been carved here and there, a few of which you recognize, others you do not.

The passageway now turns sharply to the left and continues downward in an ever-tightening spiral. Down and down you go and, just when you feel like you are about to turn right into yourself, the passage ends, opening up into a new world.

It takes a moment for your eyes to adjust to the place in which you find yourself. This is a land in shadow where light is used grudgingly. Yet, even as your torch light fades as if by some holy command, you do not feel especially afraid. For all the darkness, there is an ethereal glow about the place, and you can see ahead of you a river where spectral shapes row themselves up and down, some fighting the current, some flowing with it. Though it is hard to say for sure, you feel as though you recognize some of those beings. For a moment, some of them even seem to see you and wave a fleeting greeting as they continue along.

You walk down to the river's edge and are surprised to discover it is a much wider body of water than you first thought—almost like a small inland sea.

You now notice that someone has rowed a tiny boat over to you. You look up and find yourself face to face with a dark robed figure. Though you can see a serene face, you cannot tell if you are in the presence of a male or a female. The figure makes a gesture you recognize as being friendly, and your gut instinct is to trust this being. Without speaking, it directs you to get into the boat. With little hesitation you do as it wishes, and the figure begins rowing you silently to the distant, fog-shrouded shore.

As you near the mysterious island, you hear a ghostly chorus chanting an ancient dirge. The tune stirs something deep inside you, like some long-repressed memory aching to get out. Your mind races to place the tune in your mind. Your mouth can almost, but not quite, form the words. You are so caught up in the half-familiar song that you are surprised to feel the tiny boat bump the island's shore and see the figure motioning for you to get out.

For a moment you hesitate, wondering how you will get back if this being takes the boat and leaves you, for you surely cannot swim so great a distance. But looking up at its wise and kind face, you know that you will be cared for, and you step out from the boat onto solid ground.

Looking around, you see that the fog is gone and that the air is warm and clear, like that of a midsummer night. The sky above you is midnight black. The moon is dark and no stars dot the heavens. You can sense presences around you, but cannot make any of them out. Somehow you sense you need not fear them.

You know you would like to explore the underworld realm further. . . . (At this point you may call upon a deity, guide, or ancestral spirit to assist you, or you may explore on your own. Go anywhere you like where you feel comfortable. If you come to any barrier, like a gate or a fence, always mentally ask permission to pass through before stumbling in. And don't worry about getting lost. If you cannot retrace your steps to the boat, simply will yourself to be there. Remember that you are in one of the astral realms, a place where all thought is action. In this fluid world, that which you will to happen comes to pass with astounding speed. When you are ready to leave, return to the boat.)

. . . You find that the Summerland does not pull at you to remain in it, and you are now ready to return home. You have learned all you can for this trip, and you know you are free to return at any time.

Just as you knew it would, the dark figure with the boat is waiting patiently for you. You get in and it rows you silently back to the shore, where the entrance to the cave waits.

As the boat bumps the shore, you stumble out and step onto the ground. As you turn to thank the being who rowed you, you find both it and the boat have vanished into the fog. You raise a hand in parting just the same and speak the words: "Merry meet, merry part, and merry meet again." As the final sound of your voice fades in the fog, you swear you hear a spectral chorus chanting out your parting words. The vibrations from their voices seem to echo across the vastness of space and time, then they fall silent in the fog once more.

As you step back into the cave, you find your torch blazing brightly again, hanging on the wall as if it was expecting you. You take it in hand and start the long climb upward.

You finally reach the top and leave the cave, walking back through the woods by the same route you entered. You are astounded to discover that while you have been gone, spring has come to the woods and they are now brimming with the sights, smells, and sounds of new life. (This imagery echoes those of many myths, such as those of Persephone and Kore, where deities retreat into the Summerland in winter and return to Earth in spring.) When you are out of the woods you begin to fly swiftly home again, stopping only when you reach the outside of the place where your body lies waiting.

You feel the pulsating glow of the protective energy around you and know that you are about to return safely to your body and to your normal waking consciousness. You are looking forward to being soon able to contemplate and record your feelings and experiences from this powerful journey.

You enter through the wall of the room under which you lie as if asleep and begin to remember the sensation of being a living, corporeal human being. You again see your resting body surrounded by the golden light, the pentagram, and the shield, all of them doing their job for you just as they were when you left.

You move slowly over your waiting body, as glad to see it as if suddenly discovering an old friend, and you melt into it, saying to yourself the words, "I am home."

Feel the awareness of your physical self return—your legs, arms, back, stomach, and neck. Flex them and relish in the joy of being a living human being. You are once again part of the waking physical world, and you open your eyes and feel exhilarated, energized, and glad to be home.

Meditation for Exploring the Middleworld

. . . You decide to take the path leading into the center fissure and, holding the torch ahead of you, boldly step into it.

The passage is narrow, but not overly close, and you keep moving onward. The path leads straight out from the cave wall. Along the walls you notice small windows that show you scenes, which at first look as if they could be from your own life. But, on closer inspection, they appear to be scenes reflecting choices just the opposite of those you have so far taken in your life.

Suddenly the passage ends, opening up on a high gorge over a raging river. Over the river is a small wooden bridge swinging ominously in the wind. At the end of the bridge is a world of summer bounty, and standing there as if waiting for you is a figure swathed in the verdancy of summer. Though you can make out a serene face from this distance, you cannot tell if you are in the presence of a male or a female. The figure makes a gesture you recognize as being friendly, and motions for you to cross the bridge. You hesitate as you look at the rickety bridge, but the summer meadow beyond is more inviting than the bridge is intimidating. You set down the torch and start across.

As soon as your feet touch the bridge, the wind seems to die as if at your command, and you begin the walk across to the being in green. As you walk along you can hear a ghostly chorus chanting an ancient dirge. The tune stirs something deep inside you, like some long-repressed memory aching to get out. Your mind races to place the tune in your mind. Your mouth can almost, but not quite, form the words. You are so caught up in the half-familiar song that you are surprised to realize you have made it to the other side of the bridge.

The being smiles in welcome and motions for you to go ahead and explore this intriguing world. For a moment you hesitate, wondering how you will find your way back here if you wander too far. But looking up at its wise and kind face, you instinctively know that you have the power to go anywhere in this world you so desire, and you run off into the sunny meadow. . . . (At this point you may call upon a deity, guide, or ancestral spirit to assist you, or you may explore on your own. Go anywhere you like where you feel comfortable. If you come to any barrier, like a gate or a fence, always mentally ask permission to pass through before stumbling in. And don't worry about getting lost. If you cannot retrace your steps to the bridge, simply will yourself to be there. Remember that you are in one of the astral realms, a place where all thought is action. In this fluid world, that which you will to happen comes to pass with astounding speed. When you are ready to leave, return to the bridge.)

. . . You find that the Summerland does not pull at you to remain in it, and you are now ready to return home. You have learned all you can for this trip, and you know you are free to return at any time.

Just as you knew it would, the figure in green waits patiently for you. You start across the bridge again, then turn to thank the being who encouraged you, but you find your guide has vanished into the green backdrop of the meadow. You raise a hand in parting just the same and speak the words: "Merry meet, merry part, and merry meet again." As the final sound of your voice fades in the fog, you swear you hear a spectral chorus chanting out your parting words. The vibrations from their voices seem to echo across the vastness of space and time, then they fall silent again, blending with the sounds of summer.

You pick up your torch and step back into the cave, starting the long walk back. You finally reach the opening and leave the cave, walking back through the woods by the same route you entered. You are astounded to discover that while you have been gone, spring has come to the woods and they are now brimming with the sights, smells, and sounds of new life. (This imagery echoes those of many myths, such as those of Persephone and Kore, where deities retreat into the Summerland in winter and return to Earth in spring.) When you are out of the woods you begin to fly swiftly home again, stopping only when you reach the outside of the place where your body lies waiting.

You feel the pulsating glow of the protective energy around you and know that you are about to return safely to your body and to your normal waking consciousness. You are looking forward to being soon able to contemplate and record your feelings and experiences from this powerful journey.

You enter through the wall of the room under which you lie as if asleep and begin to remember the sensation of being a living, corporeal human being. You again see your resting body surrounded by the golden light, the pentagram, and the shield, all of them doing their job for you just as they were when you left.

You move slowly over your waiting body, as glad to see it as if suddenly discovering an old friend, and you melt into it, saying to yourself the words, "I am home."

Feel the awareness of your physical self return—your legs, arms, back, stomach, and neck. Flex them and relish in the joy of being a living human being. You are once again part of the waking physical world, and you open your eyes and feel exhilarated, energized, and glad to be home.

Meditation for Exploring the Upperworld

. . . You decide to take the path leading into the right fissure and, holding the torch ahead of you, boldly step into it.

The passage is narrow, but not overly close, and you keep moving onward. It turns sharply to the right and takes you upward in a tight spiral, which after a while begins to loosen its coil somewhat. As you continue, you notice that the passageway is widening as well as losing its circular feeling. Here the walls have lost their rocky appearance and are beginning to look crystalline, as if they possess a life energy all their own. Flashes of light catch your eyes, flashes which seem to be coming from deep within the walls. Up and up you go and, just when you feel like you have gone as high as humanly possible, the passage ends, opening up into a new world.

It takes a moment for your eyes to adjust to the place in which you find yourself. This is a land in light and color where shadow is used grudgingly. Your torch is pale in comparison with this world, and you set it down, forgotten and useless in this land of light. You can see ahead of you a vast ocean with waves of translucent blue slapping the shore. Though it is hard to say for sure, you are struck with an uncanny feeling that you have been here before.

You walk down to the water's edge and are surprised to be met by a tall figure draped in pure light. Though you can see a serene face, you cannot tell if you are in the presence of a male or a female. The figure makes a gesture you recognize as being friendly, and your gut instinct is to trust this being. It points toward an island that now rises from the mist far out in the ocean. As it appears you can hear majestic music haunting the air around you, as if the very universe is singing with joy at the appearance of this magickal isle.

Without speaking, the being in light communicates to you with its mind, asking if you would like to visit the island. Your mind tells it that you would. From the back of the being, two silver wings begin to beat the air, making a musical counterpoint to that which already enraptures you. Without hesitation you take the being's arm, and you both fly up over the ocean toward the island.

As you near the mysterious island, you hear a ghostly chorus chanting an ancient dirge. The tune stirs something deep inside you, like some long-repressed memory aching to get out. Your mind races to place the tune in your mind. Your mouth can almost, but not quite, form the words. You are so caught up in the half-familiar song that you are surprised to feel the being settling you down on the sunny shore of the island.

For a moment you hesitate, wondering how you will get back if this being leaves you behind, for you surely cannot swim so great a distance. But looking up at its wise and kind face, you instinctively know that you will be cared for, and you turn to explore this enchanting realm.

The dome of sky above you is a brilliant blue-white. All around this warm, crystalline world seem to be beings of light. You know you would like to explore the upperworld realm further. . . . (At this point you may call upon a deity, guide, or ancestral spirit to assist you, or you may explore on your own. Go anywhere you like where you feel comfortable. If you come to any barrier, like a gate or a fence, always mentally ask permission to pass through before stumbling in. And don't worry about getting lost. If you cannot retrace your steps to the ocean shore, simply will yourself to be there. Remember that you are in one of the astral realms, a place where all thought is action. In this fluid world, that which you will to happen comes to pass with astounding speed. When you are ready to leave, return to the shore.)

. . . You find that the Summerland does not pull at you to remain in it, and you are now ready to return home. You have learned all you can for this trip, and you know you are free to return at any time.

Just as you knew it would, the figure of light awaits you at the ocean's shore. You again take the being's arm and fly swiftly to the land where the entrance to the cave awaits.

As the being sets you down, you turn to say your thanks, but you find your guide has vanished into the light. You raise a hand in parting just the same and speak the words: "Merry meet, merry part, and merry meet again." As the final sound of your voice fades in the fog, you swear you hear a spectral chorus chanting out your parting words. The vibrations from their voices seem to echo across the vastness of space and time, then they fall silent once more.

You take your torch from where you left it and step back into the cave to start the long descent back to the winter woods. You finally reach the bottom and leave the cave, walking back through the woods by the same route you entered. You are astounded to discover that while you have been gone, spring has come to the woods and they are now brimming with the sights, smells, and sounds of new life. (This imagery echoes those of many myths, such as those of Persephone and Kore, where deities retreat into the Summerland in winter and return to Earth in spring.) When you are out of the woods you begin to fly swiftly home again, stopping only when you reach the outside of the place where your body lies waiting.

You feel the pulsating glow of the protective energy around you and know that you are about to return safely to your body and to your normal waking consciousness. You are looking forward to being soon able to contemplate and record your feelings and experiences from this powerful journey.

You enter through the wall of the room under which you lie as if asleep and begin to remember the sensation of being a living, corporeal human being. You again see your resting body surrounded by the golden light, the pentagram, and the shield, all of them doing their job for you just as they were when you left.

You move slowly over your waiting body, as glad to see it as if suddenly discovering an old friend, and you melt into it saying to yourself the words, "I am home."

Feel the awareness of your physical self return—your legs, arms, back, stomach, and neck. Flex them and relish in the joy of being a living human being. You are once again part of the waking physical world, and you open your eyes and feel exhilarated, energized, and glad to be home.

Three

Rituals to Assist a Dying Spirit

CHANCES ARE THAT AT SOME POINT IN EACH OF
our lives we will know someone who is terminally
ill. If that person is a close friend or a family member, he or she may come to us to ask our help in
making a peaceful transition to the Summerland.
Or, that person may ask us to arrange for the
transfer of healing energy to help prolong life. The
decision to do either of these things should be
carefully considered by both the petitioner and the
assistant, discussed in detail beforehand, and, if
this course of action is chosen, it should be followed through in full accordance with the will of
the one in need.

Warning: The two rituals in this chapter are designed to be used *only at the request of someone who is terminally ill* to assist him or her in making a peaceful transition into the world of spirit, or to help him or her have the strength to continue on. The ethics of Paganism as well as basic respect for human life and free will demand that express permission be given by the dying person before either of these rituals is enacted on his or her behalf. It cannot be overstated that these are rituals of assistance only, and that express permission for performing them must be obtained by the one who is terminally ill. I would go so far as to advise you to wait until you are approached. To avoid both karmic retribution and legal entanglements, get permission first! Any less is interference with free will at the least, and psychic murder at the most. In the case of the ritual designed to assist in a peaceful transition, it should be done out of the presence of the dying person to avoid any hint of coercion. As with any magick or ritual, it is wisest to keep the precise goal to yourself, especially in situations such as these where the emotions of other loved ones can run irrationally high.

Both rituals in this chapter, as well as some presented later in this book, require the casting of a magickal/ritual circle. For those unfamiliar with this process, as well as the creation and setting up of an altar, a format to follow, complete with explanations of each step, is presented first. Those who already have a method for doing this and who are not looking to change it may continue on with the body of the rituals beginning on page 68.

❧ Creating and Setting Up an Altar

For those who have never set up an altar for private ritual before, there is no mystery in doing so. The word *altar* comes from the Latin *altare* and means "a high place" (read "exalted"). When placed in a religious setting, the altar becomes a focal point for the ritual and is a resting place for the divine forces that are being called upon and/or worshiped. On the practical side, an altar serves as a place to organize and set out tools and other items that will be needed during the rite, or which lend ambiance to the occasion (like evergreen bows during a winter solstice ritual).

You don't need anything fancy to serve the altar's function. Any sturdy and flat surface can be used: small tables, flat stones, boxes, dresser tops, et cetera, have all been employed. After you have designated your altar, follow the six-step method for setting it up:

Cleanse

Clothe

Orient

Arrange

Decorate

Use

The first step is to ritually cleanse and purify the chosen altar by one of several means. You can wipe down the surface with a clean white cloth that has been dampened with lightly salted water (but do not use salted water if your surface is wooden), or water in which a bit of the herb mugwort has been mixed (mugwort water is often used to purify and cleanse magickal mirrors and crystals, and works equally well on altars). You might choose instead to bathe the altar in the smoke of a purifying incense such as sage, frankincense, or cinnamon. Or, you could place your hands on the top surface and visualize your personal energy pushing out the old energies of the altar and sending them harmlessly into Mother Earth.

You should always cleanse your altar before the first time you use it, but you do not have to cleanse the altar every time you use it. Let your own inner senses guide you as to when the altar needs to be psychically cleansed. This might be after a great number of others have used it and you now wish to use it for a solitary ritual, or when you feel a negative emotion has become imprinted on it, or when it is regularly used for mundane purposes such as a chest of drawers. Perhaps you just feel better refreshing it every third new moon or so, and this is fine too.

If this is the first time you have used your altar, and you plan to make using it a habit, it is traditional to offer a blessing on the altar to further align its energies with your purposes. One way to do this is by touching it, or by touching one of your ritual tools to its surface, and stating aloud your blessing. This might sound something like:

> *Blessed be now and always this altar which graces my circle. May it*
> *be a fit resting place for positive energies. May it witness only positive*
> *acts. May it serve only positive functions. So mote it be!*

The next step is optional, but commonly done, and that is to clothe the altar with some type of altar cloth. The cloth you choose does not have to be elaborate; it needs to be no more than a piece of cloth that covers the surface. This serves to create atmosphere, to protect the altar's surface, and to help mask the "real" identity of the item in the mundane world. Shutting off those mundane associations helps you concentrate on the task at hand. For instance, if you are using the work island of your kitchen for an altar, you don't need to be reminded in the middle of your ritual that you need to chop some lettuce later for dinner salads.

What color the cloth is, how it is decorated, and how far it drapes down over the sides of the surface is not really important. Many Pagans use a basic black cotton cloth for most of their rituals. Black is neutral, absorbing of light, and traditional. Cotton is usually chosen because natural fabrics are preferred to synthetics, and cotton is a lot less expensive than wool or silk. Some Pagans will change the color of the altar cloth with the changing seasons or in accordance with the specific type of rite being performed; for example, they might choose red at the winter solstice, gold at the summer solstice, white for handfastings (Pagan marriages), and black for passing-over rituals. Currently cotton print fabrics are available with stellar designs that would make attractive altar cloths or ritual robes. If you are handy with a needle and enjoy embroidering, you might consider personalizing your altar cloth with runes, sigils, symbols, or names as the mood moves you.

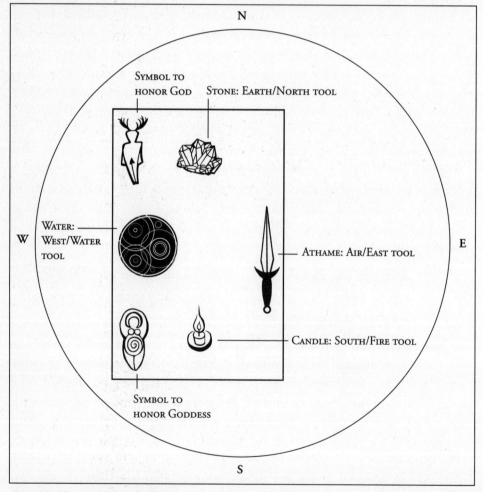

Example of a west–oriented altar.

When you are ready to perform a ritual, you will need to place your altar in the area where you will be casting your circle (if it is not already permanently placed there). Altars usually do not sit in the middle of the circle, since this can impede the traffic flow even if you are going to be the only one doing the ritual. Instead the altar is set off to the side of the circle in one of the four cardinal directions (or sometimes at a point halfway between them), and is usually facing outward (see illustration below). Some Pagan traditions dictate in which quarter the altar will be placed for all or certain rituals. For the purposes of rituals concerned with death, the altar should be in the quarter you or your tradition view as being the direction of the Summerland. In my tradition this is the west, in some others it is the north.

When the altar is clothed and in place, you may arrange your tools and/or other items on it. Again, some Pagan traditions dictate which tools will be used and in what part of the altar they will reside. If you are with a group you will have to work this out among yourselves, and if you are alone you can decide these associations for yourself. Should you need guidance, use the example given here, or read any of the books available on basic Wiccan/Pagan practice to find other ideas along with the reasoning behind them.

If you wish to decorate the altar with items of the season, or items that are symbolic of the ritual you are about to undertake, do this now. You may place on your altar any items you feel are appropriate; for example, in rituals concerning life renewal, eggs, apples, and apple blossoms are all good choices.

❧ Opening and Closing a Ritual Circle

If you are new to Paganism/Wicca and are unfamiliar with opening a circle, the following ritual will take you step by step through this process. The way of opening (sometimes referred to as "casting") and closing (sometimes referred to as "grounding") a circle presented here is not the only way in which this can be done (i.e. not the only correct words, gestures, movements, et cetera), but it is a method that follows the standard pattern used by many other Pagans, and it is one that is easy for newcomers to understand and utilize.

As was explained earlier, the purpose of the circle is two-fold: one, to protect those inside it from outside forces, and two, to contain raised energy until the ritualist(s) is (are) ready to release it toward its goal. The word *circle* has been in the English language since its earliest incarnation, and is thought to be derived from the classical Greek word *kirkos* meaning "ring." I find this etymology of the word particularly nice to think about when referring to a magickal/ritual circle because of the symbolic association of the word *ring* with trust, fidelity, and partnership—all positive attributes for those inside the circle to have.

To cast a circle you will need only yourself and some uncluttered, private space in which to work. You may choose to use a ritual tool such as an athame (a double-edged ritual knife that is never permitted to cut anything physical) or a wand to assist you, but the projected energy from your own body will serve the purpose just as well. If you are unsure of your directions, then you will need a compass to point them out for you. When you have pinpointed north, south, east, and west, mark them in some way so that they will be easy for you to find again. You might do this by placing a candle or stone at each point, or you might orient your altar in the direction of your choice so that it will be a marker to show you which direction is which. I recommend using a method that clearly marks the directions at the end boundaries of your circle, since it is wise to know just where your circle ends and to remain inside it until the rite is complete. In an emergency, or where a ritual demands temporary exit, you may "cut" a doorway in the circle to go out and reenter, but it is not a good habit to get into. The circle is not an interesting decoration, something that was fun to cast; it is there for reasons of protection and containment. To poke holes in it may allow some of the energy you are raising to leak out and it might offer an opportunity for unwelcome spirits or energies to come in. Until you are used to working within a circle, it is best to follow custom.

To begin, stand in the center of the area in which your circle will be cast. If you are with a coven or a group, your acting leader will likely take the center place and will ask the rest of you to stand around the perimeter of the circle. In either case, spend a few moments in quiet contemplation, centering your energies before beginning.

Some Pagans like to purify the circle area before they begin by blessing the area with lightly salted water or smoke from sage incense (the latter known as "smudging" in Native American traditions). Others will take a broom, which when used as a tool in Paganism is called a besom, and sweep out negative and unwanted energies from the circle area. If you wish to do either of these things, do so now while focusing on the meaning of the ritual you are about to undertake.

When you have purified the area and are ready to continue, walk to the quarter where you, or your tradition, deem the casting of the circle should begin. For many traditions this is in the east, though this may vary depending on the type of rite being performed. To keep things simple, this example will begin with the east.

Hold your tool or your power arm (the dominant one, the one you write with), with forefinger pointed out, at the starting point. Neither your tool nor your finger needs to be touching the ground. Begin walking slowly clockwise, drawing a circle around you. Clockwise is the traditional direction associated with growth, increase, construction, gain, et cetera. Most circles are cast in this direction and closed by moving counterclockwise. However, in some cases the opposite is true. For example, banishing rituals, those designed to remove some influence or problem, are often cast and closed in the opposite directions. This does not mean that the act to take place is negative; negative rituals can just as easily take place in a circle cast clockwise. Only the intent of the ritualist makes this call.

Move completely around the inner edge of the circle until you have reached the starting point again, all the while visualizing an intense blue-white light growing around you. Send as much energy into the creation of the circle as you can. Make it real, and then respect its reality. So many newcomers ignore the circle's power and tend to skimp on the steps used to cast it. Remember that in Paganism we see our minds as capable of doing anything and everything, and we know that those things it creates are as real as something we would create with a hammer, nail, and block of wood.

There is more than one way to visualize the completed circle. Some like to see this as a dome growing over them, and others as a sphere surrounding the area. Any of these is correct. Do what best speaks to you of an impenetrable barrier that sets you apart in time and space from the mundane world.

Once you are back at your eastern starting point, hold your tool or arm (with forefinger again extending up) and call out to invite the powers of the east. This process, which will be repeated at each cardinal point, is commonly known as "calling the quarters." Other names for it are "summoning the wards" (or "watchtowers"), "calling the elementals" (astral world beings who are connected to each element and whose energies can aid magick and ritual), or "calling the spirits of the elements" (another way of saying "calling the elementals"). The wording you will find below assumes this call is an invitation, though you may change it to be a summons or command if you like. If you do, keep in mind just who and what you are calling on. It is generally accepted that the watchtowers, guardian spirits of the directions, and some elementals can be commanded. The elements that come on command are usually the ones that have become traditionally associated with a particular element through contact with ceremonial magick (based on Middle Eastern mystical systems). These are sylphs for air, salamanders for fire, undines for water, and gnomes for earth. Other elemental spirits, such as faery folk, discarnate human spirits, and all deities, should be invited, never commanded.

Each element is thought to be one of the four basic building blocks from which all physical things are made. This idea is an ancient one accepted today in virtually all traditions of Pagan and ceremonial magick. We call these elements in with the quarters both as a courtesy to these powers, and to evoke their protective and magickal influences.

If you are in a group situation, it is likely that different people will be given the honor of calling each quarter. After the call, there will probably be a unison response from the group offering welcome or blessings. If you are alone, naturally you will have to do all this yourself. As you call each quarter, you may carry with you the tool of the element, the one at your altar representing that direction/element. For example, if you were calling the west, you might carry your chalice or bowl of water, and if you were calling the south, you might carry a lit candle. This is a nice addition and can further help you link yourself with the element you are calling, but it is not a prerequisite to a successful quarter call. You may go alone or with just one tool, such as a wand you use to direct energy.

Just which element corresponds with which direction, and what tools are chosen to represent them, vary from tradition to tradition. For the purposes of this example, the standard Wiccan correspondences will be used: air to the east, fire to the south, water to the west, and earth to the north. This example will also assume that you are calling the quarters either without tools or with only one tool that you will carry with you the entire way. If you do choose to use a different tool for each call, you will need to return to your altar between each call, replace the previous tool, and pick up the next one (then follow the same process in reverse when you dismiss the quarters later on).

Facing the east, say the following while visualizing your voice carrying out to the farthest reaches of that direction, covering the vastness of time and space:

> *Watchtowers, guardians, elementals, and insightful powers of the east,*
> *I* (or *we* if you are in a group situation) *ask your breezy, cleansing*
> *presence at this circle tonight. Guard, protect, and worship with me*
> (or *us*) *this night* (or *day* as the case may be). *Join me* (or *us*) *in*
> (state purpose of your rite here). *Welcome, powers of air, and*
> *blessed be.*

Some traditions require that a bell be sounded or a drum beaten as the quarter call is finished. Personally, I am not fond of this practice as I feel it frightens away certain types of spirit life who may be beneficial to your workings. On the other hand, it may also chase away spirits you do not want at your circle, so the choice is yours to make.

Walk to the southern edge of the circle (moving clockwise) and raise your arms again, saying:

> *Watchtowers, guardians, elementals, and passionate powers of the south,*
> *I ask your fiery, transformative presence at this circle tonight. Guard,*
> *protect, and worship with me this night. Join me in* (state purpose of
> your rite here). *Welcome, powers of fire, and blessed be.*

Next, move to the west and call:

> *Watchtowers, guardians, elementals, and fertile powers of the west,*
> *I ask your gentle, purifying presence at this circle tonight. Guard,*
> *protect, and worship with me this night. Join me in* (state purpose
> of your rite here). *Welcome, powers of water, and blessed be.*

Lastly, move to the north and say:

> *Watchtowers, guardians, elementals, and powers of the stable north,*
> *I ask your sturdy, comforting presence at this circle tonight. Guard,*
> *protect, and worship with me this night. Join me in* (state purpose
> of your rite here). *Welcome, powers of earth, and blessed be.*

After the north quarter has been called, walk back to the east to complete the circle before returning to your altar for the rest of the ritual. At this point, before doing anything else, you may wish to walk the perimeters of the circle again, or even twice more. Many traditions feel that a circle should be cast more than once. The number chosen is usually in keeping with the spiritual teachings of the culture on which the particular tradition is based. For example, many Celtic Pagans cast the circle three times, three being the sacred number of that culture.

When the casting is complete, you have successfully done what is termed "opening the circle." You may now call upon your personal deities, inviting them to your circle in your own words, or continue on with the body of your ritual. If you do choose to ask deities to your circle, be sure to light a candle or erect some type of statuary or symbol in their honor. This gives you a focal point for their presence within your circle and pays homage to them.

After the body of whatever ritual you are doing is completed, you will need to close the circle by the same method you cast it, only doing everything in reverse order.

Before you "un-cast" the circle, walk to the last quarter you called to begin dismissing them one by one. In the example, this would be the north. Again, the tone is not one of command, but of release, as you say:

> *Thank you, powers of the north, for your presence here this night* (or
> *day), and for lending your stable energies to this* (state purpose of ritual
> here). *Go now with my* (or *our*) *blessings and my* (or *our*) *thanks.*

You may use a bell or a drum beat to dismiss the quarters, even if you did not use it to call them. These sounds tend to raise the vibrations of an area, purifying it and banishing unwanted beings that may have become attracted to the energy you raised in your circle. Using bells and drums at this point makes much more sense to me than using them to call the quarters in the first place, since you usually want the area cleared of spirit life, both the pleasant and the unpleasant, before you dismiss your circle. If you choose to use either of these, sound them now, after the quarter dismissal is complete. Do the same at each quarter.

Next, move counterclockwise to the west and say:

> *Thank you, powers of the west, for your presence here this night, and*
> *for lending your fertile energies to this* (state purpose of ritual here).
> *Go now with my blessings and my thanks.*

Then to the south, say:

> *Thank you, powers of the south, for your presence here this night, and*
> *for lending your passionate energies to this* (state purpose of ritual here).
> *Go now with my blessings and my thanks.*

And lastly, to your starting point in the east, say:

> *Thank you, powers of the east, for your presence here this night, and*
> *for lending your insightful energies to this* (state purpose of ritual here).
> *Go now with my blessings and my thanks.*

Starting in the east again, take your tool or forefinger and begin walking the perimeter of the circle counterclockwise. You are now grounding or closing the circle, and you should be visualizing the energy you raised to create it either being sent into Mother Earth or being reabsorbed into your finger or tool. You may do this only once, or you may walk the circle again as many times as you did to cast it. I find that once is sufficient, but you may prefer more.

Once the circle is closed, you may make a statement acknowledging this; a simple phrase such as, "The circle is closed but always part of me," works well. Groups often have their own unison statement and response, sometimes ending with the traditional Wiccan closing, "Merry meet, merry part, and merry meet again."

A Ritual to Help the Dying Live to Fight Another Day

This ritual is designed to give someone who is dying the boost of renewed energy needed to remain alive in the face of a life-threatening illness or an injury. While some terminally ill persons opt to refuse medical treatment and thus hasten their demise, others refuse to give up the fight to remain in this life. While both paths are difficult choices for someone terminally ill to make, particularly if he or she is suffering from pain, there are many reasons why someone might choose the latter path. Perhaps there is a project they wish to complete first before letting go, such as a book to finish writing or a musical composition to complete. Perhaps they just want to live a few more months to see a child married or graduated from college, or see a first grandchild born. Perhaps there is a promising new treatment for their ailment which won't be available for a few more months and they are determined to be around to give it a try. Maybe the dying person just wants to extend life for as long as possible.

This ritual can be done by one person alone, but is most effective with lots of help. Covens or groups with members skilled in sending energy can do the best job; group directions will be given here, but a solitary person may enact this ritual as well. The rite works in much the same way as many healing rites in which a massive supply of energy is sent into the person who needs the healing. This goal has traditionally been accomplished by using one person, or a gathering of persons, in a circle as a channel. The collective energy is then sent, either through touch or imagery, into the body of the person who needs it for healing, who is usually, but not always, present in the circle. Several methods can be used to affect this transfer. Sometimes energy is drawn up from Mother Earth or down from above (by visualization and will, a process that grows easier with practice) and transferred to the sick person. Other times energy is raised within the circle itself by chanting, dancing, singing, et cetera. In these cases the energy is sent swirling around the cluster of people in the circle in a clockwise motion and, at the appropriate time, is sent inward in a spiral motion to reach the person at the circle's center who most needs the healing.

As with other types of healing rituals, Pagan ethics demand we get express permission for the ritual from the dying person in need of our help. Do not assume on behalf of someone who cannot clearly make their wishes known that you should do this for them. And do not assume that just because someone does not believe in the power of your ritual, and will not ask for your help or grant you permission for it, that you have the right to step in and make this choice for them. If you were in their position, would you want someone making this decision for you? Probably not.

You need no special tools for this rite, only your physical selves as channels for life energy. You will also need a leader to help direct the action and cue everyone else as to when to raise and send energy, et cetera. If you have a regular priest or priestess you wish to have fill this role, that is fine. If not, try to select someone in your group who is either skilled in energy manipulation or who has the requisite psychic abilities to sense when the energies you raise are ready to be directed toward their goal.

Whether the ill person will physically be with you or not during the rite, cast your circle in your usual manner, calling on the quarters, deities, et cetera, all as you normally would. Having the ill person present and participating is the best case scenario, but sometimes severe illness or disability can prevent this from happening.

After the preliminary rites of circle casting are concluded, the leader should state aloud the purpose of the ritual so that everyone can align their personal energies with the goal. After that, at the leader's direction, everyone should begin to work together to raise as much healing, life-sustaining energy as possible. Dancing, stomping, kicking—any expansive movements which make people feel fully alive—will work. A chant might even be chosen to accompany the action, such as one of the following:

> Life is precious, life is rare,
> A part of life we come to share.
>
> Raise we now the life and power,
> To send to one in need this hour.

The chant might even be personalized to include the name of the person on whose behalf this ritual is being done.

To avoid cluttering up the text with too many uses of "his or her" and "he or she," I will designate the leader of the first ritual in this chapter a "she" and the one on whose behalf the ritual is worked a "he." In the solitary rite which follows, the gender roles will be reversed. This does not reflect on the ability of either sex to lead or perform the rituals; it is merely a device to smooth out the text for easy reading.

If the Dying Person is Present

When the leader has decreed that the energy in the circle has peaked, she will signal for the terminally ill person to stand in the circle's center. Circles are always conceptualized as a time and a place set apart from "normal" reality. They are places at the center of all worlds and at the meeting point of all times. The ill person should sit in the center of the circle representing that he is within reach of all that ever was, is, or will be.

The rest of the group or coven should form a tight circle around the person and place their dominant hands onto the ill person's head. With their non-dominant hands they should reach upward, as if trying to grasp onto the life force of the universe (or, of you prefer the term, the divine). The dominant hand is the one to which you are oriented, i.e. are you right-handed or left-handed? If you are right-handed, then your right hand is dominant. The dominant hand is the one usually thought best for sending out energy, and the non-dominant hand is the one usually thought best for receiving energy.

As this is happening, the ill person should be visualizing all the deadly sickness flowing from him and being channeled harmlessly into the ground under which he sits. He should feel this negative energy vacating his body and making room for the positive, life-sustaining energy that will take its place during the remainder of the ritual.

At the leader's direction, each individual should draw down the life-giving energy from above, using whatever visualization works best for the individual. As the energy flows into the group through the raised non-dominant hands, it should be visualized as being directed out through the dominant hands and into the dying person. Keep this mental picture going for as long as you can: the more energy you give, the better for the person who needs it.

Do not worry about depleting your own personal energy stores during this rite. One of the "secrets" experienced magickal folk know is that you can only dangerously weaken yourself if you are giving out large doses of your own energy. In this ritual, you are drawing down energy from the universe/divine that is merely being channeled and focused through you—it was not yours to begin with, you are only the tool shaping its flow. You cannot weaken yourself or expose yourself to illness or harm by drawing down and passing along this energy. In fact, by using yourself as a channel for positive energy, when the rite is done you will most likely find that you feel a renewed burst of energy and well-being.

When the leader senses that all the energy that can be absorbed by the ill person has been given, she will direct everyone to finish sending out the energy that has already been drawn down. Everyone will then take their hands off the center person, who will remain where he is as the rest of the group joins hands in a circle around him.

Everyone should visualize the sick person being filled with a brilliant light, which symbolizes and contains the life energy that has been given to him. Then, see a beam of God- or Goddess-inspired gold-white light coming straight down from above, passing through the person and into the earth, providing a beam of energy on which that person can draw in the days to come. Allow everyone, including the one in need, to visualize good wishes for the future of the sick person, extra time brought thanks to this ritual.[1]

The leader should allow this to go on as long as she senses it is productive. Allowing the visualizations to begin fading in intensity will weaken the rite. At this point, the leader should voice the results of the rite aloud, and always in the present tense, as is traditional with positive magick. To phrase the desired outcome of any spell or ritual in the future tense is thought to keep the need in the future, always just out of reach. For this ritual, the affirmation of the results might sound something like this:

> (Name of person), *the light of health and life shines in and through you. By the will of those who love you, including our Lord and Lady, arise and live. So mote it be!*

The ill person should stand, but remain in the center of the circle. If it is desired at this point, the leader may go around the circle asking each person present to voice a special blessing for the dying person. This is optional and should be done with careful consideration for the personal feelings and level of tiredness of the one for whom the ritual was performed (you don't want him to spend all his renewed life-energy just enduring the rest of the ritual). The blessings may be given along with tokens or talismans, which can help the person draw on the energy of the rite when it is needed. These blessings should be simple and sound something like: "I bless you with inner strength," "I bless you with sparkling good health," or "I bless you with unlimited willpower."

When you are finished, the circle should be closed in the usual manner, and any excess energy grounded.

You might consider having a small feast after the ritual. This, of course, must be done with consideration to any dietary restrictions the ill person may have. Within these limitations, a light and well-balanced meal focused on further raising healing energies works very well.[2] This ritual can be repeated as often as is needed. The only prerequisite is that the dying person give consent for it to be performed on his behalf, and that those present feel they are up to the demands of the rite.

If the Dying Person is Present, but Bedridden

The ritual can be done in the same manner as above, but the dominant hands of those doing the rite should be placed on the non-dominant hand of the ill person. If this is not possible, place the hands on the solar plexus or heart area, both of which are chakra (energy) centers that can readily absorb your gifts of energy.

If the Dying Person is Not Present

As the energy is raised, it should be visualized as a growing cone rising high over the group. This tower of energy is known in many Pagan circles as the "Cone of Power." When the leader recognizes that the energy in the cone has reached its peak, she will direct that the action stop and the cone be sent to the ill person.

Methods of sending the cone vary from group to group. Some raise their arms in unison to send it, others collapse. Some shout, while others turn from facing the inside of the circle to facing the outside. One group might symbolically cut a hole in the ceiling over the circle to allow it to escape, and another group might make throwing motions as they send it away. Whichever action signals to the group mind the idea of sending energy is what is best to use. Of course, all of these physical actions must be accompanied with the clear visualization of sending out the cone.

❧ A Ritual Prayer to Help Release
the Spirit of One Who is Dying

Warning: Again, Pagan ethics demand we get express permission for this type of rite. Even if you feel you are the person closest to the one dying, and feel you absolutely know her wishes, you still have no right to perform such a ritual on anyone's behalf without their express consent. Just as it is accepted Pagan practice to ask permission to send healing energy, et cetera, to someone else, we must also ask for permission to help someone pass over.

The following is a ritual constructed to assist the spirit of someone terminally ill to gently leave the earthly body, if this is the conscious choice she wishes to make. You might at first think of it as a Pagan form of assisted suicide; however, this ritual is not designed to be used to "kill" anyone. In fact, it will not function this way because the decision to leave the body remains the free will of the person who is dying; this ritual might best be viewed as a prayer to request a peaceful transition. During this rite you will only be opening the door of opportunity from a remote location. The choice of whether or not the spirit passes through it will not be up to you.

Deciding to do this ritual, even when you are requested to do so by someone with all their faculties who clearly knows what they are asking, is not always easy. Most of us rebel at the thought of a loved one dying, even when he or she is hopelessly in pain. And we have all heard enough of those last-minute miracle recovery stories to make us leery of encouraging a quick end.

For both legal and psychological reasons, this ritual is best done from a remote location—in other words, away from the presence of the one who is dying. Consider the option: someone sees you in a hospital or hospice room brandishing a ritual knife and calling on deities to come take the dying soul. This could easily land you on the bad end of a wrongful death suit. Also, if the dying person changes her mind about wanting your help making the transition, she will not need to be faced with your ritual in a weakened condition. Such an act—especially if the dying person is no longer in a position to stop it—could be viewed as coercive, and this takes us into the no-no realm of manipulative magick.

Begin this ritual at the precise time selected for you by the dying person who, though she will not be present, will nonetheless be aware that the rite is taking place and can mentally tune into it if she chooses.

Erect your altar and cast your circle in your usual manner. Be sure to orient the altar to face the direction you feel marks the direction of the Land of the Dead. In addition to other items on your altar, for this specific rite you will need to have on your altar one tool with which you can direct energy and symbolically cut a doorway in your circle, two unlit candles, and some matches. Wands and ritual knives are popular choices for this, but you may use whatever feels right to you. All other items at this time are unnecessary, but they may be included as you wish.

It is perfectly permissible to have other persons inside the circle with you if they feel close to the dying person and can agree to stay there until the ritual is complete, but my personal feeling is that privacy works best here. Keep in mind that you are performing this rite at the request of the dying person—and for no other reason—and that if privacy is requested, then you must either respect that wish or decline to do the ritual. There are also the practical considerations: you don't need people unfamiliar with the rules of the circle passing haphazardly in and out of it while you are trying to work, and you certainly don't need them questioning later whether you somehow "murdered" the dying person, even though you were not in her presence at the time and you had express permission.

When you are ready to begin, stand before the altar and spend as much time as you need meditating on the cycles of life, death, and rebirth. Allow yourself to sense your place in this great circle of time. When you are ready to continue, lift your chosen tool in the air above you to connect it with the energies that propel the universe. If you like, you may evoke a deity who is special to you to watch over the proceedings.

Next, point the tool in the general direction of the dying person and speak to her announcing your intent. "Speak" in this case is a metaphor for any sort of communication you feel is appropriate. Certainly mentally going through the dialogue is just as effective as speaking aloud, particularly since you are doing all this at a location away from the dying person. Perhaps she will even request which method she prefers you to use.

> (Name of person), *though your earthly shell is feeble and tired, your spirit is strong. Let it feel and know my words. The gates of the Summerland are open to you, as are the gates of life. Two paths, full of love and adventure, await your command. The choice of the two is yours. Those who love you, in this world and in the next, want only what you want. Noble spirit, eternal and strong, possessed of free will: your choices are respected here, they are ever yours to make. At your bidding, I open now the gate to the Summerland that you may either gently and peacefully pass through its portals into joy and warmth and love of new adventures at your will. Or, if you choose instead the path of life, to know that the other path is still open to you at any time you decide to explore it. May the path you take be*

a gentle one on which you never hunger, never thirst, and all your
dreams come true.

If the dying person has a patron deity, and you have discussed the role of that deity in this ritual with the person beforehand, you may call upon the deity now to comfort the dying person. Perhaps the deity will become an escort into the Summerland, or perhaps he or she will counsel the person to remain in this life a bit longer and will impart her the strength to do so. To allow the choice of function to be the deity's and not yours, be sure to word your invocation to this deity in non-specific terms, ones which do not clarify a role for it. You may then allow yourself some time to pray to the deity, stating your desire for the dying person to be able to exercise her free will.

After this, continue by addressing the dying person:

> *Your loving* (insert name of deity)*, who had been with you*
> *throughout this life, is at your side to comfort you now.*

Pause in silence for a time to allow the person to commune with the deity in whatever manner she sees fit. Though you will not be present to witness this, trust that the person for whom the rite is being done will know the patron deity is present.

If you are not calling upon a patron deity, you will still need some time in silence to allow the spirit of your dying friend to acquire the sense of peace this ritual is ultimately designed to give. Remember, this is not a ritual to force death, only one which softens the transition, whenever it may take place.

When you get a mental sense that it is time to continue, address the dying person once more:

> (Name of person)*, know that you will be missed when you travel on,*
> *but, like myself, take comfort in the knowledge that you shall return*
> *to this plane by and by. Love never dies, but seeks its own over and*
> *over again. The gates are both open, the paths are illuminated.*
> *May all your transitions be blessed with peace, joy, and abiding love.*
> *So mote it be!*

Take the matches and one of the unlit candles and go to the west end of the circle (or another end if that is where your tradition views the Summerland) and cut a doorway with your tool. Light the candle and place it in the doorway. The candle not only serves to protect the opening in the circle, but symbolically lights the pathway to the Summerland. You may sing, hum, chant, or meditate on the path leading to the Summerland.

Next, take the other unlit candles and go to the east end of the circle (or another end if that is the one your tradition associates with life or new beginnings) and with your tool, cut a doorway. Light the candle and place it in the doorway. You may sing, hum, chant, or meditate on the path of physical life.

Now that you have opened both gates for your friend, you may close down the ritual. Without re-closing either of the portals you have cut in your circle, close down the circle and end your ritual in your usual manner. Allow the candles to burn for as long as you can be present to watch them—never leave a candle burning unattended. When the time comes that you must leave the area, extinguish them.

Whether the person you are doing the ritual for chooses to pass through the gates of the Summerland at this time is unimportant. You have opened the doors and made her transition easier, which is presumably what that person wanted you to do for her in the first place.

Four

Grief: A Universal Emotion

AT THIS POINT IN OUR LOOK AT PAGAN DEATH, we need to digress long enough to look at the universality of the grieving process. Nearly as inevitable as our own death is the fact that, at some time during our life span, we each will be faced with the death of someone we love. This may be a family member, a close friend, a cherished pet, or even someone famous whom we never met but to whom we have felt close because that person somehow managed to touch our lives on a deep and personal level. Hence it is fair to say that grieving for a loved one is likely the greatest common denominator among those of us yet living.

Whether it is our own bereavement or someone else's, grief never fails to move us, and coming face to face with it makes almost every one of us uneasy in the extreme. If you think you are immune to this discomfiture, just call to mind the last time you happened to catch a funeral party coming out of a funeral home, or the last time you watched a newscast with footage from a war zone complete with parents searching for their children through bodies on a battle-field. Chances are you looked away, changed the channel, or quickly found something else on which to focus your mind.

Being uneasy with open displays of grief is part of our cultural conditioning. Nearly all societies seek to coerce their members into properly channeling or curbing raw emotions to keep them in their "proper" place out of sight and earshot of everyone else. Chances are that no matter how untimely or difficult a death you mourn, if you allow yourself to get carried away by the emotional overload in public, there will be more than a few people who will never forget it, and they may never let you forget it either.

Of all the control measures society uses to force us to pigeonhole our grief, the public funeral has been the most efficient. The entire process is set up to get it all out and over with so that mourners can walk back into civilization without any bottled-up emotions that might carry over into "normal" life, erupting in embarrassing ways. In most funeral homes the room where the formal services take place is divided so that the family and closest friends—those most likely to give way to histrionics—are separated visually from the rest of those attending the services. This is done presumably to protect the privacy of the family, but it is also done to protect others from the sight of disagreeable emotional outbursts.

Within the bonds of the mainstream religions, followers are often told just whom they may mourn and for how long. For instance, Judaism dictates precisely how long the mourning period for each family member must be, and mourning beyond this customary cut-off date is not indulged. Another example is losing control over your emotions at the loss of a pet. This is not only unacceptable to our society, but is even considered a heresy by some Christian fundamentalists.

The mainstream religions have also not been above exploiting the period of mourning, a time when human mental resistance is at its weakest, to further their hold over their congregants. In both Christianity and Islam, mourners are reminded that the spirit of the dead is in a "better place" than it was on the nasty old earth. And considering the firm belief in both a perfect heaven for those who followed the religion's rules, and a miserable hell for those who did not, this does not say much for their views of Mother Earth. In Judaism mourners are required to chant the *kaddish*, a ritual prayer for the dead, several times a day for a specified period of time depending on the mourner's relationship to the deceased. The prayer has nothing to do with death or the afterlife; it merely reasserts the supremacy and arbitrary will of the all-powerful God and the mourner's subjugation to that will.

Fortunately these dismal views and ethics are not held by all adherents of mainstream religions, but the fact remains that the funeral legacies they have left to us do not usually sit well with Pagans. Fortunately, we are now looking to our own history and to our own hearts for guidance, and we are changing this model to suit ourselves. The first step in doing this is to come to an understanding of the mourning process.

⚜ The Eight Stages of Grief

The stages of human grief have been written about at length in articles and books dealing with the mourning process. We tend to speak of working through these stages as a process because it involves a necessary sequence that takes us from the emotional low of the initial shock to recovery and the resumption of our lives. Each psychologist or clergy author usually puts his or her own spin on the succession of events, but on the whole the process from grieving to recovery is very similar in all of us, though there are individual variations in the time scale needed to pass through each stage. Each stage has many manifestations, some physical, some emotional, and some social.

Keep in mind that these are generalities gleaned from studies done by professional psychologists and sociologists, and that a certain amount of deviation from them is normal. When judging whether you or someone you love needs outside help in dealing with their grief, each individual situation must be considered fully.

In general, the eight stages of grief are:

Stage 1: Shock

Time Frame: The first few hours after learning of a death. In some cases this shock may last for several days.

Watch how actors on film react upon hearing news of a death. They pause, mouths agape, then they blink once or twice. For a moment or two they appear speechless. Then, eventually, with a great gulp, they begin to ask pertinent questions. Beyond that, their reactions depend on the character's relationship to the deceased. All in all, the actors present a pretty good mirror image of our natural reaction upon hearing news of a death. No matter how surprising or expected, our first response is one of shock.

Stage 2: Denial or Disbelief

Time Frame: The same day until several weeks after the death.

This is a feeling that may come back for short periods long after the death. Close on the heels of shock comes a sense of surrealism, which is our mind's way of protecting itself against any stunning news. Occasionally this feeling can continue for several weeks, particularly in cases where the death was sudden or the person involved was very young. Children can often carry denial out for years, insisting each day that the dead person will be coming home soon.

Stage 3: Active Emotional Mourning

Time Frame: From a few hours after the death to several weeks. In some cases it may extend for several months.

This is the period of intense emotional upheaval, the tears and pain felt when the reality of what has happened is fully absorbed. During this time it is not unusual to spontaneously burst into tears regardless of the situation in which the mourner finds himself, and for a while these outbursts are tolerated by the larger society. When they extend beyond the limits of a few weeks, people grow intolerant of the grieving and can even become hostile toward the mourner. This does not, however, mean that the mourner is in the wrong. When active emotional mourning continues for more than a year, professional help should be sought.

Stage 4: Guilt or Blame

Time Frame: From a week or two after the death to about a year. Perhaps significantly longer without therapy.

It is human nature to look about for a convenient scapegoat to cast blame upon when something unpleasant occurs. In the case of a death, this blame might be cast upon someone else or upon our own heads. This is a natural reaction, and as long as the feelings do not embitter the mourner or continue for many years, there is little need to seek outside help.

Stage 5: Anger

Time Frame: Same as for guilt or blame: from a week or two after the death to about a year. Perhaps significantly longer without therapy.

Closely related to guilt/blame is the experience of anger. A surprising number of mourners find that, when their emotions finally settle, they are angry, not with themselves or anyone else close at hand, but with the person who died. Feelings of being abandoned are part of this stage, and mourners often lash out at the deceased for "leaving" them. Fortunately these feelings usually pass within a year or so. Persistent and active anger beyond this point requires professional counseling.

Stage 6: Depression

Time Frame: From several weeks after the death to several months. Longer depressions during which the mourner cannot function normally require professional intervention.

Genuine clinical depression is not always a recognizable part of the grieving process, but feelings of despondency are nearly always felt for at least a short while. These largely depend on the circumstances of the one who grieves. If the mourner is left all alone by the death, the depression may be more pronounced. If they remain with a close circle of live-in friends or family, the period and severity of depression will likely, but not always, be lessened.

Stage 7: Acceptance

Time Frame: Several months after the death to a year or more.

Eventually the mourner comes to accept the death—not to like it, but to acknowledge its truth. This is the first step in fully recovering one's own life.

Stage 8: Full Recovery

Time Frame: One to two years, depending on the relationship to the deceased and the manner of death.

Though emotional scars will remain and memories will never wholly fade, mourners eventually recover from their losses and return to living their lives. After this point, the passionate trials of the active mourning period are well behind them and spontaneous outbursts of grief should not be occurring. It is all right to think about the passed-over loved one, and even to continue to hold annual memorial services in their honor. It is normal if tears come then, but in daily life, active grief should not be keenly felt.

How We Deal with Specific Types of Grief

The precise relationship we share with the person we lose to death will often determine not only how intensely and for how long society finds our mourning acceptable, but may affect the way we feel about ourselves and the world around us. Of course, the manner of death is another matter that affects our feelings and impacts upon our mourning period. Certainly someone elderly who has been released from life following a painful, terminal illness provokes different emotions within us than the loss of a child who is the victim of accident or abuse.

The following are only general guidelines to help you further understand and explore the nature of grief in its variant forms.[1]

The Loss of a Pet

Be warned if you love an animal that, though society may applaud the care you give it in life, to mourn its death will be frowned upon. Recently a coworker of mine had to leave work early because her family dog had died. I was stunned at the ridicule which sprang up from our coworkers as soon as she walked out the door, most of which was just plain heartless. Worse still was the fact that most of them were unaware (though I feared it would have made little difference in their attitude) that the dog had been the couple's "first baby," and that the children, aged four and six, were also extremely attached to it and were already emotional wrecks. Perhaps the ridicule was merely a bit of posturing intended to convey to everyone else that they knew the unwritten rules of what was and was not acceptable even though, deep down, they may have actually felt some sympathy.

The loss of a pet can be devastating, and yet it has only been recently that specialty books have become available that address this issue. Children are especially affected by this loss, and this is often their first experience with death. With their needs left unaddressed, they can become confused and even frightened that other family members may die, too.

Couples who have no children, or whose children have left home, face special problems. One study, published in the late 1970s, went so far as to equate the loss of pets in these households with the loss of a child, and presented evidence that the strain on a couple's marriage was just as severe. Persons who live alone, who own assistance animals (i.e. seeing eye or hearing dogs), who are elderly, or any others for whom the pet is the only companion or means of function in society, also have a harder time dealing with this loss.

The Loss of a Grandparent

Most of us expect to lose grandparents to death either while we are teens or young adults. We can accept this as part of the natural cycle of life—that the old should die and the young live on—and we can more easily deal with this even if we do not like it.

Our grandparents are our link with the past, just as children are our link with the future. When the elder members of our families die, we are often forced to think about the passage of time in terms of what has been left behind that is no longer reachable. For instance, this is the time when grandchildren often find they have questions about their family's past that can only be answered by a grandparent who is no longer living.

For children, the death of a grandparent may be their first experience with a human death, and the way those around them react to it may color their feelings about dying for the rest of their lives.

The Loss of a Child

Without any doubt the death of a child is the hardest of all losses to endure. All parents expect that they will outlive their children. We accept this as part of the natural cycle of life, and this seems as orderly and sensible to us as it is to lose older grandparents. When a child dies from either illness or accident, a parent will often blame him- or herself. This attitude can destroy a marriage or other loving relationship, estrange the grieving parent from their own parents, and can have a profound effect on the way the remaining children feel about themselves and their place in the affections of the parent.

My husband lost his only sister to a car accident when she was eight years old. For years he felt as if perhaps his mother, who had been driving the car, would rather that he, the younger and less well-known child, had died instead. Though she loved him dearly, and certainly harbored no death wish for him, she clearly had no idea how he felt until one night when she was teasing him with the baby-talk phrase, "Who does mommy love best?" My husband, with all the brutal honesty of a five-year-old, answered, "My sister."

Another couple we know lost a seven-year-old to cancer. Although expected, this death was no less devastating to the couple and to all those who knew them.

Because no other loss has such far-reaching effects, there are literally thousands of support groups for bereaved parents (see Appendix B for some addresses). This is also one of the few deaths over which society is fairly forgiving in the time it allows you to openly mourn.

The Loss of an Adult Child

No matter how old or young a parent may be, or how sick or well a child is, all parents fully expect that their offspring will outlive them, and losing an adult child is nearly as hard as losing a youngster. When an uncle of mine died after living for more years with a bad heart than anyone expected, I was surprised at how profoundly my grandmother was affected. Normally a very strong woman who weathered a lot of heartaches in her life, my grandmother suddenly became very fragile and ill, and for a while we all began wondering if she would survive the mourning period herself.

Older adults who have had to face this loss, even when presumably prepared for the death, often manifest symptoms of physical or mental illness. Illness, depression, loss of appetite, and disinterest in the world around them are the most common aftereffects.

It is important that other family members be around for the older parent to help pull them back into life, especially other children and grandchildren. Allow the bereaved parent to decide just when and how much they want to talk about the deceased offspring and follow this lead. With time and love, recovery will occur.

The Loss of an Unborn Child

For those who have never experienced a miscarriage or stillbirth, it is hard to fully comprehend the vast feeling of emptiness felt by the parents. In these cases, mourning proceeds just as it does when a living child dies, and often continues until it becomes an ugly obsession. Sometimes the parents, the mother in particular, will develop a bitter view of the world, especially if she has trouble conceiving again. She may burst into tears when around an infant, become hateful toward young mothers in her acquaintance, or express paranoid feelings about the entire cosmos being turned against her.

Many support groups have sprung up in response to the need for meeting with others who can fully understand just what has been suffered (see Appendix B for group listings).

The Loss of a Parent

Losing one's parents to death is considered by many adults to be a milestone in their lives, albeit an unwelcome one. Suddenly we find we are the senior members of the family, the elders of the tribe so to speak, with all the responsibility that goes with the job suddenly settled on our shoulders. We also begin to think about our own mortality, usually centering on the concept that we are in the generation who will be "the next to go."

Regardless of how well we did or did not get along with the departed parent, there is usually a sense that a very special part of us is irretrievably gone. In many cases, the parent was the one person we could always feel free to brag to about our accomplishments without fear of censor, the person who stood by since birth and cheered each goal we reached.

Because western societies give us unrealistic expectations about the parent-child relationship, fantasies to which few families can measure up, adult children are often left feeling as if something was missing in their lives, even in the best of relationships. Because of these expectations, children who did not bond well with their parents are often at greatest risk for depression as feelings of "it's too late now to do anything about it" overtake them. Counseling is the best course of action if these feelings persist.

When children who lose a parent are not adults themselves, the emotional problems can be even more pronounced. Young children may become fearful that the remaining parent will be taken too and may become clinging and fretful. A close friend of mine since high school lost her husband last year to a sudden illness. Though she is lucky in that she has a high-salaried job, supportive family nearby, and access to the best child counselors, she is aware that her daughters (aged 7 and 10) often sneak in from play just to look at her, as if needing to assure themselves that she is still there and is all right.

If both parents are lost in a mutual disaster and the child must live with other relatives or a foster family, the insecurity can bring about a whole range of emotional disturbances that are best dealt with by professionals.

There are numerous books on the market discussing the death of parents, particularly when younger children are involved, and these are well worth reading, such as *The Orphaned Adult* by Marc D. Angel (Washington, D.C.: Human Sciences Press, 1987) and *How to Survive the Loss of a Parent: A Guide for Adults* by Lois F. Akner (New York: Morrow, 1993).

The Loss of a Friend

Perhaps the death of a friend makes us look at our own mortality more than any other kind of loss. A friend is often a peer, someone of the same age and general socioeconomic background as ourselves. Being born at a similar time and in similar circumstances, we naturally presume a similar life expectancy. When this does not occur as expected we are forced to question how we look at our own existence.

Children and teens who lose a friend or classmate can be particularly upset and need special guidance. A number of award-winning works of juvenile fiction have been written that have been found to be a great source of self-help; for example, *The Bridge to Terabithia* by Katherine Paterson (New York: Crowell, 1977). Ask any librarian or bookstore employee for more information on similar books. Another source of assistance for youngsters is The Good Grief Program (see Appendix B), which helps train school officials to deal with the mass effect of the death of a peer.

The loss of a friend arguably becomes harder to take as we grow older. As we age it is likely that, aside from our spouse or mate, a friend is someone with whom we have shared our most intimate thoughts and secrets over the course of a lifetime. With them goes a special outlet, one which is not likely to be fully replaced in this incarnation.

Elderly persons often become despondent when acquaintances in their peer group begin to die of what we call (for lack of a better term) "old age," and they may find themselves habitually reading the obituaries and counting the heads of old friends as they pass. Again, the issue faced here is one's own mortality and, even when one does not overtly fear death, one's own demise is never wholly comfortable to contemplate, and the loss of a friend seems to force the issue.

The Loss of a Sibling

As with the loss of a friend, when a brother or sister dies we are faced with the immediate sense of our own mortality. We may even have concerns about our health if the sibling perished from a disease that could be genetic in origin.

Because the quality of the relationship with a sibling varies so greatly from person to person, it has been hard for researchers to categorize and map out this mourning process. Certainly the age at which we lose a sibling, and if that sibling is older or younger than us, has a lot to do with our feelings.

The Loss of a Significant Other

At the time you become part of an official couple, you usually do so expecting to spend the rest of your lives together. Yet we all know it is almost a certainty that one partner will pre-decease the other. We plan for this by making wills and buying insurance policies to protect both the one who is left behind and any off-spring who might still be dependent on the surviving parent. But even with all our careful planning, nothing we do can ever prepare us for the feelings of emotional vacancy which come with the death of a partner.

Children, pets, parents, and friends may all come and go in life, but a partner is expected to remain through it all. With this person you share the burdens of each day, your tragedies and triumphs, your dreams and failures. Aside from a trusted friend, your life partner is probably privy to more of your confidences than anyone else in your life. Over the course of those lucky life-long marriages/relationships, this amounts to a significant investment of time and shared secrets. When that person is suddenly taken out of your life, the loss is most keenly felt. The surviving partner may think they hear the other's voice in the house, or hear the familiar footfalls, or they may find themselves turning around to see if the mate is there, purely out of habit.

When the relationship has been exceptionally good, the survivor may express feelings of being torn in two, or complain that he or she no longer feels whole. This engenders extreme feelings of loneliness that can rapidly lead to depression and a tendency to withdraw from the world. My grandmother experienced all these feelings after she became a widow. She only wanted to stay inside, often complaining that the world seemed made for couples, and would often have to be coerced into accompanying us to places because she hated feeling like a fifth wheel. She even burned photos and gave away her treasures, almost as if she expected to die soon.[2]

Like losing a child, the loss of a significant other is one from which we never fully recuperate, but we can recover and go on with life, perhaps even finding new love. No one is ever too old to love again. My formerly widowed father-in-law happily remarried at age sixty-five, and literally became young again as he and his bride set out to enjoy their golden years together at a pace that would exhaust most folks half their age.

This is also a loss over which society is more tolerant of prolonged grieving, particularly when the relationship has been one of long standing.

The Loss of Someone Famous

Never allow yourself to feel that you have no right to mourn someone, even someone you never met. When anyone who has touched your life—even from afar—dies, you may feel genuine grief that needs to be expressed.

When noted Wiccan author Scott Cunningham died in March 1993, the publisher of this book reported a deluge of calls from grieving readers wanting to know how and why. Most of us who read Scott's books never met him, never spoke with him, and probably never even wrote him a letter to tell him how much his work meant to us. Still, in solitary and coven rituals all over the world, Scott's spirit and memory were honored with honest feelings pouring forth from those of us who felt his loss.

When someone famous dies who has been a fixture in your world for a long time, it can affect you similarly to the loss of a parent or grandparent by making you conscious of the swift passing of your own life span. A few years ago an actor died on whom I had developed a hopeless crush at age 12. His reported age at death seemed quite incredible to me twenty-five years after my heart first turned over at the very sight of him. His demise made me very aware of my own age, the passage of time, and my generation's place in the pecking order of death.

The loss of someone famous sometimes evokes concerns over our own mortality. Psychologists tell us that those we admire often seem larger than life, indestructible, even immortal. This image is unconsciously reinforced by the motion picture and recording industry, which preserves for us a "living" image of those we admire long after they have passed. When we discover that these folks are mere mortals after all, people who actually can and do die, we are made to consciously realize that we can die too.

Enduring Secret Grief

One type of bereavement on which I could find no information is that of facing the death of someone you care about but whom no one knows how close you were in life. Certainly we have all known persons involved in relationships where, for one reason or another, those involved felt the need to keep a closely guarded secret. These griefs are probably most common in romantic relationships that people wish to keep hidden from their families or coworkers, such as homosexual, interracial, or multi-partner relationships. Other secret griefs may come when you mourn a pet or someone you didn't really know, but who still meant a great deal to you.

You may feel the need to keep your feelings a secret from fear of ridicule or of exposing too much of your inner self to others. Or you may feel that you have no right to be mourning this person in the first place. This is a ridiculously heavy burden to place on yourself. Your feelings are what they are, and therefore they are valid whether or not others think them silly, ill-conceived, or out of place. You should never think you must hide them or apologize for them. Even without the psychological experts to guide us in this matter, it is easy to assume that, without any acceptable social outlet for the grief, the bereavement period is extended and there is greater risk of falling into a clinical depression.

Fortunately, Paganism as a whole is open to alternative lifestyles, and also accepts other attachments and relationships the mainstream tries to ignore or belittle. Within most traditions, Pagans harboring secret griefs will find acceptance and an outlet for their frustrated grief. If you are now facing any type of secret grief alone, I urge you to go to Appendix B for addresses of Pagan counselors who can assist you through the painful process.

At this point it seems that some discussion is needed about the questions children have about death. I have no children and have never had to deal with this tricky subject, so the suggestions I make are based largely on what has been successful for others. This is not intended as advice in its strictest sense, just as suggestions. I have taken the prevailing feelings of the child psychologists and what has worked for my friends with Pagan children—giving them a Pagan slant where possible—and tried to coalesce them into something which might be helpful to anyone struggling with this issue.

☙ Explaining Death to Pagan Children

How you choose to explain death and the afterlife to your own children is largely a personal matter, and most Pagan parents probably try to explain these concepts as they themselves understand them. Some Pagan parents try to discuss reincarnation, others the great cosmic oneness of all life, while others talk of the brevity of the human life span.

Very young children have no grasp of final endings. If you exist then you must always exist, you must always be *somewhere*, they reason. They have learned this through conditioning because of other separations they have endured: Grandma going back home, Mom and Dad going out and leaving the kids with a sitter, et cetera. In their world, these people who have been with them recently have not vanished off the edge of the earth. They are still somewhere even if they are unseen, and they always return. Because of this experience one of the first questions children usually ask about death is, "Where do people go when they die?"

The answers to the "where" should not be too difficult for Pagan parents. Simply take your cue from your own spiritual tradition and personal beliefs. You might also consider, if the child is old enough to understand that not everyone believes as your family does, briefly encapsulating some of the other ideas people hold about where the dead go that he or she is likely to hear from playmates. Hearing it from you will be a lot less confusing than leaving the child trying to puzzle it out on the playground with other kids who are just as confused.

The second most commonly asked question from children about death is, "Why did they die?" Pagan children are usually taught all about the life cycles of humanity at a young age through exposure to seasonal rituals, and are probably less likely than mainstream children to ask why someone died. However, if this does come up, the best bet is to stick to your assertion that death is simply a part of life. The psychologists advise strongly against trying to get into physical details or abstractions with children because the wording chosen can sometimes cause more fear and confusion. For instance, saying that someone "got sick and died" will only induce terror the next time you or the child comes down with a cold. Saying someone "got old and went away" only provokes feelings of abandonment and may prejudice them against the elderly.

Very young children tend to see anything that is taken from them as being part of a punishment, something which has been denied them as the result of misbehavior. They will often try to understand what the deceased might have done to be given this "time out" or—even worse—what they themselves might have done that was so bad it caused the person to leave them. It is important to reassure all children that death is a natural part of life, one which we all must eventually face, and that it has nothing to do with punishment or being naughty.

Older school-aged children who experience a death will begin to question aloud their own mortality and that of those who are close to them. Psychologists caution parents to use explanations that will allay fears without making false promises (such as "I'm not going to die") or offering assurances that may not be able to be met (such as "You're going to be around for a long time yet"). Though it is second nature for parents to want to reassure children, and it sounds brutal to hold back, it is certainly kinder than making statements which could prove sadly untrue in the long run.

It is my opinion that Pagan children whose parents have home altars or hearths where ancestor spirits are regularly honored will likely grow up with a healthy attitude toward death (see Chapter 6 for more ideas). They will be able to see for themselves the continuity of their family line and feel themselves a part of that great unbroken chain. They will grasp early on the abstractions of death by knowing that they can still share with Grandma the picture they drew in school and will be better able to feel her loving presence even though her physical shell is absent.

❧ A Guided Meditation for Help in Overcoming Unreconciled Grief

The following guided meditation is based on an experience my grandmother had a few months after the death of my grandfather, and I have found it extremely helpful in dealing with unrelenting grief. Though I took the liberty of smoothing out some of the action and adding some psychic protection, it is very much like her original vision. In it you will meet with your passed-over loved one, be allowed to say your good-byes, know that he or she is well, and then return to your normal consciousness. Have some tissues handy—this will likely be a powerful emotional experience.

About a week before you want to do the meditation, go to sleep each night by mentally reaching out across the universe to your passed-over loved one. Ask him or her to speak to you, to give you some sign that he or she can hear your cries. If you are having trouble letting go, chances are that the spirit of your loved one is quite near. Even professional parapsychologists generally accept the idea that emotional turmoil over the passing can bind a spirit to the earthly plane. After a few nights you should receive some sign, usually in the form of a dream vision, or, more common still, by hearing the familiar voice whisper in your ear.

Like myself, my grandmother was one of those people who was psychically wide open in the minutes between full wakefulness and actual sleep. Both of us often experienced hearing the voices of loved ones, some living and some passed over, while floating in this netherworld. Though this experience may at first be startling, try to will yourself to accept it, to know that this is a loved one and that you are in no danger from its spirit.

After you feel this basic contact has been made, select the night you will do the meditation. On this night, cast a circle of protection around yourself and your sleeping place, then go to bed as usual. But, instead of attempting to fall asleep, take yourself down into a sleep-like altered state of consciousness, one in which you are fully aware of what your mind is doing. This can be accomplished by the progressive relaxation of your body (i.e. consciously relaxing your feet, then ankles, then legs, et cetera, on up to the top of your head), and by focusing your mind on one item or issue to the exclusion of all else. For this experience you can either count your breaths or visualize a closed door, one you will be using to meet with your loved one.[3] Doors are used symbolically as dividing points between two realms of existence. Note how many times in metaphysical circles you hear the term "door between the worlds" expressed to describe such a portal. Chances are you've used it yourself in passing-over and Samhain rites.

When you feel you are ready, visualize your own astral self (a spirit-like etheric body) stepping out of your physical body and standing in the room you are in just inside your protective circle. From this point on, you should try and see the meditation happening from the point of view of your astral double.

Visualize a closed door forming in front of you. It can be a french door, a metal door, an old wooden door, one with symbols or medieval carvings on it, et cetera. Nothing is wrong so long as it appeals to you as a portal between the world of matter and the world of spirit.

Once the door is in place, visualize the heavens above you opening up and a golden-white light descending upon you and the door, just a wide enough circle to illuminate you and whoever might be standing on the other side. This is to be perceived as the light of your own loving deities blessing your experience and offering you their protection. It is also a guiding beam by which your loved one can safely navigate the trip from the Summerland and back again.

When this is done, think about the person you want to see, and wait patiently for a knock on the door. After you hear this, open the door, but *do not* go through. This is a portal, one which can take you into the realm of the dead just as easily as it can bring the dead to you. This is a magickal place between places where you and your loved one can safely meet and talk without either one of you being dragged unwillingly into the other's world.

After the door is open, look to see who is there. In the event that you are facing someone or something you do not want to see, simply shut the door and close down the meditation. Though it rarely happens, a meditation of this sort can go awry, so you must always remember that it is your choice whether to continue or not. You alone are in control of the process. However, keep in mind that, if you are faced with the spirit of a passed-over person other than the one you called out to, perhaps this is a restless spirit who has something to settle with you before he or she can rest. Keep an open mind about dealing with this spirit, but don't feel coerced into interacting. As long as you do not go through the door or invite the spirit to cross the magickal threshold into your world, you cannot be hurt.

One sensation you should be aware of ahead of time is that of wind currents that may seem to be pulling at you from the doorway. Recall how ghosts are portrayed in nearly all the spooky movies you've ever seen, how their hair and clothing looks as if it is being buffeted about by a gentle wind. The only explanation I can think of for this phenomenon is that you and the spirit are both standing at an opening between two worlds, the atmosphere of each having different qualities of density, temperature, and pressure which, when they meet, must work to stabilize themselves. A very dramatic analogy for this effect is when a window is opened in an airplane at 30,000 feet and everything not bolted, tied, or nailed down goes flying out the opening.

Hopefully, when you open the door, you will be face to face with only the loved one to whose demise you are having trouble adjusting. You may now initiate dialogue, or you may wait for the spirit to speak, whichever you prefer. When my grandmother found herself facing my grandfather's spirit she was completely dumbstruck. He initiated the conversation by insisting that he was just fine, and that he was glad she had moved into the retirement apartment near our family home. He told her he loved her and to please, please stop crying all the time. He also promised they would be together again someday, but not for a while yet.

As long as your feet are firmly planted on your side of the door, you may touch the spirit. Hold hands, even embrace. Do whatever you need to do to ensure that you are both feeling acceptance about the parting until you too cross over to the other side of existence.

When all has been said and done, close the door. See the light from the heavens closing down, taking the spirit back to the Summerland. Then visualize the door starting to fade from sight. When the images are completely gone, allow your astral self to return to your body.

After this you may wish to wake up and record your experience in your magickal diary or Book of Shadows, or drift off to sleep and worry about recording the experience later if you think you can retain it all. You may even want to take some time to think about all that happened before you attempt to write it down and analyze it. My grandmother was never sure just what took place either, but her attitude toward losing my grandfather changed after this experience. Though she continued to question whether it was "real" or not, she could not deny how much better it made her feel . . . and neither should you.

Five

Dancing with the Grim Reaper

FESTIVALS HONORING FERTILITY, THE HARVEST, and various deities are easily the most numerous spokes on the Pagan Wheel of the Year, yet our traditions still have a notable history of festivals and feast days to honor the dead; though relatively few in number, they comprise some of our best-loved holidays. The imagery they present to us of death and renewal are deeply ingrained in our psyches and, because they involve those we love, they are profoundly meaningful. It is for these reasons Pagan celebrations have survived since antiquity and are still with us today, and why many—like Halloween—are also celebrated in the mainstream, albeit in a slightly altered form.

Not all death festivals known to humankind are listed here—not even close. Only a few of those that are well-known, or are in some way unique, are presented in this chapter. Part of the problem in compiling a larger listing is that many celebrations merely go by the generic title "Feast of the Dead," and their imagery and manner of observance vary little to their counterparts in other cultures. Because of this, they tend to go unnoticed by many modern Pagans who seem to like a significant name to attach to their celebrations. Other death imagery can be found in those festivals honoring the crone Goddess, such as in Scotland's Festival of the Cailleach and Greece's Feast of Hecate; and in the feast days of Goddesses who resurrect themselves each spring, such as Kore, Persephone, or Inanna. Still other festivals of the dead focus on ancestor spirits, and these will be discussed in Chapter 6.

Feeding the dead, or feasting with them, is an almost universal theme within these festivals. When seeking to work out your own commemorative rituals, this is one aspect that should not be overlooked simply because several million of our ancestors thought it so important to our Pagan faith that it became a practice that has survived to this day. When seeking to commemorate the lives of your beloved dead, or for honoring the concept of death/rebirth, these death festivals can be a great source of fresh, meaningful ideas.[1]

⚜ The Feast of Sekhmet

Egyptian/January 7

Sekhmet is not actually one of the many death and underworld deities of the Egyptian pantheon, but a sun Goddess. Yet her feast day commemorates the deliverance of humanity from death and marks the start of the old Egyptian new year.

Sekhmet once became so thoroughly displeased by humanity that she sought to destroy all human life. Her efforts were halted by Ra, a sun God who tricked Sekhmet into drinking seven thousand vats of red-tinted beer and fruit juice instead. The drink both appeased her desire to consume the blood of humanity and sent her into a deep, drunken sleep. When she awakened, she no longer felt the need for vengeance and allowed humankind to live in peace for yet another year.

As you enjoy your own Feast of Sekhmet, you might wish to add fruit juices—spiked or not—to your own feast, particularly ones in a vivid blood red, in honor of Ra's quick thinking. Grenadine, cranberry, cherry, and many grape juices will provide this coloring.

❦ Carmentalia

Roman/January 8-12

The five-day long Carmentalia honors the trio of faery or nymph prophets known collectively as the Carmenae. Their leader, Carmentis, is a Goddess of prophecy and childbirth who is conceptualized as a hinge on which the door of life swings.

On the first and last day of her festival she is concerned only with life, particularly in the form of newly born, or soon to be born, babies. Pregnant women make offerings to her to ensure a safe and healthy delivery, and older folk ask her blessings upon their lineage. Carmentis has her priestesses, called Flamines, who act in her stead as skilled midwives and seeresses. On this day their talents are sought out and their services contracted for the coming year.

On the second through fourth days of the festival, the focus is on death—conceptualized as the door of life swinging in the opposite direction. These days honor Mania, one of the Carmenae who is the patron Goddess of human discarnates. Legend tells us that on the first of her three nights, Mania and her legions of dead prowl the earth, appearing to the living in grotesque forms in an attempt to drive them insane. Those who succumb to the shock are fated to die within the coming year, their spirits being imprisoned in the capped well at Rome's center where Mania's legions reside (the well was opened several times a year in order to allow spirits to pass in and out as needed).

Because it is believed that Mania attempts to appear to at least one person from each household, families make straw effigies of themselves, including all servants and slaves, and tie them to the door posts. Legend tells us that the brave indulge in divination practices to induce Mania to reveal how much longer they will live. Mania can also bring with her to the earthly plane the spirit of passed-over loved ones so that families may visit.

The associations of Carmentalia with Mania make it a good time to renew the joy of life and perhaps to experiment with strengthening your own life force, or, if you are terminally ill, to come to terms with approaching death.

❦ The Feast of Februus

Roman/February 1

Rome was well-known for adopting its deities from other cultures, and Februus appears to be of Etruscan origin. He was a God of the dead and of ritual purification. When his name was first given to February it was nicknamed "the cleansing month." It is likely that rituals of personal and home purification took place on this day, and probably ritual purification of burial sites as well.

This is a good day for taking some *lightly* salted water (overdoing the salt can damage wood and fabric, so use it sparingly) around your home and casting away all negative influences. As you go through your home, lightly flick droplets from your fingertips and pray to Februus, or another favored deity, to shed his or her blessings on your home. You can also take this purification process into a nearby cemetery and ask blessings on the resting places of your loved ones.

❧ The Feast of Manes

Roman/February 18-20

In the Roman Pagan tradition, the Manes are benevolent spirit guardians who watch over burial grounds. On this day they are honored in communal festivals held in the cemeteries. The priests and priestesses of the death cult sacrifice black sheep and pigs at the graveyard's entrance. The collected blood is gathered in chalices of precious metal and poured over the graves in offering. Food libations are left for the Manes, as well as for any spirits who happen to join in the festivities.

The Feast of Manes is a good time to make friends with the guardians of your nearby cemetery, to anoint the graves with precious oils, and to leave gifts for the Manes and the spirits (see Chapter 8 for more on anointing rites and gravesite offerings).

❧ Lantern Festival

Chinese/Last Full Moon before the Chinese New Year (January-February)

The three-day Lantern Festival is the last holiday of the Chinese year. As the name suggests, it is a day for the hanging of colorful lanterns in every conceivable space. Lantern-making in China is a cherished art form, and many of these craftsmen's offerings are awe-inspiring in their elaborate and intricate design. Though this is now viewed as a preparation for the New Year's celebration two weeks hence, in the distant past it was an act of sympathetic magick intended to lure back the waning sun to the earth, much as Imbolg is celebrated in modern Wicca. Of course, it is also a festival to pay tribute to the spirits of those who have passed over during the previous year.

Vendors sell moon foods—particularly those decorated to look like the moon or which have long-standing lunar associations—to persons who are out to decorate temples and graves or to see the fireworks which light the night sky. Later, some lanterns are gathered and placed in small toy boats and sent floating down the river in memory of the spirits of those who passed over the past year.

Like the Chinese Lantern Festival, the Thai people make elaborate paper lanterns and float them down rivers in memory of passed-over loved ones, or to help escort them back to the Land of the Dead at the festival's end.

❧ The Feast of Cybele

Mediterranean/March 22-24

Cybele is a Goddess of the earth and of vegetation, and her festival is best characterized as one huge fertility rite to ensure that the land will continue to produce. Yet the theme within this festival is that of life springing from death. During the first two days of the festival, an evergreen tree, Cybele's symbol, is taken into her temple and wrapped in burial shrouds. This effigy is buried in sacred earth and mourned by the entire community.

The last day of the festival is known as the Day of Blood. At the burial site, a priestess of Cybele takes some blood from the willing arm of a priest and tosses it over the burial site. This is both an offering/sacrifice to Cybele and an ancient act of fertility in which the life's blood of a priest, as the representative of God on earth, is sacrificed for the Goddess through whom he, and all life, would be reborn.[2] At the end of the ceremony the community confirms their belief in regeneration by celebrating the rebirth of Cybele's son Attis. The Feast of Cybele is a good time to reflect on the meaning and unity of life and death.

❧ Anthesteria

Greek/New Moon of March

This three-day festival honors sexuality and wine, celebrating the God of the vine, Dionysus, but it also has its death imagery. On the last day of the festival, a special food paste made of legumes and fish is offered to the spirits and to Hermes so that he will guide the souls of the dead safely into the underworld.

Anthesteria is a perfect time to pay homage to the death deities of your tradition, seeking their help and good will. It is also a good time to ask Hermes to help a wandering spirit find its way home.

❧ St. Mark's Eve

English/April 24

Many of the festivals and feast days of Christian saints fall on or near popular Pagan holidays. This one, dating to around the fifteenth century in England, falls near the Celtic fertility festival of Bealtaine, marking the end of the Celtic winter season. On this same day the occupying Romans of the first century C.E. began their spring festival of Floralia.

As early as the fourteenth century, English folklore tells us that if we sit inside an open church door at midnight on St. Mark's Eve, we shall see the spirits of all those in the town who will die in the coming year walk past. Some legends go so far as to say that those walking east to west (in the direction of the Celtic Summerland) will unquestionably die, but any walking west to east (the direction of sunrise and new beginnings) will only suffer extreme illness and be spared death.

Divinations predicting who will die in the year to come are not unknown. Even in modern southern Appalachia such rituals, performed at specific times of the day or under certain conditions, are reputed to yield excellent results.

❧ Feast of Lemurs

Roman/Full Moon of May

In ancient Rome, ancestor spirits were held in high esteem and festivals to honor them were held throughout the year. But the unfortunate lemurs, the spirits of those passed over who had no surviving descendants, were to be pitied and feared and, of course, had to be given their own feast day to make up for their lonely state.

On this night the lemurs walked the earth, and the entire community was expected to take time out to pay them honor in the same way they would their own ancestor spirits, the lemures. Though homage was paid them at the cemeteries, the Romans did not want these wandering, unattached spirits to find their way into their homes. To this end, black beans were burned to keep them at bay and no joyous family events, such as weddings, were permitted since these might attract the attention of the unhappy spirits. Some brave folk among the community would even try to place items on the graves ahead of time that would keep the lemurs inside where they belonged. Burned beans were used in this effort as well as homemade talismans.

On the Feast of Lemurs, gather your clan to feast and to pay your respects to the forgotten spirits.

❧ Garland Sunday

Irish/Third Sunday in September

Though I have written about this little-known Irish celebration several times before, it bears repeating since it is first and foremost a celebration of death and rebirth. The festival probably grew out of Mabon (the autumnal equinox) celebrations, which contain similar death imagery.

The day before Garland Sunday, all unmarried girls in the community help construct a long garland of native vines that is decorated with apples. In Celtic myth and folklore, the apple is a sign of both death and rebirth, a fruit sacred to the Triple Goddess. Along with the community's unmarried men, the garland is carried in a long procession to a local cemetery. Townsfolk follow behind watching for any dropped apples. It is believed that if any of the apples fall from the garland during the procession, it is an ill omen for the community, perhaps even heralding a death in the near future.

Once inside the cemetery the garland is broken apart and strewn over the graves amidst loud keening, a traditional mourning wail said to have first been used by the Goddess Brighid as she mourned her son/lover's demise in battle. After the crying and mourning is over, feasting and dancing follows at some point near the cemetery, perhaps even in the meeting hall of a local church.

On this night it is also obligatory to show hospitality to strangers, since they may be spirits in disguise.

Even if you are not part of a coven or a group, you can still take apples to the cemetery and mourn death while you celebrate life.

❧ The Feast of Lights

Egyptian/September 14

Though the original lunar date of this festival is lost to us, this festival has been kept alive for centuries in many parts of the Nile Valley on September 14. During the last hour of daylight, families carry great feasts picnic-style to the local necropolis (meaning "cemetery" or, literally, "city of the dead"). As soon as night falls, thousands of candles are set alight in the necropolis so that the spirits of those interred there may be guided back to enjoy the festival meal with their former community.

The imagery here is one of a very striking communal festival that could easily be recreated in any burial ground, providing proper permissions are first secured.

✣ Mabon

Celtic-Teutonic/Autumnal Equinox

Today, as one of the eight Wiccan Sabbats (solar festivals), Mabon is widely celebrated by modern Pagans from a variety of traditions. In Celtic countries, the
autumnal equinox gained popularity as a spiritual holiday only after the Norse
and Saxon invasions of Britain and Ireland brought them into prominence. The
holiday is named for Mabon, the God who symbolizes the male fertilizing principle of the divine in the Welsh myths. Some mythologists equate him as the
male counterpart to Persephone, the Greek Goddess who returns on this day
each year to her underworld exile, a place from which she will emerge in spring.

Again, we see both the images of death and rebirth in this old festival. The
death imagery is easy to notice simply by observing the world around us. This is
a night of balance after which the power of darkness will overcome the power of
light, each day becoming progressively shorter as the nights become longer. The
majority of the harvest is in from the fields that now lie fallow, and the trees
wither and die.

In many Celtic lands it became customary on Mabon to visit burial mounds
or gravesites to honor dead ancestors, particularly one's female ancestors. This
was due to a Summerland place known as the Land of Women, an idea based on
the belief that, upon death, all human souls must first be reabsorbed into the
wombs that bore them before they can be reborn. By Celtic custom, it is the
women who are responsible for adorning the graves while the men prepare the
feasting site.

Legend tells us the Druids, the Celtic priests, cut wands from willow trees at
Mabon that were thought to be powerful tools for magick involving the conjur-
ing of spirits. Because willow is a tree associated with death, we can surmise
some of their rites involved using the dead for divination purposes.

✣ The Feast of the Departed Worthies

Tibetan/October 17 or Full Moon after the Autumnal Equinox

In the temples of rural Tibet a blurred line separates the modern religion of
Buddhism from the Pagan practices of the past. Though this feast is intended to
honor the martyrs and leaders of the Buddhist faith, it also retains its aspects as a
Pagan festival to honor all the beloved dead.

On this day images of the dead are placed on altars and homage is paid to them
through prayer so that they will intercede on behalf of humanity with the deities.

The best way to adapt this feast day into your Wheel of the Year is by honoring our Pagan martyrs (see Chapter 8, p. 150, for ritual text).

❧ The Dumb Supper

Anglo-Celtic/October 29 or 30

Just nights before the major Celtic festival of Samhain, a ritual feast that has been dubbed the Dumb Supper is held in honor of the dead who walk among us ("dumb" in this case refers to the state of muteness, not a state of mind). Traditionally the meal is eaten in complete silence, with a place set at the head of the table for the spirits.

Any foods are appropriate for the feast, but breads or cakes are traditional. So are drinks which are red in color, symbolizing blood, the substance our ancestors believed contained the essence of life. Certainly red wines may be used for this, but cranberry or cherry juice or drinks reddened with grenadine can also serve, especially in family settings.

In recent years the Dumb Supper has become popular among those following family traditions, settings where particular Pagan traditions are being passed down through a single family line.

❧ Samhain

Celtic/October 31

There is little that can be said about this popular Sabbat that has not already been said. Entire books have been written on the Sabbat holidays—including one written by me[3]—with a great amount of space given over to Samhain. Of all the European Pagan festivals, this one has survived most intact thanks to its modern incarnation as Halloween. For the sake of saving space, I will address only those points of the holiday that focus on death.

Samhain has always been described as a night when the veil separating the world of the living from that of the dead is very thin. On this night spirits may pass through the veil and roam the earth, visiting old friends, family, and favorite places. Naturally they must be made welcome—window candles and/or jack-o'-lanterns are set out to light the journey of the spirits, and to guide them to the feast and ritual sites. Plates of food are also left out as a libation to the dead, a custom still observed in rural Ireland today.

Though death is very much a part of Samhain's symbolism, this Sabbat also celebrates the triumph of life over death. Samhain celebrates and mourns the death of the Harvest Lord, the God of the passing year, with the assurance that he will be reborn again in spring and that the cycle of life, death, and regeneration will continue.

As one of the eight Wiccan Sabbats, and arguably the most popular of them, Samhain is celebrated widely in modern Paganism. Trying various divinations, making spirit contact, and doing past life regressions are all excellent ways to connect with the essence of this festival.

❧ The Day of the Dead

Mexican/November 1

The popular mind thinks of Mexico as a land thoroughly immersed in patriarchal religion, but because the Catholic Church based its conversion efforts upon the native spiritual traditions of the region, many Pagan beliefs and practices are still in evidence.

In Mexico it is not hard to find people who believe in spirits, manifestations of the divine, and magick. With this in mind, it is not surprising to find that they are a people who honor their dead in what has become a national holiday, the Day of the Dead (*El Día de los Muertos*). Despite the death imagery, this festival is never solemn until it moves into the church at midnight. Images of skulls and skeletons are used to decorate homes and villages, and *calveras*, curios with death themes, are sold in market squares amidst music and revelry. In smaller communities the central plazas are often overtaken by vendors and revelers who dress up in costume, drinking and eating in honor of Death himself. The Mexicans believe that this is Death's one day off during the entire year, a twenty-four-hour period when they are exempt from his prowling.

On the Day of the Dead most businesses close so that families may go to the cemeteries to decorate the graves in anticipation of the main portion of the festival, which comes after sunset. As sunset approaches, families take the favorite foods and drinks of their ancestors, a handful of candles or colorful lanterns, and make the walk to the local graveyard. Here a lively atmosphere reigns as the feast is held in the cemetery. Few graves are undecorated and unattended by loved ones, and lively music plays in the night.

By tradition all revelry must be finished by midnight, when a mass for the dead is given at the local church, after which everyone returns home. The plate, which had earlier been set out in the graveyard for the ancestors, goes home too. It is placed lovingly at the head of the kitchen table or on a family altar overnight so that any spirits who wander in for a late-night snack will know they are welcome. Though the remainder of this food may be eaten the next day, most Mexicans insist that it has no taste because the flavor (the "astral" part of the food) has been eaten by the dead.

If you live in Mexico or in the American Southwest you can easily find a community where the Day of the Dead is celebrated. Some Mexican towns welcome tourists for this festival, so ask your travel agent about these. If this is not possible, feel free to adapt its customs to your coven's or family's needs.

❧ All Soul's Day

English/November 1

All Soul's Day is the Anglo-Saxon version of Samhain, one which became the All Saint's Day of the Anglican and Catholic Churches. On All Soul's Day it is believed that the spirits of all those passed over come to walk the earth, and that they can turn the tide of fate for the better or for the worse, depending on how they are treated.

Feeding the dead is the primary way by which one shows respect and asks for blessings, with cakes being the favored offering. Children dressed as spirits once went door-to-door begging for one of these "soul cakes," knowing they would not be denied just in case a real spirit was among them. This practice is one of the origins of our modern day Halloween custom of trick-or-treating.

As Christianity became the accepted religion of England, the practices of All Soul's Day were relegated to the role of folk customs, and All Saint's Day moved the observance into the churches.

If your kids go trick-or-treating, you are already observing an All Soul's Day custom. If you wish to do more, leave soul cakes out on which your wandering spirits can snack.

❧ The Resurrection of Osiris

Egyptian/November 13 (approximately)

Though the exact date of this ancient feast day is questionable, its imagery is not. As the brother/husband of Isis, the Goddess of life, Osiris' image as a deity of vegetation and of death and rebirth is fitting and natural. As Isis rules the heavens, Osiris rules the underworld and takes care of all aspects of the afterlife for those passed over, looking after them as if they were his own children. It is he who passes judgment on the souls about to enter his kingdom, granting immortality to those

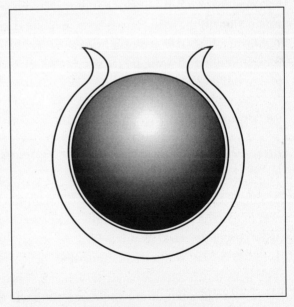

The crescent-shaped (bovine) Horn of Isis.

he finds deserving and punishment to those he judges to be in error. This day, which is one of several Osiris festivals in the Egyptian year, celebrates Osiris's restoration to life at the hands of Isis. It is also a day the living hope to appease him to help pave their way into a pleasant afterlife, or help one already passed over, by paying tribute to him.

Before the resurrection is cheered, ritual dramas are enacted that commemorate Osiris's death and embalming. A mummified effigy is laid to rest with a crescent symbol to represent the bovine-like horns of Isis and her regenerative powers (cattle being symbolic of abundance in Egypt). Boats bearing this "body" are floated down the Nile on barges decorated with candles and barley, a food linked to fertility rites and, therefore, to rebirth.

The festival meal is traditionally held in the fertile fields Osiris also rules, with offerings of vegetation left in burial grounds and in temples. Celebrate Osiris' feast by leaving offerings to him at burial grounds and performing unselfish acts of service that will win his favor.

✺ Feast of Hecate

Greek/November 16 or the Dark Moon of November

Hecate, the crone aspect of a powerful Triple Goddess, appropriately has three festivals of her own during the solar year. This one, the second of the three, marks Hecate's aspect as a deity linked to death.

As a Goddess of the crossroads, she symbolizes old paths coming to an end and new roads taken—including those leading to and from the Otherworld. Her totem animal, the toad, often serves as a blood sacrifice at isolated crossroads.

On her feast day it is traditional to eat blackened breads and goat cheese soaked in olive oil—the oil most often selected in the Middle East for anointing graves and corpses.

✺ The Snake Festival

Indian/First Full Moon after the Winter Solstice

The snake is viewed in many cultures as a symbol of rebirth and has often served as a representation of the Goddess. Though not a part of modern Hindu practice, in eastern India at the Hindu Temple of Manasa an ancient Pagan ceremony honoring the snake is still held.

India's Snake Mother is the guardian of all who have passed over, and she is their personified hope for a gentle rebirth. A priestess of the snake cult leads the worshippers in a wild song and dance until she falls into a deep trance. A priest then calls the spirit of the Snake Mother into her body so that she may speak with the worshippers, sometimes offering words of comfort from those passed over who have not yet returned to the earthly plane.

Snake Mother Meditation

An innerworld journey to meet with the Snake Mother is very appropriate at this time. To begin, allow yourself to fall deep into a meditative state of mind. When you are ready, visualize yourself heading deep into the Indian jungles. Soon you come to a clearing where your eye is caught by a large round hole in the center of a rocky outcropping. The opening is not as large as a cave, but is still big enough for you to squeeze through if you desired. As you study the opening you notice that it is a sacred place: on the rocks are drawings and carvings of sacred symbols and nearby are items which have clearly been left in offering to a beloved deity.

You decide you would like to enter the sacred place and see where it leads. Cautiously you step inside. The entryway is dark and close, but miraculously you find that you can see. The tunnel is narrow, but you continue as it begins winding its way downward, deep into the earth. The path continues to narrow and you find you must bend over in order to keep walking, then you find you must crawl on your hands and knees. Finally you discover that if you are to continue on that you must crawl on your belly. Realizing that there is no turning back now, you do this as the tunnel continues downward.

Without warning the tunnel ends in a small space which looks like the inside of a large, hollow eggshell. As you sit there, huddled in a fetal position, you wonder what to do next. Before you can make a decision you hear a loud tapping at the egg and, looking up, see a fissure appear as if something is trying to break in. The pieces of shell keep falling around your head as the opening grows larger.

You can hear a strange hissing noise coming from the creature trying to break into the egg. Whatever is out there is enormous!

Soon the egg is opened enough for you to look up and see the largest, most beautiful serpent you have ever seen. She regards you almost lovingly, as if you were one of her precious babies emerging from the egg. You step outside and into the underworld of this Goddess. At this point allow yourself a visit with the Snake Mother, then go back into the eggshell and return by the same route you entered.

Six

Honoring the Ancestor Spirits

WHEN WE THINK OF HUMAN INVOLVEMENT WITH ancestor spirits we generally think in terms of the Native American, Roman, or southeast Asian cultures. Most Pagan cultures honored their deceased family members in some way as well. They sought their guidance, tried to contact their sentient spirits, built shrines for them, held festivals in their honor, or paid some sort of homage to them.

In former times, the word *ancestor* had a much broader meaning than in today's mainstream culture. Today non-Pagans tend to use this term exclusively to denote direct-line antecedents, while many Pagans take cues from the distant past and use it to refer to all their relatives and/or tribal members who have passed over. By this definition not only is your grandmother an ancestor, but so is your passed-over sister or great-aunt.

❧ A Legacy of Pagan Ancestor Festivals and Worship

Holidays are the most common times for communal honoring of ancestors, while the anniversary of a birth or a death is the time most often chosen by individual families. The previous chapter mentions several of these holidays that honor the dead in general, but another host of festivals exist that function specifically to honor the ancestor spirits.

It is as much a fallacy to believe that Pagans worshiped their ancestors as it is to believe that they worshiped trees, or rocks, or any other items of the physical world. As we do with nature, most Pagans worship through and with our ancestors, giving them due honor just for being what they are, but we do not worship them as deities. Part of the confusion over this comes from the practice of necromancy, or divining with the dead. The idea behind this is that, once passed over, a spirit somehow becomes a know-all and can speak to us like a God who has the answers to all our problems. Anyone who has ever worked with divinations involving spirits knows that this simply is not true. Because Pagans interact with the dead and seek to communicate with them (though we do this more for our own enjoyment than to divine the future) we have been accused of worshiping the dead, just as we have been accused of worshiping trees simply because we also interact and communicate with them.

One notable exception to this is in the old Hawaiian culture, where the most ancient of the ancestor spirits have been semi-deified. Known as the *aumakua*, they are often sought for special homage and asked to intercede with the higher Gods on behalf of their descendants. They were believed to watch over their families and shower blessings or punishments as deserved. The Etruscans deified their dead by making living sacrifices of their enemies to their Gods. In other cultures, like that of the Celts, we have mythology that tells us of the mating of deities and humans creating a semi-divine race of heroic ancestors. But these hybrids tend to have many human failings, and are not the infallible, perfect Gods usually noted in the mainstream/patriarchal religions.

The ancestors are honored in modern Paganism, as they were in the past, because it is they who are responsible for our being here today. It was their wars that shaped our world, their ethics we lived by, their religions that gave us our moral character and collective worldview. When we throw our beliefs about reincarnation into the mix, those whom we call "they" just may be us. By honoring the memory of the ancestors, we celebrate the unbroken chain of life linking us to the past and to the future. We become for one brief moment like our ritual circles, the sacred space in which all time and place meet.

The Chinese kept household altars for the ancestors, and made pilgrimages to the burial grounds at festival times to tell their ancestors how the family was getting along and to make offerings to them.

In China, the new moon in November is known as the Moon of the Ancestors. At noon, the eldest living male in the family leads a procession to the family burial ground, where they picnic with the spirits of departed loved ones. These burial grounds are most often part of the fertile fields that provide the family's living. Gifts of coins, clothing, or hair are left behind. At nightfall, the entire community gathers to place colored paper lanterns on the river so they may float gently downstream, carrying good wishes to loved ones in the Land of the Dead.

In Japan, where the native Pagan religion of Shinto is still followed, there is a minor celebration each summer called the Doll Festival, or *Hina Mastsuri*. In this festival, little girls are encouraged to dress up their favorite dolls as the ancestor mothers.

Japan also has a very old festival to honor the ancestor spirits known as Obon, or the Bon Festival. Since long before recorded history, these eighteen days at the end of August (13-31) have been the time when the Japanese know the veil separating them from the spirit world is thin. During this period the spirits of the ancestors, or *shugoray*, come to visit their families.

Gardens are carefully tended beforehand with particular care being paid to the *jizo,* or ancestor shrines. Because the spirits favor the gardens, offerings are often left there for them ahead of time, but few people venture there during the festival itself for fear of seeing spirits.

As with Halloween, ghost stories are a popular pastime during Obon, often involving entire communities. It is traditional for one hundred candles to be lit before the storytelling begins. One hundred stories will be told, and, as each story is completed, a single candle is extinguished. Naturally this is great for building suspense since, eventually, the group is left in a totally darkened room.

Circuitous dancing is another multicultural phenomenon in death festivals, one which takes on an interesting twist in Japan. Called the *bonn odori*, each person in the circular configuration dances alone as energy to summon the ancestor spirits is raised by the group. Eventually all the dancers expect to be joined by a family member or other loved one. Parapsychologists who have studied the psychic phenomenon present at the dance have come up with many interesting sound recordings and photographs containing the disembodied voices or physical images of wraith-like creatures.

Prayers for the souls of the dead are part of the festival, and the giving of pairs of raw fish is also popular (fish representing new life). In pairs, as is seen in the astrological symbol of Pisces, each swims in a different direction, one symbolic of the past, the other of the future.

Before Obon ends, families make a pilgrimage to their *haka*, or family grave, where sometimes hundreds of the ancestors are buried. They clean the area, plant fresh flowers, and leave behind decorations and whatever favorite foods and drinks they can carry. A very old tradition, one which is seen less and less often, is to leave behind the image of a horse, so that the spirit can use it to travel between worlds. This belief that the horse's spirit is easily able to traverse the distance between the seen and unseen realms is part of the mythology of many cultures, not only the Japanese.

On the last night of the festival, the spirits are encouraged to return to the Land of the Dead in huge communal rituals where bonfires blaze brightly to light their way. In some communities the last night of Obon is so lavish a spectacle that they have become tourist attractions for curious westerners.

In Thailand, the ancestors are honored with small spirit houses that are placed near family altars. These resemble miniature Asian temples where the spirits can reside comfortably within the home. If you like the idea of this type of dwelling

A birdhouse as a Thai spirit house, painted with symbols of magick, rebirth, and eternity.

place for your ancestor spirits and you cannot locate an authentic spirit house at an import shop, you can make one from an unpainted, wooden birdhouse available at most garden stores or craft fairs. Using acrylic paints, decorate the house with symbols of rebirth and Paganism and set it in a quiet corner of your home, preferably in a communal room so that all family members may stop by to pay their respects.

Many African tribes believe that ancestor spirits continue to watch over their former communities after death and that they can act as intercessors with the deities. Whenever a major question comes before the entire community, specific rituals are followed by the tribal priests and shamans in order to either ask the ancestors' permission for an action to be taken or to ask for guidance in the matter.

Insofar as extant evidence can tell us, most European Pagan cultures did not keep altars to the ancestors inside their homes. The noted exception to this are the Romans, who not only had home altars dedicated to the ancestors, but several festivals in their honor. This does not mean the ancestors were forgotten or ignored in other cultures, only that the shrines to them were kept away from the home.

The Romans kept permanent altars to the ancestors erected in their homes, a custom which is rapidly regaining favor among modern Pagans, particularly those who work and worship in family traditions. The *lares* and *penates*, household guardian spirits and ancestor spirits, were given their own festival in early January. The lares, from an Etruscan word for "lord," were thought to live under the homes of those they looked after in subterranean burrows, for there was a persistent belief that they would perish if exposed to sunlight. At night they came out and looked after the exterior of the places in their care. The penates were thought to live above the house or in trees and brush. They had to be back in their lairs before sunset, and therefore they took care of their household and household tasks during the day. These spirits were also seen as caretakers of the lives and well-being of those in the household, and great care was taken to attract and keep their loving concern. This was done by making offerings of bread and wine to them, and by keeping lights burning all through the night on the home altar.

Once a year, on January 8, a family ceremony would be held in their honor. Every member of the household gathered near the altar and offered thanks for the continued concern of these household spirits. New libations would be made to them and fresh straw (to be used as bedding) would be set out for them to take as they needed. All commerce closed for the day and, at public buildings, concerned citizens and city officials alike would gather for public ceremonies.

For nine days beginning on February 13, the Romans celebrated Parentalia, the root word "parent" within the name of the holiday underscoring its significance as a festival to honor ancient, direct-line ancestors. Small houses were built in out-of-the-way corners of the home so that the spirits might have a place to stay while watching the festivities, which included the festivals of Lupercalia (a mating festival) and Feralia. Feralia fell on the last night of Parentalia, and was a night to honor all the dead who were believed to be visible in spectral form floating over their burial places. Naturally, this was a time when offerings were made to the ancestor spirits and their graves were lavishly adorned. Afterward personal purification rites were held, as well as the annual purification of the ancestor altar.

Another Roman festival honoring ancestors was the Feast of Sacrifice (now dated to March 28, though it likely once had a long-lost lunar date) during which lights or candles were placed on the tombs of family members, and the graves were anointed with oils. Food libations were also presented, and often a token of personal esteem that was of some actual value in Roman society. The purpose of this appears to be appeasement of the dead as well as a payment of personal homage.

On October 5 the Romans again honored their ancestors in the Feast of Mania. On this night it was believed that the passageway to the underworld was unguarded and wide open so that both spirits and incarnate humans could pass through. In recent years those following Roman Pagan traditions have adopted this festival as a shamanic one that facilitates innerworld journeys to the Land of the Dead.

The popular Roman festival known as Saturnalia (December 17-24) was not specifically a time to honor one's ancestors, but a period to honor the God Saturn and celebrate the new year. On the last night of the five-day celebration, gifts were exchanged in memory of loved ones who had died during the previous year. Early Roman explorers and conquerors spread this tradition throughout Europe, where it has remained a part of the Yuletide celebration.

The Celts honored their ancestors by honoring the earth on which they lived, and by worshiping the deities who once mated with the children of the earth. Oral stories passed down from parents and grandparents are especially cherished links in the eternal chain of life. The storytelling tradition is especially strong in Ireland, where people are still consciously aware that whenever the old stories are retold the ancestors are being honored.

In the Norse traditions the *idises*, or household ghosts, are the spirits of the ancestors. The idises watch over their families, and may also be assigned to carry them to death when the time comes.

In another Norse tradition, the *Disir* are a Triple Goddess form similar to the Three Fates of the Greco-Roman tradition, only these take the form of ancestral mothers. Sculptures of these women, who usually appear in a trio, can still be seen in Scandinavia and are inscribed to "the mothers." On October 14, during the celebration known as Disirblot, the Disir are honored in homes with a feast featuring pork, the same dish believed to be served to the warriors who reside in the afterworld of Valhalla. Apples and ale are also in evidence, and lavish toasts are made to the "grandmothers" in hopes that they will bless the home in return throughout the coming year. The women of the household perform divinations for querents, secure in the knowledge that their matriarchs are guiding their skills.

In the spiritual ceremonies of the Native American Lakota tribes, the phrase *mi taku oyasen* is often heard in ritual. It means "all my relations" and reaffirms the Lakota's belief in the unity of all life, particularly in the family/tribe, both incarnate and discarnate. This honors not only the memory of the ancestors, but of all the tribal dead.

On the first full moon after the winter solstice, the Hopi tribes of the American Southwest celebrate the return to the earth of their ancestor spirits, the *kachina*, in the festival known as Soyal. The kachinas settle themselves in spruce tree shrines built for them by the tribe. They remain to help see their people through the end of winter and to ensure their harvest. On the last full moon before the summer solstice, they return to the Otherworld in the festival Nimman Kachina. Both of these events are nine days long, considered to be some of the most sacred times in the Hopi Wheel of the Year.

Outside of festival times, the most often chosen time to honor the ancestors is at the anniversary of a death. Many people believe that on these anniversaries the spirit is free to travel to earth again and visit family. Since before recorded history the Jews have honored their dead on the anniversary of the death, which in Yiddish is known as the *yahrzeit*. As in the distant past, today memorial candles are lit on these anniversaries and prayers offered, though the synagogues have wrested control of the latter and now control what and with whom prayer is done.

Death anniversaries as triggers for spectral sightings are well documented, though little understood.[1] Certainly the date on the solar calendar alone cannot be a significant trigger since it is out of sequence with the actual celestial alignments of the solar system. The most likely cause of spirit sightings at these times is due to the fact that the date and its meanings are pressed into our subconscious minds. For instance, on the anniversary of my grandfather's death for many years I experienced some sort of contact with him, either through a dream message or by hearing his voice speak to me as I started to fall asleep. Many times I was not consciously aware of the date until the event happened, and since this was not happening on the death dates of my other grandparents I was forced to examine the reason why. When I remembered that the date of this particular grandfather's death was firmly fixed in my mind by a grandmother who dreaded its coming each of her twelve years as a widow, it is not hard to conclude that my mind was reacting to the date and probably not to a spirit presence. On the other hand, deep feelings engendered by the date of a tragic event might very well attract spirits. Obviously if the deep mind can be affected to the point that it conjures up unbidden images from the repressed subconscious, perhaps it can call out to the Summerland as well.

Offerings placed on ancestor altars have been made both at festival times and on these death anniversaries. Food, drink, blood, and precious stones have all been used in this manner.

A little-known altar offering that was immensely popular in the past was that of hair. Hair offerings have been found in Roman burial sites and are still placed on family altars in Polynesia. In ancient Israel and among some Native American tribes, cutting the hair was a sign of mourning done immediately upon learning of a death. Perhaps it has been used sacrificially during times of grief because hair, like bone, is slow to grow and slow to decay. The slow growth makes giving it up a true sacrifice since it cannot easily be replaced, and being slow to decay makes it a good memento to keep. The Victorians were fond of clipping hair from the dead and weaving it into broaches or entwining it with flowers for framing.

Birthdays of the deceased have also been times to honor them, though this has been done less often than at the anniversary of the death. My father, who did his graduate work in comparative religion, used to tease that on our birthdays my brother and I should follow the customs of other peoples and not only give gifts to him and our mother, but should exempt them from household chores in thanks for them giving us life. As a child I refused to believe anyone would celebrate their birthday in this manner, and I thought he was making up the whole thing. I later found out that in some cultures this is indeed the way in which birthdays are celebrated.

Today even the most mainstream people engage in acts that border on what they would call "ancestor worship" if done by Pagans. Remembering the anniversary of a passing by looking at old photos, sharing stories of the deceased's life, or visiting the cemetery and leaving an offering of flowers are to be found among these.

❧ Erecting and Consecrating an Ancestor Altar or Shrine

An ancestor altar or shrine is a space for the spirits of the ancestors to rest and be honored when they come to your home or yard (see Chapter 3 for a basic discussion of an altar's function and instructions on how one is traditionally set up for Pagan ritual). If there is any difference to be noted between an altar and an ancestor altar at all, it may be generalized that the former is a functional place for ritual while the latter is more like a memorial, but both can serve as places to hold your rites if you wish them to be. The ancestor altar is symbolic of your respect for, and belief in, the ancestor spirits. Through setting apart a place for them, it reaffirms yourself as a pivotal point by marking your ties to the past and the future.

You can use the altar/shrine to make offerings to your ancestors, to help you adapt to a bereavement period, to allow your children contact with grandparents they otherwise would never know, or to hold rituals that honor them. The altar/shrine can be a permanent fixture in your home or yard, or it can be erected and dismantled as needed. Those following family traditions usually prefer to leave their altars up year-round, and other traditions make this choice by personal preference.

You can create a shrine virtually anywhere. Outdoors, you may wish to paint the names of your ancestors on a rock along with symbols of rebirth and eternity. You could also use a simple stone mask representing a deity to whom you feel close (often seen in garden shops) and place this outdoors, where you can adorn it with fresh flowers or herbs when you like. Or you may wish to place some symbolic statuary at the base of an old tree. Trees are excellent symbols of your lineage when you view yourself as the trunk with your ancestors in the vast root system below you and your descendants in the tall branches above. This is not a new idea—in fact, this imagery is exactly where the term "family tree" comes from.

A rock memorial.

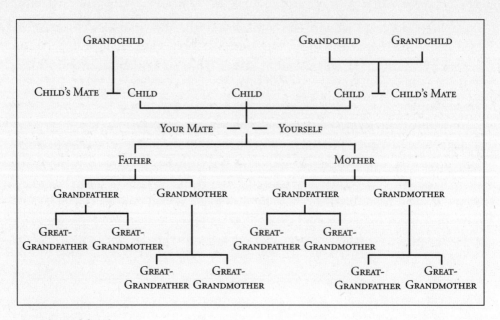

A traditional family tree.

No matter how much or how little you know about your family history, you can create a family tree to grace an ancestor altar as well as help the rest of your family understand their connections to those being honored at this place. Even if all you know is one ancestor's name, you can fill in blanks to represent simply "mother" or "father," et cetera. Or you can draw a tree showing your connections to your siblings, mate, children, friends, or coven.

Indoors, you can create an ancestor altar/shrine on a table or dresser top, on a wall shelf or empty bookshelf, or in the most traditional place: over the mantle near the fireplace. In old Europe fireplaces were literally the heart of the home, the center point that was considered sacred space and where the fire of life was left burning night and day.

On this ancestor altar you should place old photographs, jewelry, or other mementos and reminders of your antecedents. You should also include a candle (which should not be lit unless you are where you can keep an eye on it) since flames have been central to memorial altars since before recorded time, a theme we still see carried out on the graves of famous leaders in the form of an eternal flame. The grave of slain U.S. President John F. Kennedy boasts such a flame, and they are also present in modern synagogues near memorials for the martyred dead.

If you are short on floor space but still want an ancestor altar in your home, try using a blank wall. Hang old photos of your family up in a pleasing arrangement around a wall sconce, one with either a candle or an oil lamp. On death anniversaries the lamp can be lit in honor of the one whose memory you are recalling.

After you have created this sacred space, you will need to consecrate it to its purpose so that your ancestors may feel free to rest there at will once you begin actively honoring them. For this rite you will need some purifying incense or oil and a single candle. Good purifying fragrances include frankincense, bay, sandalwood, cinnamon, sage, benzoin, lemon, rosemary, vervain, and cedar.

When you are ready to begin, cast your circle around you and call the quarters and any deities, et cetera, you wish to have present. Light the single candle, saying:

> *Behold the flame of memory:*
> *A light of hope in the darkness.*

Take the oil or incense and, using your fingers to dab on the oil or taking the incense and allowing the smoke to flood the altar/shrine, say the following:

> *I purify this altar* (or *shrine*) *that it may be*
> *deemed a fit resting place for all my relations.*

When you are done, put down the oil or incense. Then, holding your hands up over the altar or shrine with palms down, visualize a purifying beam of sacred energy coming from them and filling your altar/shrine. This is the final act of "de-programming" to remove any other energies that the items in it may have absorbed. You want the altar/shrine to be free of energies that your ancestors would not be comfortable with or that they might reject. Any unwanted or negative energy that you feel coming out of the item should be grounded, directed harmlessly into Mother Earth by your visualization and will, or by absorbing this into your hands and then placing your hands on the ground to disperse the energy.

When you feel that this clearing of the altar/shrine is complete, you may say before closing your circle in the usual manner:

> *For all my ancestors,*
> *So mote it be!*

A Solitary Rite to Honor the Ancestors

This ritual can be converted to group use, but naturally works best in solitary or family situations where the ancestors being honored are all closely linked to the persons participating in the rite. This rite should be done centered around the altar or shrine you have made for your ancestors because, at the end, you will be inviting them to reside there if they choose to do so. This means new ones may come to your home, and old ones may leave or return again. This will be their choice, but you must make the invitation if you want them there.

For this ritual you will need one single candle and an incense formula designed to evoke friendly spirits or to act as a portal between worlds. Try any of the following incense formulas:

Incense Formulas to Evoke Friendly Spirits

❧ To Help Open a Portal between Worlds 1

2 parts lavender

1 part cinnamon

pinch of wormwood

❧ To Help Open a Portal between Worlds 2

2 parts lavender

1 part mastic

1 part cinnamon

pinch of wormwood

❧ To Help Attune Your Senses to the Spirit Realms

1 or 2 parts sandalwood chips

1 part Balm of Gilead

1 part sage

❧ To Assist in the Seeing of Spirit Manifestations

1 part mastic

1 part amaranth

1 part yarrow

pinch of sage

As you mix the incense, focus on it being a portal for only your own loving family. This will help minimize the chance of bringing in a lower entity you do not want. You may also wish to add a touch of frankincense, basil, or black pepper to the blend. These are highly protective substances that will hold lower entities and unwanted spirits at bay. Any psychic self-defense techniques of which you are fond can also help make this a safe, pleasant experience.

When your altar is set for whatever rituals you plan to use, light your incense charcoal but keep the incense off of it for the time being. Whether you wish to place this portal inside your circle, or just outside of it, is up to you. There are two schools of thought on this (both discussed in detail in Chapter 10) and neither is right nor wrong. If you start out one way, and find you are uncomfortable with it, shut down the rite and begin again at a later time using the other method.

Cast your circle in your usual manner, call the quarters, then light the single candle, saying:

> *Hear me this eve, spirits of my lineage,*
> *Shattered fragments of my own soul.*
> *United by blood, love, and kinship,*
> *I light the flame of life to honor you this night.*
> *My circle, as my heart, is open to you.*

At this point, take a look at the incense charcoal and make sure it is smoldering. If not, pause long enough to fan it to life or to re-light it if necessary. Say:

> *Mothers and Fathers, hear me as I add my own joyful voice*
> *to your ancient ghostly chorus as it echoes down to me over*
> *many centuries past, singing the soul-song of oneness, of love,*
> *of life, of death, and of rebirth.*

Toss the incense on the coals. As you do this, visualize the door to the Otherworld opening and your loved ones spilling forth. Then turn and face the direction where you view the Otherworld being and say:

> *Goddess of the Otherworld, Mother of all Life,*
> *part wide the veil and close the deep chasm*
> *separating world from world that my cherished*
> *ancestor spirits may be here with me in this place*
> *and time. God of the Otherworld, Lord of Death,*
> *I hear now the bay of your hounds, the beat of*
> *hooves pounding the night sky, riding hard with*
> *the immortals. In this sacred moment in time,*
> *in this sacred space, the old ones join me now.*

You should feel a tangible presence in the air around you, and you may even see ghostly shapes arising inside your circle. The presence should feel loving, but if you feel the least bit uneasy, you should dismiss the spirits—by command if necessary—douse the incense, and stay inside the protection of your circle until the uneasy sensation goes away.

The energy around you may make you want to dance or sing. Follow your impulse to join in these ancient rites with your family/tribe. This is as valid a way to honor them as any physical offering you could make.

When you have worked through this energy, say some words of welcome to your family. Then make a statement of your identity in relation to them. If you are female, start with a listing of your mothers as far back as you can recite. For example, mine would sound like this:

> *I am Edain, daughter of Billie, daughter of Doris, daughter*
> *of Estella, daughter of Suzanna, daughter of Mary.*

My brother might say:

> *I am Richard, son of Donald, son of William,*
> *son of Edward, son of Liam, son of Henry.*

You can also align yourself with your other lineages as you choose, perhaps saying daughter of, son of, daughter of, et cetera. For example:

> *I am Edain, a daughter of Donald, a son of Veva, a daughter*
> *of John, a son of Mary, a daughter of Desdemona.*

If you do not know your heritage, or do not wish to recite it, you can simply make a statement such as:

> *I am* (Craft or secular name), *a daughter* (or *son*) *of my mother*
> (or *father*, et cetera), *who is the daughter of another mother,*
> *who is the daughter of another mother, who is the daughter*
> *of the Goddess* (or *God*).

After you make your lineage identity, continue speaking these affirmations:

> *I am the trunk of the tree. I am the end product of many*
> *generations. I am the point at which the past ends and the*
> *future begins. I am what I am because of the past. I am*
> *the future unborn. All time and space meet in my aspect.*
> *Through me all life and all death are united as one.*
> *Blessed be all my relations. Blessed be the ancestors.*
> *Blessed be my tribe. Blessed be all souls. We are one.*
> *We are I.*

You may make an offering or give a libation to your ancestors at this time, and spend as much time in the circle with them as you like. When you are ready to end the rite, you should tell the spirits that they are free to reside in your shrine/altar and remain an active part of your family. Allow the incense to burn a while longer so that any who wish to leave may do so, then dismiss your quarters and close your circle in your usual manner.

❧ A Ritual to Maintain Personal Ties after a Death

One of the primary reasons death is hard for us to accept is because of the images of eternal parting that have been ground into our heads by our society. Even in Paganism, which embraces the doctrine of rebirth, it is sometimes hard for us to truly believe that we and our loved ones will meet again. And even when we do firmly believe in this promise of a life to come, we certainly know we will not have the exact same type of relationship simply because we will not be the exact same people.

The following is a ritual my husband and I have experimented with on Samhain, a night when the past, present, and future are all nearest to us, and when we can most easily work the magick to keep ourselves close to our loved ones. I once referred to this ritual as a way of "strengthening karmic ties," but in reality it is more a way to reaffirm one's closeness to departed loved ones. Through this ritual you unite your spirits in hopes that your love for each other is strong enough that you will recognize each other when you meet in another life, either past or future.

Remember that since time is not linear, but is only perceived that way, the idea is not really to "come back again together." This is only an overused metaphor for our limited, linear perceptions. The idea is to open the inner eyes of your many selves who are living in other times and places so that they will consciously or subconsciously recognize the passed-over one with whom you work the ritual so that you can reunite in another loving relationship in another time and place.

For this ritual you will need only two candles and some oils or perfumes. The oil will be used to anoint the candles, one representing yourself, and the other representing a passed-over loved one. Choose an oil that to your mind best represents each of you, or buy a commercial perfume if this works better for you. Scent is a powerful trigger to deep memories, which is why we use it so liberally at festival times (mainstream ones too) and in romantic situations.

Before anointing the candles you should carry the one that will represent yourself around with you for about a week, so that it will absorb your energy and truly become an extension of yourself. The other should be wrapped up with an item belonging to the passed-over person with whom you wish to strengthen your ties. If this is impossible, try placing it near a photograph of the person, or on or near an item with which that person once had contact. Naturally, the greater the contact, the better the catalyst.

When you are ready to do this ritual, cast your circle as usual and begin to anoint the candles, doing the other person's first. As you anoint be sure to focus on the person, summoning up in your mind all the associations you can about that person, making the face and spirit as real as possible. Set the candle at the far side of your altar or circle, then anoint your own candle. When you are finished, place this candle near yourself.

Close your eyes and, with your mind, call out to the ancestor with whom you are going to work. Visualize your call going out across the vast reaches of the universe, across time and space. You do not have to call their spirit to the circle itself, but you must establish an emotional link. You need only to awaken their spirit so that it is aware of you on some level of its being. Do this by focusing on shared memories and on the images of people you both love. After each one you clearly visualize, mentally reaffirming your goal, all the while leaving the spirit with the free will you would want for yourself. After each memory and reaffirmation of the goal, move the spirit's candle a few inches closer to your own.

When the two candles are side by side, take one in each hand and say the following words:

> The flame of love burns bright, drawing two souls together
> across the universe. Time and space is ours to conquer if we
> so desire. As each so wills it, so may it be with (your name)
> and (spirit's name). May the eyes of our souls be opened to
> each other's presence; may our hearts be wise in their choosing.
> In love I join our life flames that we might recognize these
> opportunities as they appear to all of our selves.

Place the flames together so that the two candles make one flame. Hold them there for moment or two while visualizing the touching of your souls. Get a sense for the essence that is the flame of the spirit's being so that it will be easily recognizable to you again. Hopefully the spirit is getting the same feedback from your candle. When you have done this, say:

> May the soul see and know,
> May the heart feel and show.
> Two souls, one goal.
> In love we are eternal.

While the flames are still as one, extinguish the candles by blowing them out. Visualize this act as the much-touted "breath of life." As the smoke rises from the wicks try to see this as a friendly messenger carrying your need to the hearts of the deities. Then say:

> By the free will of all,
> So mote it ever be!

You may want to experiment by trying this ritual between yourself and someone who is still with you on the earthly plane. In this case, both of you would anoint and use your own candle in the rite. My husband and I have tried this and later found, when practicing past life regressions, we were drawn to explore many more lifetimes where we believe we had some type of emotional link. While it is true that these "lives" could be discounted as a psycho-drama for which we had conditioned ourselves, we still found it interesting and hope that somewhere in time we are together again in some type of loving relationship. If you do try this, leave the choice of being together again or not up to the free will of your other selves. Binding yourself karmically to one who is living now with the intent of reincarnating repeatedly together may send you into a cycle of misery. If your relationship sours, you will have a mess trying to undo that spell and all your selves will suffer for the error in judgment.

If you have experience with past life regression, you can begin to find out just how well your spells have worked by seeing if you recognize the person you did your spell with in subsequent efforts. If not, you may need to work more on opening the eyes of your soul so that you can know other beloved souls when they appear to you.

Seven

Honoring The Animal Spirits

WE PAGANS CHERISH OUR ANIMALS JUST AS WE DO all the other manifestations of nature through which we worship. We have never forgotten that the fate of the animals is linked to our own. No matter where we look in our past, the animals have been there for us as friends and teachers, and as such, they deserve a place in our rites when they no longer share our world.

Within the mainstream religions it is generally accepted that animals have no place in the afterlife and that no heaven awaits them, especially not one shared with human souls. There has even been debate as to whether or not animals have souls at all. The arrogance leading humans to believe that, of all living things, we alone possess an eternal spirit has inevitably led to the type of denigration that makes it all too easy to exploit our animal friends and their environment.

It is only in modern times that the sacred trust between animals and humans as co-inhabitants and caretakers of this world has been breached. We do not have to look very hard or deep into our collective past to see the high esteem in which animal life was once held. Such veneration should never be confused with the modern day animal rights/animal welfare movement, which is often spear-headed by people who have little understanding of the nature of the animals they seek to protect. A sad example of this ignorance occurred a few years ago when a group professing to care about animals' lives went to dog shows and poisoned animals claiming, as their justification, that the dogs were better off dead than at the shows. They based this judgment on some erroneous personal convictions that went against what we know is the nature of canine behavior.

In general, it is safe to say that Pagans have never worshiped the animals themselves, but use their images and energies as a focus for worshiping deities whose essence and energy they share.

Our ancestors killed game willingly and often. This was how they fed their tribes and families. They did their killing with a conscious awareness of the interconnection and interdependence of all life. They killed with respect for the spirit of the animal they hunted. Most hunting took place after lengthy tribal rituals in which the hunt was acted out—a use of sympathetic magick to ensure success—and the animal's spirit pacified. After making the kill, it was not unusual for hunters to offer a prayer of thanks to the animal's spirit for its sacrifice. In some cultures it was customary for hunters to consume the heart of the animal so that its spirit would live on within themselves. Other tribes finished their hunting rituals with animal fertility rites, more acts of sympathetic magick to ensure the perpetuation of the species from which they took their kill.

Tribal people around the world knew how precious their animals were, and the manner in which they used every single part of a carcass is legendary. After everything which could be turned into food and clothing was used, the sinew became thread, the teeth decorations, and the claws talismans of strength and potency.

The concept of having a totem animal, one who shares its attributes with a human, is common to the shamanic practices of virtually all nature-based religions. The practice has regained widespread popularity among today's Pagans, and many books on modern shamanism provide rituals and guidelines for discovering and working with these animals.[1]

Many animals figure heavily in creation myths. In these, the deity who is credited with the creation of the universe (or with a specific segment of it) is depicted as a particular type of animal, one usually held sacred within that culture. For example, Hathor in Egypt was one of the creation deities, and she is seen as a winged cow. Cow Goddesses Bo Find and her two sisters first brought the animals and vegetation to Ireland. In Wales, Cerridwen the sow Goddess bestowed wisdom, death, and rebirth.

A great number of other Gods and Goddesses—perhaps as many as a quarter of all Pagan deities still known today—are either guardians of a particular animal species (like Ireland's Aine and her cattle), have animals symbolic of or sacred to them (such as China's Fu-Hsing and his bats), are skilled shapeshifters who can take animal forms at will (like Wales' Cerridwen), or are made of up mixed animal parts, taking the best from each to create a unique balance of power (as seen in Rome's Pales). A few were designated as Lord or Lady of Beasts, or as the deity of all animals, such as the Incas' Sigu or the Greeks' Artemis. Below is an abbreviated list of some of these deity/animal associations:

Cultural Deity and Animal Associations

Deity	Gender	Culture	Animal(s)
Abul	female	Sudanese	serpent
Acca Larentia	female	Roman	wolf
Aige	female	Irish	deer
Aine	female	Irish	cow
Akerbeltz	male	Basque	goat
Amalthea	female	Cretan	goat
Amphitrite	female	Greek	sea mammals
Anubis	male	Egyptian	jackal
Apedemak	male	Sudanese	lion
Arachne	female	Greek	spider
Artemis	female	Greek	all animals
Artio	female	Celtic	bear
Atargatis	female	Middle Eastern	dolphin
Badb	female	Irish	crow
Bast	female	Egyptian	cat
Biliku	female	Andamanese	spider
Blodeweudd	female	Welsh	owl
Bo Find	female	Irish	cow

Continued on next page

Deity	Gender	Culture	Animal(s)
Bran	male	Celtic	raven
Budhi Pallien	female	Assamese	tiger
Cerberus	female	Greek	dog, lion
Cerridwen	female	Welsh	sow
Cernunnos	male	Celtic	stag, all animals
Ceto	female	Greek	whale
Chinigchinich	male	North American	coyote
Dechtere	female	Irish	crane
Diana	female	Roman	all animals
Durga	female	Indian-Hindi	lion
Echidna	female	Greek	serpent
Edain	female	Irish	horse, butterfly
Epona	female	Celtic	horse
Fintann	male	Irish	salmon
Fu-Hsing	male	Chinese	bat
Gansesa	male	Indian-Hindi	elephant
Garbhog	female	Irish	serpent
Gengenwer	male	Egyptian	goose
Gucumatz	male	Mayan	serpent
Gunputty	male	Indian-Hindi	elephant
Hanuman	male	Indian-Hindi	monkey
Hapi	male	Egyptian	dog
Hathor	female	Egyptian	cow
Hekt	female	Egyptian	frog
Herne	male	Anglo-Saxon	stag, all animals
Hippia	female	Greek	horse
Horus	male	Egyptian	falcon
Hunahpu	male	Mayan	tapir
Huntin	male	Central African	fowl
I Kaggen	male	West African	praying mantis
Inari	female	Japanese	white fox
Io	female	Greek	cow
Ituana	female	South American	scorpion
Ixchel	female	Mayan	serpent
Julunggul	female	Aboriginal	serpent

Deity	Gender	Culture	Animal(s)
Kherty	male	Egyptian	ram
Khons	male	Egyptian	hawk
Khophra	male	Egyptian	beetle
Khors	male	Slavic	horse
Koojanuk	male	Inuit	bird
Kurwaichin	male	Slavic	sheep
Kurkil	male	Siberian	bird
Kurma	male	Indian-Hindi	tortoise
Kuzu-No-Ha	female	Japanese	fox
Lahar	male	Sumerian	cow
Le-Hev-Hev	female	Melanesian	rat, crab, spider
Liban	female	Irish	fish
Macha	female	Irish	horse, raven
Mafdet	female	Tibetan	mongoose
Mahakh	female	Aleut-Inuit	dog
Medusa	female	Greek	serpent
Mehen	male	Egyptian	serpent
Melusine	female	Breton-Cornish	serpent
Meuler	male	Incan	lizard
Moccus	male	Gaulish	boar
Nagas	male	Indian-Hindi	serpent
Nasa	female	Persian	fly
Neglam	male	Irish	bird
Nekhebet	female	Egyptian	vulture
Nekhebkan	male	Egyptian	serpent
Norwan	female	North American	porcupine
Ningyo	female	Japanese	fish
Oloso	female	West African	crocodile
Onnioni	male	Huron	serpent
Ophion	male	Greek	serpent
Orore	female	Chaldean	fish, fly
Osiris	male	Egyptian	bull
Ossian	male	Celtic	deer
Pales	male	Roman	sheep, cow, goat

Continued on next page

Deity	Gender	Culture	Animal(s)
Pamphile	female	Greek	owl
Pan	male	Greco-Roman	goat
Quetzalcoatl	male	Aztec	serpent
Rainbow Snake	male	Aboriginal	serpent
Rhea Silva	female	Roman	wolf
Rhiannon	female	Celtic	horse
Saba	female	Celtic	deer
Sarapis	male	Egyptian	bull
Scylla	female	Greek	dog
Sebek	male	Egyptian	crocodile
Sef	male	Egyptian	lion
Sesha	male	Indian-Hindi	serpent
Sigu	male	Incan	all animals
Siris	female	Babylonian	bird
Sun Hou-Tzu	male	Chinese	monkey
Taksaka	male	Indian-Hindi	serpent
Tarvos	male	English	bull
Tauret	female	Egyptian	hippopotamus
Tepeyollotl	male	Aztec	puma
Thalassa	female	Greek	fish
Tsan Nu	female	Chinese	silkworm
Turrean	female	Irish-Scottish	dog
Uairebhuidhe	female	Irish-Scottish	bird
Vajravaraki	female	Tibetan	sow
Wakantanka	male	Lakota	eagle, buffalo
Waluthanga	female	Melanesian	serpent
Zonget	female	Siberian	bird
Zotzilaha	male	Mayan	bat
Zu	male	Babylonian	bird

When dealing with animals on a more mundane level, we find numerous occurrences where pets or special guardian/totem animals were entombed with their owners. Cats were so cherished in ancient Egypt that their bodies were mummified just like those of their human owners. The burial sites of the Pharaohs contain not only cat mummies, but elaborate depictions of anthropomorphic animals offering protection and guidance to the passed-over spirit, or interceding on their behalf with the deities. Clay figurines of guide dogs, called *colimas*, were buried with the Incas to provide conduct to the Otherworld, and food animals were not unusual grave offerings in most ancient cultures.

Mythology and folk legends make much use of animals to teach lessons to humans, or to provide otherworldly guidance where necessary. Two excellent examples of this from the Celtic world are the White Hart, a stag which is archetypally linked with divine messages, and Gelert, the faithful hound of a Welsh prince who was rashly killed when the King thought the dog tried to kill his infant son when, in reality, he was fighting off a marauding wolf.

🌿 Making and Consecrating an Outdoor Animal Shrine

If you have a small, unused place on your property—even a corner of your back porch will do—you can set up a permanent shrine to the animal spirits. All you need is a place of focus such as a large rock, a statue, a staff thrust into the earth, or a bird or wild animal feeder.

Bless this place as being a sacred site by purging it with incense and saltwater and stating aloud your intent for the site. This can sound something like:

> (Name of place), *I bless and consecrate you this day to be*
> *a holy vessel to honor the unselfish spirits of the animals who*
> *have passed before. I bless you with elements of air and water*
> *that the animal souls of both the upperworld and underworld*
> *be welcome at your side. May all who come to worship and*
> *meditate here feel blessed and comforted. With loving intent,*
> *and harm to none, so mote it be.*

As you speak, visualize the shrine becoming pure and new, a sacred place for honoring passed-over animals. Naturally, once the shrine is dedicated to the animal spirits it should not be used for mundane purposes, such as a place to set your garden tools.

After you have purged the shrine, you can begin to collect items honoring the animals. For instance, keeping the shrine stocked with bird seed or small animal food is a nice touch. Another is to add items, such as fossilized bones or arrowheads, which remind you of how animals fed and sustained your ancestors.

You can also make a shrine to a special animal who has meaning for you. Perhaps you might feel moved to do this for your totem animal or for an animal who is sacred to a personal/patron deity of yours. In the large sycamore in our backyard we have an inconspicuous shrine to birds, animals sacred to sun Gods and Goddesses in many cultures. The shrine consists of a wooden sun wheel wrapped in gold yarn (a solar color) with tassels attached in the colors of the Triple Goddess (white, red, and black). At the end of the tassels we have attached feathers we find while out walking along the country road near our home. Nearby in the same tree is a bird feeder we keep stocked summer and winter, and at Yule we string popcorn strands on the tree as a special treat.

If you feel moved to do so, you can go to your shrine and make special offerings. You may want to do this on a pet's birthday, on the anniversary of its death, or when seeking a new totem animal to assist you.

A sun wheel for an animal shrine.

❧ Making and Consecrating an Animal Memorial Altar

As mentioned previously, the difference between a shrine and an altar is that the altar is a place intended for active worship and ritual, while the shrine is not, though it can be used as such if you want it to be. Many do use a shrine in this manner and, as always, there are no right or wrong ways to handle this. An animal altar can be set up permanently as separate from any other altars you have, or it can be set up and taken down as needed. Whichever option you choose depends on your personal tastes and space considerations.

My own animal altar is set up only when needed, usually at the anniversary of a pet's birth or death, depending on when I feel moved to honor its memory. No item in my magickal cabinet is exclusively used for my animal altar. In fact, accoutrements from the animal altar often grace my regular ritual altar at Samhain, when all the beloved dead are to be remembered. One item I always include in both animal and ancestor altars is a symbol of the cat, the animal fabled to possess nine lives, which makes him a perfect personification of our beliefs in reincarnation.

An altar to honor your pets and familiars—or any memorial altar for that matter—need not have all the working tools you would normally have set out on a ritual or magickal altar. I have never set these out on any memorial altar, whether for people or animals. What is most important is that you have as many mementos of your pet or familiar as possible—favorite toys, photographs, ribbons, trophies, papers, collars—anything you hold as a cherished keepsake will do. You will also need a single candle to represent the light of rebirth and hope.

After you have set up the altar, you should consecrate it to its purpose before enacting any rites there. With a stick or a pot of incense, circle the altar three times (more or less if your tradition has a sacred number other than three), letting the smoke from the incense purify the area. Allow the smoke to wash over the altar without getting it close enough to ignite anything; you want to be very careful not to scorch or damage any of your precious keepsakes.

Set the incense down and hold your hands, palms down, a foot or two above the surface of the altar, saying:

> By my will be transformed, you items of mundane life.
> You are now honored to serve as a resting place for the
> sacred spirits. May no negative thought or feeling be
> permitted at this holy site. As I will, so mote it be.

The altar can be used for passing-over rites for a pet, to honor animal spirits at Samhain and other death festivals, or to hold memorial rituals for a pet on the anniversary of its birth or death.

❧ A Solitary Passing-Over Ritual for a Pet or a Familiar

Creating and enacting a rite to say farewell to a special animal in your life can be very therapeutic. As mentioned in Chapter 4, society still does not condone the mourning of pets, and this self-help rite may be the only way you can express your bottled-up grief. Fortunately many support groups have sprung up over the past few years, both to meet this need and to try and change society's ridiculous taboo. Look in Appendix B and in the Bibliography for the names of organizations and books that can point you in the direction of these groups.

Passing-over rituals for pets follow a form almost identical to that of passing-over rites for humans. After all, our souls are on the same journey, heading in the same direction.

For this rite all you will need is your altar, set up as recommended above or in any other manner which suits you; a single candle and a match; and keepsakes to help you focus your attention. If you have other living pets or familiars who appear to wish to join in this rite, even if only by their mere presence, you should not discourage them. Animals know so much more than we arrogant humans ever credit them with, and sensing etheric presences is certainly high on their list of talents. If they choose to come and go during the ritual, you should allow this too. Like small children, they are able to pass over the boundaries of your circle without harming either it or themselves. Since they have not been conditioned to divide their perceptions of existence with the sharp lines of demarcation we adults draw on life, their minds see sacred space everywhere they want it to be.

After you have cast your circle and called your quarters, or done whatever else is traditional for you, you will want to call upon a deity for assistance. This divine presence will be the one that comes to take your pet to the Summerland, so you may wish to choose one of value to the animal rather than one of your own personal deities. If none readily comes to mind, refer to the list found earlier in this chapter to find a God or a Goddess with whom you feel your pet would be comfortable, or one whom you think will take an interest in your particular type of pet. In the instance of a dog, your evocation might sound like this:

> *To the farthest reaches of the upperworld, to the darkest depths*
> *of the underworld, to as far as my voice may carry, through time*
> *and space and all the universes, I call upon you, Scylla, loving*
> *Goddess of canines, to come to this sacred space this night. One*
> *of your children who has passed over into spirit needs your*
> *assistance at this hour. We both welcome you here. Blessed be.*

Light the candle on the altar. Think of this as the light of divinity, a focus for the spirit of your pet. Next you will call the presence of your pet's spirit. As you do this rite, do not be surprised if you actually see, sense, or even hear the animal moving about just beyond the boundaries of the circle. These occurrences seem to be more common to rituals involving beloved animal friends than with humans. This phenomenon may again be credited to the fact that animals cannot compartmentalize their thinking as we do, and do not as readily recognize our arbitrary boundaries. Using the example of the dog, the invitation might sound something like:

> (Name of animal), *beloved canine friend and trusted companion*
> (or *familiar* if this is how the pet functioned in life), *bring your*
> *wandering spirit to this place where you have always been loved.*

Let the light of the divine and the light of love radiating from my
own heart be your guide. You are welcome and wanted here, as
you always have been, and as you always will be. Come, if you will,
old friend, so that I may serve you one last time, as you have so
nobly served me.

When you sense the animal's presence, you should speak aloud to it, thanking it for sharing its life with you and for choosing you to be its human companion through this incarnation. You may share memories, good wishes for its time in the Summerland, and even issue an invitation to reincarnate in your life as another pet if it so desires. As you would with a person, you should assure it that it has nothing to fear in making this transition because there is a loving guide present to lead the way. This may not seem important, but remember that the animal probably relied on you in life to look after it and make choices on its behalf. It may have hopped up in your lap during thunderstorms, or may have come to you for a reassuring stroke when things around your home became hectic. Never doubt that your words of comfort can greatly soothe its soul. Then say your final farewells, concluding with words such as:

Be well, old friend. Take with you my love and my good
wishes for a joyous afterlife. We shall surely meet again.
Brightest blessings, gentle beast.

At this point you may ask the deity to take the animal into its loving charge. As you do this, extinguish the candle and attempt to close down the loving energies emanating from you. This is so that the animal's spirit cannot confuse the light of the divine who has come for it with those of yourself and the candle.

You may conclude this rite with other rituals to honor all animal spirits if you so choose, perhaps even making a special offering at your animal shrine in memory of your pet. When you are ready, you may close the circle in your usual manner.

Remember that you can communicate with animal spirits just as you can with human ones, though the way in which these communications come about is very different simply because the animal cannot transmit its thoughts in human language. Yet many, many stories abound about pets whose ghostly voices are heard by their owners when they are in need of comfort or protection. As a gesture of good will, and to reemphasize the importance of the animal in your life, don't forget to leave libations of food and drink for it at death festivals (such as Samhain) just as you do for your discarnate human loved ones. You can also use the feast day of the deity who came to take your pet's soul as a special day to remember your pet, perhaps making offerings to the deity in exchange for him or her keeping a special eye on its well-being.

❧ Respectfully Disposing of a Pet's Remains

As society slowly comes to accept the validity of mourning for a pet, we see a corresponding increase in the number of pet cemeteries, crematoria, and other businesses that cater to the needs of grieving pet owners (i.e. pet caskets, pet memorials, pet urns, grief support groups, et cetera). Appendix B gives the addresses of several of these businesses and groups. Others may be located through the classified ads of animal/pet-related periodicals or through a referral from your veterinarian.

As a final show of love for your pet, consider making a donation to your local humane society or animal welfare organization in its memory so that other animals may have a chance to live as happily as yours.

Eight

Personal Acts of Remembrance

WE ALL CARRY THE MEMORIES OF THOSE WE LOVE in our hearts. When the memories are of someone in the Summerland they can bring pain as well as joy. From time to time we may feel compelled to do something on the physical plane to honor these memories, to help alleviate the pain, and to allow us to feel a connection to the person now in spirit. Oftentimes we are unsure just what to do; or, when we are moved toward a specific action, we may feel it is silly and find ourselves insecure about seeing it through.

Paganism may be the fastest growing religion in North America today[1], but it is probably also the most misunderstood by those in the mainstream. Thanks to almost two millennia of persecution at the hands of those who worship other deities, the popular image of us as wicked old Witches or eccentrics is a hard one to dispel. Because of this, it is sometimes impossible to include acts that are meaningful to us in funeral services or at other times when we might wish to commemorate the life of a loved one. If one is a solitary Pagan, one not part of a larger group, the sense of isolation can make the problem worse.

Fortunately there are a number of ways to honor our departed loved ones within our own spiritual framework, and many of them need not have the knowledge or consent of others. The purpose of these small rites is to offer comfort to the living person performing these rites and to let the spirit of the deceased know it is still loved and its memory cherished.

℣ Offerings at the Gravesite

Aside from the home altar, the gravesite is the place most of us tend toward when we want to pay special homage to a passed-over loved one. This is natural since our minds more readily grasp the idea of the physical rather than the ethereal. Whether the spirits of our loved ones are actually there or not is immaterial. The gestures are noted, the magick is made, and our minds and our hearts comforted and linked to the spirit world just the same.

Many items left at or found in graves are meant to conjure up images of death in the mind of the one who left them there. These humbling death images and icons are known collectively by the term *memento mori*, a Latin phrase meaning "remember you must die." Following is a list of images that function as symbols

Grave offerings.

of death and/or regeneration, so that appropriate ones can be chosen for ritual work or for grave offerings (specific ideas for using many of them follow in this chapter). Because of the close ties between death and rebirth, both in mythology and in the Pagan mindset as a whole, you will find that many of these are interchangeable. One example of this interchange is the cauldron, which in Celtic mythology is seen as both a symbol for the Summerland, where all life returns after death, and as a womb, where it begins again.

Pagan Symbols of Death or Transition

apples	mirrors, when covered
autumn	the Moon
belladonna (toxic!)	owls
birds	Pluto (the planet)
black (in Western traditions)	ravens
bones	Raido (the Rune)
burrowing animals	roses, white
cairns	scythes
cauldron	skulls
crone Goddesses	spades and hoes
cypress trees	toads
dark moon	the Tower (Tarot card)
dogs	tuberoses
fire	water
hair	wheel
hourglass	white (in Eastern traditions)
jasmine	willow trees or branches
Laguz (the Rune)	winter
lotus	worms
mandrake (toxic!)	yew (toxic!)

Pagan Symbols of Rebirth

Aces (Tarot cards)	new crescent moon
ankh	the Phoenix
acorns	pomegranates
Berkana (the Rune)	red
black (in Eastern traditions)	seeds
burrowing animals	serpents

Continued on next page

Pagan Symbols of Rebirth (Continued)

cats	spirals
cauldron	spring
Death (Tarot card)	summer
eight (the number)	the Sun
egg	urns
green	water
Laguz (the Rune)	wheel
lilies	white (in Western traditions)
melons	wreaths
mother Goddesses	virgin Goddesses

It is no coincidence that grave offerings denoting rebirth are used most often in Pagan faiths. These offerings include many items found entombed in prehistoric burial sites. Apples, eggs, and wreaths probably have the most potent Pagan symbolism in this respect, but because they are not the usual offerings by mainstream standards they are the ones most likely to be picked up by groundskeepers and quickly disposed of as being too unusual. You may want to check with the authorities at the cemetery in which you wish to make your offerings and see what regulations, if any, they have about leaving non-organic items. If there are none, you might consider leaving a lantern of some kind. Lanterns archetypally represent illumination and hope, and will light the path of the spirits as they traverse between worlds. If you are not going to be there the entire time to supervise, do not use a lantern with an open flame. Instead, consider purchasing one of the small, battery-operated candles so often seen around Christmas. These cost no more than a few dollars and, powered with two 'C' cell batteries, should stay lit through a single night.

Another very old Pagan grave offering is blood.[2] To the ancients, blood was synonymous with life. In Wicca we keep this belief alive at Lughnasadh through our annual symbolic "killing" of the God/king, whose blood is spilled on the ground so that the land will remain fertile.

Oftentimes blood grave offerings were collected from animals in sacrificial rites, other times it was human blood that may or may not have required the donor to perish. If you do not wish to use blood as an offering, you can substitute wine or grape juice and make the gesture symbolically. Don't feel as if you're cheating if you do this—substitution is probably the most common way in which blood offerings are made by today's Pagans, and since ours is a religion powered by symbolism, your rites will lose nothing in the process.

Certainly offering a few drops of your own blood taken from a pricked finger can make a fitting statement of your belief in rebirth without endangering anyone. To keep the offering as sanitary as possible, consider buying a small packet of the lancets used by diabetics to test their blood sugar.

Blood offerings can be made in group situations too, but caution must be exercised. Unfortunately the reality of AIDS has made many of us rethink not only our lifestyle choices, but our ritual choices as well. Many years ago I was part of a passing-over ritual held at a gravesite where we concluded by each of us placing a drop of our own blood in a chalice of wine that was passed around the circle. When we were through, the Priestess took the cup and, with a gentle blessing, poured it over the ground in front of the headstone. We all felt very connected to the deceased and to each other at that moment, and it was easily one of the most meaningful final rites in which I have ever taken part. Now, ten years later, I hesitate to work with blood rites or to recommend them to others. If you are in a situation such as this you have every right to demand certain standards be met for everyone's safety, such as insisting on the use of sanitary, individually wrapped lancets. If blood is spilled on the outside of the chalice, or anywhere else where you will have to come into contact with it, insist that the ritual either be brought to a halt or that you fall back on an alternate plan that you have prepared ahead of time. Such precautions are not meant to cast aspersions on anyone's health or character, it is merely a matter of showing concern for the well-being of everyone present. This concern is mandated to us by the "harm none" directive in our Pagan Rede, and it should offend no one.[3] It also fits in with our concept of a coven as being a unit of "perfect love and perfect trust." If you have perfect love for each other, then you should be able to trust each other to work together for the good of everyone concerned.

Fresh flowers are easily the most often used grave offering today, an offering that is seen in many cultures. Though it has been long-forgotten by the masses, this too was Pagan in origin. Numerous neolithic gravesites have been found with fossilized flowers in them.[4] Flowers symbolize spring, which is why they are used liberally in spring rites rife with the imagery of rebirth and fertility, all of which are symbolized by the innocuous flower. You may wish to look through a book on the language of flowers and flowering herbs to help you pick out ones that will have special meanings for you. On the following page is a partial list of flowers and their meanings:

Flowers[5] and Their Meanings

apple blossom	romance
azaleas*	nearness
bachelor buttons	work, fidelity
buttercup	friendship
bluebells	protection
cactus	protection
camellia	company, gatherings
celendine*	fidelity, eternity
clematis	security, steadfastness
cowslip	secrets
crocus	birth, rebirth
daffodil	communication of secrets
daisy	simplicity
dogwood	love
gladiola	prosperity, new beginnings, wishes
goldenrod	prosperity
hawthorn	divination
heather	divinity
heliotrope*	wellness and vitality
honesty	honesty, innocence
honeysuckle	prosperity
hydrangea*	abundance, romance
impatiens	steadfastness
iris	frailty by strength
jasmine	night rendezvous, death
lady's slipper	wealth
lily	purity, life or death
Lily of the Valley*	death, change, happiness
lotus	death
lupin	passion
magnolia	unfolding events, fidelity
morning glory	new beginnings, quickness
mum	affection
myrtle	remembrance

orchid	promises kept
pansy	weakness
petunia	gentleness, shyness, steadfastness
primrose	modesty, guardianship
Queen Anne's Lace	quiet strength, willpower
rhododendron*	in waiting, passion
rose, pink	youth
rose, red	love, fidelity, passion
rose, white	silence, death
rose, yellow	friendship
snapdragons	power, man
snowdrops	children
sunflower	power, strength, watchfulness
thistle	unity
trillium*	good luck, blessings
tulips	constancy
verbena	motherhood
violets, purple	fidelity, passion
violets, white	betrayal, romance
water lily*	other worldliness, dreams
wintersweet	eternity
ylang-ylang	peace, serenity

*Warning: Use caution when handling those marked with an asterisk (*): some are quite poisonous.

Stones of various types have also been left at graves, though this is a less common offering than jewelry or precious metals, which are usually buried with the deceased. Stones of all types have been piled on graves or placed on top of headstones, and occasionally one sees evidence of this even today. Whatever the original meaning behind this gesture, it has been lost to us. In all likelihood some of these gestures were probably not offerings at all, but ways of the living protecting themselves from the spirits of the dead rising from the grave.

On the following page is a list of some stones and metals along with their meanings, and which might make appropriate grave offerings:

Stones and Metals and Their Meanings and Uses

amethyst	Associated with the element water, it is used magickally to induce peaceful sleep and to impart courage. It is also used in necromantic rites.
aquamarine	Also associated with water (the element of death and birth), it imparts peace and can help make contact with the dead easier to achieve.
beryl	Another water-related stone.
bloodstone	Among its many associations is that of birth/rebirth. The imagery of blood in its name makes it a good stone for leaving as a grave offering in lieu of blood.
chalcedony	A moon and water stone used in travel spells. May be a good stone to see your loved one on a safe journey to the Summerland.
copper	Used in travel spells. May be offered to assist the spirit on its journey to the Summerland.
diamond	A stone of transition.
emerald	Protection, exorcism, and prosperity. A stone of the faeries.
garnet	Rich red stones which can be used as a substitute for blood.
geode stones	Linked to fertility, rebirth, and the hidden underworld. Sometimes used as a catalyst for opening past life memories.
gold	Found in the graves of kings, such as in the pyramid of Egypt's King Tutankhamen.
hematite	A volcanic stone thought to belong to the underworld realm.
holed stones	Stones with naturally occurring holes in them are linked to fertility and rebirth.
iron	Protection from faeries and evil spirits.
ivory	Has been used as a grave offering in Africa, but is not recommended—to take ivory requires the taking of a life (the endangered elephant).

lava	A volcanic stone thought to belong to the underworld realm.
moonstone	Stone of the Goddess linked to all the moon's attributes, including birth and death.
obsidian	Like Hematite and Lava, this is a volcanic stone. It has deep associations with death, the underworld, and death deities. Knives made from obsidian were used by the Aztecs in sacrificial rites.
opal	Aids in astral projection and spirit contact.
pearl	Another stone with moon/water attributes.
rhodocrosite	Imparts peace.
rose quartz	Brings peace and love.
sapphire	Related to the moon and water, it imparts peace, wisdom, protection, and stimulates spiritual impulses.
silver	Metal associated with the moon, water, and the Goddess.
tourmaline	Imparts peace and symbolizes eternal friendship.
turquoise	Stone of spiritual knowledge.
zircon	Used in spells for protection from thieves and vandals.

Three other substances, often erroneously classed as stones for magickal purposes, have had their place as grave offerings. These are salt, sulphur, and coral. Salt and sulfur have been placed on graves usually to protect the living rather than to honor the dead. Salt has enjoyed a long and cherished history in Paganism as an element of grounding and protection. Making a circle of salt around a grave was believed to keep the spirit bound to the tomb. Sulfur is deeply linked to the underworld (recall how Christian legend says that Hell smells like sulfur) and has been similarly employed. Coral is not a stone, but the skeletal frames of sea creatures. Polynesian mythology tells us that coral contains the spirit of the Goddess. It has been placed on burial sites in the South Pacific to impart peace and wisdom and to ask the blessings of the Goddess.

If you are drawn to the custom of using death masks (as discussed in Chapter 2) and for whatever reason were unable to bury your loved one with one, you can leave one as a grave offering. The mask can serve both as an offering, a memorial, and as a token of protection.

Many cultures created death masks by making a casting of the face exactly as it reposed in death, while others created the mask separately from the body, relying on their intuition to guide them. The latter is the easiest and most practical way to make a death mask today, and will reflect the deceased's personality, achievements, family ties, et cetera, rather than physical characteristics.

To make a mask of this type you might want to draw one on posterboard and paint or color it to reflect the focus you wish it to have. If you want to do something fancier you can make a mask from papier-mâché. To do this you will need to cut a posterboard form to work with, leaving eye holes and nose holes if you wish to wear it yourself at some point. Then, take old newspapers and tear them into long strips about an inch wide. Next, mix up a thick paste of flour and water (you may have to experiment to get the right consistency). Dip the newspaper strips into the paste and begin laying them over the posterboard base for forming cheeks, orbital sockets, or any other feature you like. Don't pile the wet paper too thickly without allowing it to dry overnight. When you are finished and the piece is dry, it can be painted.

If you are skilled in woodcarving, you can carve your own mask, painting it when you are through. If you like using wood, but have no carving skills, look in craft stores for oval-shaped wood pieces that you can paint.

Another offering you can make at the gravesite requiring nothing but your own presence is a prayer. Because our religion is so ritual-oriented, and because we speak to our deities through these rituals, Pagans sometimes balk at the idea of praying, thinking this is better left to the mainstream folks. It is quite likely that our ancestors prayed to the Gods or Goddesses when they needed comfort, a favor, or just someone to listen, and we should feel free to do the same. Prayers can come spontaneously from the heart, or can be written out if this is a form with which you are more comfortable. Either way, they can help purge feelings of grief and offer you the comfort of your deities.[6]

The anointing of graves with perfumes or precious oils is another very old tradition whose precise meaning has been lost in time, though it is likely this was done either as an offering to the spirit/deity/guardian of the graveyard or as a way to offer protection to the final resting place and to pay tribute to the spirit of the deceased. In fact, in my experience, anointing seems to be the only acceptable form of protection to offer to a grave or a cemetery. Because cemetery vandalism is not uncommon, I tried several times to offer some added protection to the small country graveyard where my family has been buried for generations. I was informed in no uncertain terms that my interference was not welcome. In my protection visualization I kept seeing an image forming, which I now believe to have been the guardian of the cemetery trying to tell me to stop what I was doing. While at the cemetery I was very uneasy. I felt as if I was unwelcome, and I had the sensation that someone was carefully watching me, waiting to pounce if I made a wrong move. When I stopped trying to protect the cemetery in my own way, all these manifestations ceased.

Olive oil was the anointing substance of choice in the Middle East, where it was used to purify temples and altars. Perfumes were used in Africa and the Caribbean, and are still used by followers of the Old Religions of these regions and in New Orleans where Voodun and Santeria still flourish.[7] Essential oils have also been used, with patchouly and jasmine being among the favored fragrances. Others have bought expensive perfumes from the fragrance counter at department stores and used these instead.

Virtually any oil can be used to anoint a grave. The following is a list of some common anointing oils and their magickal associations to help you choose the best one for your situation:

Oils and Their Uses and Magickal Meanings

acacia	A purifying oil used in the Middle East to anoint temples and to fuel sacred flames.
benzoin	Has purifying and banishing properties reputed to eliminate lower, negative entities while attracting higher, positive ones.
cedar/pine	Protective and purifying. Also used in fertility and prosperity spells.
cinnamon	Has many magickal uses, including those of protection, psychic ability, and exorcism. It was a key ingredient in both the anointing oil of ancient Israel and in the embalming formula used in Egyptian mummification.
clove	A protective oil used magickally to silence wagging tongues that may be spreading gossip about the deceased, and for raising the positive vibrations of an area.
frankincense	An excellent choice for protection and exorcism still used as a base for incenses made for religious rites the world over.

Continued on next page

Oils and Their Uses and Magickal Meanings (Continued)

jasmine	From a night-blooming plant associated with the entity Death. One of its primary uses is to raise the spiritual consciousness.
lavender	Among its many magickal properties is protection. It is also used medicinally and magickally to increase longevity.
lotus	Like jasmine, it has links to the entity Death. Among its magickal properties are healing and psychic ability.
myrrh	Was burned in Egyptian temples to honor the Sun God Ra and to purify the area. It imparts a high spiritual awareness to anything it touches, and it can protect and exorcise as well.
olive	Used in the Middle East to anoint bodies, graves, and altars. Also used extensively as a fuel to burn sacred flames. Its primary functions have been to purify, or to serve as a base for other oil blends.
patchouly	A heady scent with strong links to the earth element. Used in fertility and passing-over rites. It is also used as a magickal substitute for the herb mullein, which is sometimes known as "graveyard dust."
rosemary	Among its many attributes are protection and purification. It has also been used in spells to enhance spiritual and physical healing, and to promote a peaceful sleep.
sage	True sage oil can be hard to find. It is an excellent purifier that can also exorcise.
sandalwood	Related to the moon and to enhanced spirituality, this is also a good purifying oil.
tuberose	A costly oil, but one long linked to death rites.
ylang-ylang	A moon-related oil linked to death rites and sometimes to the entity Death.

If you choose to use a perfume instead of an oil, you may be able to find out something of its magickal character by asking for descriptive material at the fragrance counter of better department stores. These cards, intended for use as sales tools, will often tell you the primary "notes" (dominant scents) used in making the perfume. With this in mind, you can check into the history of a particular herb or flower to determine its place in your anointing ritual.

Before anointing a grave, stop in front of the cemetery gates with the offering in hand, close your eyes, and mentally call out to the guardian of the cemetery, asking if you may perform this rite. Most often permission is granted. If not, try again at another time. If the cemetery is situated so that you must drive into it to be there, or if there is nowhere else to park, you may drive in and then walk back to the entrance to ask permission to go ahead with the rite. Keep in mind that in many places and in many traditions, the graveyard guardian is considered a being you do not want to thwart. If he tells you no, accept his decision and move on.

After permission is secured, go to the grave you wish to honor and stand before it with the oil uncapped so that its fragrance is set free. Kneel on the site and say the following, or similar, words. As you say them, place a drop of the oil at the base, top, and two sides of the headstone or crypt entrance, moving in a clockwise motion:

> *Blessed be the resting place of the earthly shell.*
> *Blessed be this memorial to one who has gone before.*
> *Blessed be the spirit that is freed from its shell.*
> *Blessed be this sacred space, this place between worlds*
> *in which I kneel.*

Next, add your vocal offering of protection, love, and honor, and pour the rest of the oil over the stone, saturating it as well as you can. As you do this, visualize the scent enveloping the resting place in a protective cocoon, and see the spirit of your loved one anointed by it.

When you are done, back away a few steps from the grave without turning your back to it. This is simply a show of respect, one which is usually reserved for royalty in most modern societies.

You may then turn around and leave. When you pass back through the gates, turn and thank the guardian/deity for allowing you to visit. Offer your blessing and then conclude the ritual with words such as "So mote it be" or "So be it," then go about your business.

🌿 Lasting Tributes

Lighting candles is a time-honored way to memorialize someone you love (as mentioned in Chapter 6), one which is even accepted in the mainstream. Old photos can be looked at and memories shared anytime you like as well. In the privacy of your home these small memorials are easy, common to all people, and should not be overlooked. But there are other ways to pay homage to a passed-over friend, ones which can better keep the loving energy of your loved one in your own mind and heart, and in the minds of others whom he or she touched in life.

One of the best ways to pay tribute to a passed-over loved one is to carry on work or a cause that was important to him or her. For instance, if a friend of yours died who was deeply concerned about animals, you might make a donation to your local humane society in memory of that person, or, if the loved one worked to assist the homeless, you might volunteer to replace him or her at the local shelter.

🌿 A Solitary Ritual to Honor the Pagan Martyrs

There has been a movement in Paganism over the past several years to include memorial rites for the martyrs in our death festivals. The martyrs are those who died for our religion, whether or not they were actually practicing Paganism. The list of offenses that caused someone to be accused of practicing Paganism/ Witchcraft is well-known to most students of either Paganism or history, and includes such innocuous crimes as having knowledge of healing herbs, walking alone in the woods, and humming to one's self. These dark years of persecution and execution are known in Paganism as the Burning Times, though, in truth, most Witches were hanged, drowned, or strangled rather than burned. This killing began in earnest around the twelfth century and continued until the very early nineteenth century.

Aside from the fact the persecutors gave Paganism/Witchcraft a diabolical slant that just doesn't exist, the real atrocity was that the vast majority of those executed were not actual practitioners of Pagan faiths, but wrongly-accused adherents of Christianity or sometimes even European Judaism. These martyrs deserve to be remembered and honored as much as the actual followers of Pagan faiths who were caught in the Witch hunters' dragnet. Many of the non-Pagan accused could have saved themselves the punishment of death merely by "confessing" their guilt, yet they refused to compromise their firm beliefs in their God and faith even to spare their lives. This is a stance many Pagans can admire, particularly those who follow the Nordic tradition known as Asatru, which has a feast day set aside to honor one such martyr known as Ruad the Strong.

The modern solitary, regardless of tradition, should also feel free to honor the ancient martyrs with a private feast and a ritual. For this simple ritual to honor those who perished in the Burning Times, you will need only your altar with its usual accoutrements and items of significance to you, a bell, matches, something with which to snuff a fire, and a small flame. The flame can be a single candle or a small bonfire contained in a heat-resistant dish. Sitting on your altar you will also need a white, unlit candle covered with a black cloth.

Open your circle in your usual way, call your quarters and do any other preliminaries which you or your tradition follow, then begin the body of the commemorative ritual.

Standing in front of your altar make the opening statement of your ritual's purpose:

> *I am a Witch*[8] (or *Pagan/Wiccan* if you prefer the term). *I have a proud spiritual heritage, the oldest known to humankind. My faith was born in the marriage of a single soul (the God and Goddess), nurtured on a pale crescent moon, and weaned on the coming and going and coming again of the seasons. I am a Witch. I stand here today able to freely worship the Old Ones because of the sacrifice of the many who came before me. I am bound to the past by blood and spirit, and bonded to the future by the steadfastness of my ancient faith. I am a Witch. Part of an ancient lineage and proud tradition, one which has known joy and sorrow, pleasure and pain, triumph and tragedy. I stand here tonight in this place which is not a place, in this time which is not a time, to pay homage to those who perished for love of the Old Ones that I might be free to live for that love. I am a Witch.*

Take the bell from the altar. Bells have been used in all religions as a signal to the mind and to the spirits who have gathered that something profound is taking place, to ward off unwanted entities/forces, and to herald special moments in ritual.

> *The roll of the strong and steadfast who have gone before is long and sad. Tonight their names and deeds are recalled with honor that their sacrifice should never be forgotten . . .*

Begin to read a list of some of the names of those who were persecuted or executed as Witches. You may even wish to include the names of those who died for other faiths who are not part of your heritage. If you have trouble finding these names, just look into the history of Salem, Massachusetts, or into the folklore of any European country. You may include as many or as few names as you like. After you read each one, ring the bell once. As you go through the litany of names you should begin to feel the presence of these martyrs at your circle and an undeniable building of the kind of energy which comes with unity of purpose surrounding you.

The following is a sample list of the roll call containing the names of both the falsely accused and those who were probably our coreligionists:

Ruad of Norway (ring bell once after each name)
Elinor Shaw
Mary Phillips
Bridget Bishop
Martin Tulouff
Colinette Gascoing
John Stewart
Florence Newton
Janet Mean
John Reid
Janet Pereson
John and Elizabeth Proctor
Elizabeth Francis
Margaret Barclay
Elizabeth Sawyer
Joan Waterhouse
Catherine M'Calmont
Sarah and Dorcas Good
Agnes Sampson
John Couper
Dame Alice Kyteler
Francoise Secretain
Rebecca Nurse
Claire Goessen

In some cultures it is taboo to ever mention aloud the names of the dead; many Native American traditions still observe this old code. In other traditions, particularly some Middle Eastern and Slavic ones, the names of the dead may only be mentioned on either the anniversary of their passing or on special high holy days during specific memorial rituals. If you follow a Pagan tradition that keeps to this custom, or if you just simply do not like intoning the names of those passed over, you can modify this ritual by placing the unnamed martyrs into categories or sub-groups. For example, if you choose to divide on ethnic lines, you may want to say something like:

> *For all the martyrs of Romania.*
> *For all the martyrs of Estonia.*
> *For all the martyrs of Latvia.*
> *Et cetera . . .*

Or you might choose to honor them by the way in which they perished:

> *For all the martyrs hanged.*
> *For all the martyrs burned at the stake.*
> *For all the martyrs drowned.*
> *Et cetera . . .*

Or you might choose to honor them according to the outbreak of hysteria in which they were caught up:

> *For all the martyrs of the Spanish Inquisition.*
> *For all the martyrs of the Salem Witch Trials.*
> *For all the martyrs of the Crusades.*
> *Et cetera . . .*

Whichever way you chose to verbally honor the martyrs, don't forget to conclude the roll call by including words to honor all the many other martyrs who remain unknown to us, or who could not be mentioned during this ritual due to time considerations:

> *And to all those nameless, unremembered souls who gave of themselves*
> *to secure the future of their faith* (ring bell). *May their spirits be bound*
> *up in the loving arms of the Goddess whose cause they cherished enough*
> *to die for, and may they soon return to their people on the earthly plane*
> *to enjoy with us the harvested fruit of their gallant sacrifice* (ring bell*
> again).

Allow the last chime of the bell to fade away to silence, then set it back down on your altar. Next, focus your attention on the flame in front of you, and say:

> *The fires of the Burning Times blazed strong and hot, but it*
> *consumed only our bodies, not our spirits. Martyrs live on in spirit*
> *and in the hearts of those who share and recall their painful sacrifice.*
> *By remembering them, may I have the strength to stand up for my*
> *faith whenever and wherever needed, and may I always strive to*
> *preserve the laws which protect my right to worship the Old Ones*
> *as I choose. As we say in this new generation of the Craft: "Never*
> *again the Burning!"*

Say this last sentence loud and strong, then quickly extinguish the flames. When they are out, take hold of the edge of the black cloth covering the white candle, and say:

> *From old pain comes new hope. As that which was hidden reappears,*
> *as our faith removes itself from the shadows of its hiding places . . .*

Remove the cloth; set it aside. Strike a match, hold it over the candle, and say:

> *. . . A new flame now burns brightly, one which ignites truth instead*
> *of terror, and illuminates the darkness of ignorance with the light of*
> *knowledge. It burns with hope for us all.*

Light the candle and say:

> *To all those in all ages who have perished for their faith I say to you:*
> *Blessed be! Never again the Burning; so mote it ever be!*

You may end the ritual and close your circle in your usual manner.

✣ Methods of Spirit Contact and How to Learn to Use Them

Another way passed-over persons are remembered by magickal folk is by contacting their spirits after death. A detailed discussion of how spirit contact is made by any of the methods mentioned here lies outside the scope of this book. Entire works have been written devoted to the study of some of these methods, and they are noted below wherever they apply so that you can pursue this course of study further if you choose.[9]

The Astral Projection Method

Astral projection is the art of sending one's consciousness (some say one's soul) forth from the physical body at will. This is called "traveling on the astral (or inner) plane of existence," a world conceptualized as being an unseen realm parallel to our own. While in this detached state, the astral traveler can encounter beings from all times and places since neither time nor space have any meaning in the astral world. Naturally, this means you can also meet up with your passed-over loved ones, providing they also wish to meet up with you (yes, free will is allowed for the dead as well).

Numerous methods abound for achieving this state that all take practice for success. My two favorite books on the subject—both with lots of practical advice—are J.H. Brennan's *Astral Doorways* (Northamptonshire, UK: Aquarian Press, 1986), and Melita Denning and Osborne Phillips' *The Llewellyn Practical Guide to Astral Projection* (St. Paul: Llewellyn, 1990). Another book is *Flying Without A Broom* by D.J. Conway (St. Paul: Llewellyn, 1995), which is very thorough.

The Automatic Writing Method

This method uses a simple pen and paper to allow the deceased spirit to pass messages through to the writer. Techniques for achieving the necessary receptive state of mind vary somewhat, but all require that the medium (the person contacting the spirit) be in an altered state of consciousness and remain mostly unaware of what is being written until the process is complete.

My own book on the subject, *How to Do Automatic Writing* (St. Paul: Llewellyn, 1994), outlines in detail one method of this art and provides lots of tips for jump-starting should you get stuck. If you respond better to aural or visual aids than to the printed page, Valley of the Sun carries both audio and video hypnosis tapes to take you through the process (see Appendix B for address).

Direct Voice Channeling

Direct voice is the sort of mediumship most people are familiar with thanks to the portrayal of the formal séance (a name for the event at which people gather to contact the dead) in movies and television. This is when the medium allows a discarnate spirit to speak through his or her body, using human vocal chords to communicate directly with any who are present. The process requires a mid- to deep-level altered state of consciousness during which the medium, or channeler, invites in the spirit.

Several methods are popularly in use, particularly among adherents of the Spiritualist Christian Churches, which regularly use spirit contact in their services. Two books discussing this art are Raymond Buckland's *Doors to Other Worlds* and Ivy Northgate's *Mediumship Made Easy* (London: Psychic Press, 1986).

The Dream Contact Method

A great many persons have reported having exceptionally realistic dreams of passed-over loved ones. The imagery of these dreams can be harnessed into planned, guided meditations to facilitate the same contact in an altered state of consciousness (see the guided meditation in this book at the end of Chapter 4). Those who can control their dream details (called "lucid dreamers") learn to take control of these types of dreams as they happen and can communicate with spirits during dreams if they so choose.

Several books are available that teach lucid dreaming, many of them found in libraries. Astral projection techniques can also be used to facilitate dream contacts.

The Oracle Board/Talking Board Method

The trademark name by which these boards are best known is Ouija Board®. These boards have an alphabet and numbers printed on a slick surface. A planchette, a pointing device with felt feet so that it can glide smoothly over the surface, is used to spell out the messages. Usually at least two people are needed to work the board, but more may participate. Each person participating gently places a fingertip on the top of the planchette and asks a question out loud.

Though the boards have gotten an unduly sinister reputation, extra caution should be maintained during this communication because the persons working the board have little control over who or what comes through.

Two books that look at this oracle in detail—and from two opposing viewpoints—are Raymond Buckland's *Doors to Other Worlds* and Stoker Hunt's *Ouija: The Most Dangerous Game* (San Francisco: Harper and Row, 1985).

The Pendulum Method

A pendulum is a heavy object that is balanced at the bottom of a string or a chain. It works by being suspended over a circular layout of letters or objects that are then singled out by the movements of the heavy object, much like the planchette of the oracle board. The pendulum may move in a manner indicative of a specific response without the assistance of a letter board. This is done while focusing on a question and inviting a discarnate spirit to direct the pendulum.

Different practitioners have their own ideas about just which movements of the pendulum have what meanings. For example, for some a counterclockwise spin is a negative answer while a clockwise spin is a positive one. For other mediums, these answers are reversed.

Though I have been told that at least one book devoted to the art of the pendulum is in print, I am not familiar with any of them. Several books on magick and Paganism have smaller sections which discuss using the pendulum, including my own book, *The Sabbats*.

The Psychometry Method

Psychometry is the art of seeing and hearing through touch. It works on the principle that all living beings emit an energy field that can imprint itself on inanimate objects with which they have had prolonged or intimate contact. If someone who has been trained to read these energies holds an object owned by someone passed over, they can often make contact with that person's essence. The skilled medium may see entire scenes of that person's life played out before his or her eyes, or hear complete audio transcripts of important past events.

Persons who are missing or dead through violent means often leave exceptionally strong imprints. Psychics working with police have employed this technique successfully to locate the missing and the dead.

Ted Andrews' *How To Develop and Use Psychometry* (St. Paul: Llewellyn, 1994) is a detailed book wholly devoted to teaching this art.

The Table Tipping Method

Because table tipping became a parlor trick habitually attempted at parties in the late 60s and early 70s, people tend to forget it was once considered a valuable means of spirit contact. This practice requires at least two persons, but four or more work better. All who are participating place their fingertips lightly on the surface of a small table and ask a question out loud. The table rocks to the medium's left to answer no, or to the right to answer yes. Rapping sounds may also be heard, and these too can spell out answers, depending on what signals have been decided upon ahead of time.

Raymond Buckland's *Doors to Other Worlds* discusses table tipping as an oracle and shows how fraudulent mediums have faked the tipping.

The Spirit Guide as Mediator Method

Some people—including some Pagan folk—ascribe to the belief that living beings all have at least one personal guide in spirit who looks out for us and assists us through life. Some believe that through their intervention we can have contact with those who have passed over, either by the guide passing messages back and forth or by escorting the spirit into the living person's presence. Sometimes this contact occurs through dreams, other times through special astral meeting places the spirit guide and person have worked out for themselves ahead of time. See Ted Andrews' *How To Meet and Work With Spirit Guides* (St. Paul: Llewellyn, 1992) for further discussion.

Nine

Looking Back at a Life Lived

MOST OF US FEEL THE URGE TO REFLECT ON the life of a loved one after his or her passing. This is a healthy way for us to cope with our grief. We often seek to understand how our passed-over loved one fulfilled or failed in life's purposes. Sometimes we wish to convince ourselves that the person was happy and satisfied with the course of life, and—for magickal folks—we seek to discover how that life stacks up against past and future incarnations. By using astrology and other divination tools we can begin to assess the meaning behind a spent lifetime.

🐟 The Astrology of the Death Chart

Just as the heavens are in a specific configuration when we are born, the same is true at the time of our death. And just as we can look at a natal, or birth, chart to help us determine unknown things about ourselves and the path we will take in life, the same can be done in retrospect with a death chart.

The following guidelines provide some broad generalities about the meaning of various astrological death times in relation to the spiritual and emotional aspects of the life lived. Keep in mind that these are guidelines only, and that many astrological influences can mitigate the exact shade of meaning.

The best way to look at a life using astrology is to have both a birth and a death chart on hand. If you have the precise times and places of both birth and death, you can take or mail this information to a professional astrologer, or an astrology service, who can provide a complete and detailed reading. Astrologers often advertise their services in New Age and Pagan magazines and catalogs, and usually do their best work when asked to rectify two charts, as they often are asked to do with the natal charts of lovers. To find an astrologer locally, you might consider looking in your phone book, check ads placed in whole-life living publications often found in health food stores and metaphysical book shops in larger cities, or by asking at these types of stores or looking on their community bulletin boards.[1]

🐟 Basic Death Chart Interpretation

The death chart relies heavily on the concept of "aspects" to make its determinations about the life lived. Aspects are the mathematical relationships between two planets at any given time. Though several dozen of these configurations have been noted by professional astrologers, we will only make use of the six most influential when looking at a death chart. These six aspects are listed on the following page.

When looking at a death chart, the two principal planets to consider are the Moon and Saturn, both planets with strong links to death, karma, and the afterlife, and which concern matters/things hidden. Reading their aspects in relation to each other and their aspects in relation to the Sun (the planet of the self/ego and life force) is the most revealing.[2]

Influential Aspects in Death Chart Interpretation

conjunct

Considered the most potent of the aspects, a conjunction occurs when one planet is within 12 degrees of another. This causes the energy of the two planets involved to merge. It often heralds the start of new matters or indicates the completion of an event or cycle.

square

Two planets are squared if they are within 9 degrees of 90 degrees of each other. At this time the astrological influences of each planet are in direct conflict with each other. This is not necessarily negative, but often indicates that forces beyond our control are in operation.

sextile

Two planets are said to be sextile if they are within 5 degrees of 60 degrees of each other. During this transit two planets are in inner harmony with each other, each of their most positive energies bringing out the best in the other.

trine

A trine occurs when two planets are within 8 degrees of 120 degrees of each other. At this time the planets work in harmony with each other to the point where we can become overly confident or complacent about our actions.

opposition

Two planets are in opposition when they are within 9 degrees of being 180 degrees apart. This produces a challenging disharmony between the opposing planets.

semi-square

A semi-square aspect occurs when two planets are within 2 degrees of 45 degrees of each other. In general, if the energies of the two planets are normally compatible, their mutually beneficial qualities are enhanced. If they are not easily compatible, they merely cancel each other out.

Astrological Aspects and Their Possible Meanings in a Death Chart

Moon conjunct Sun	Person has reconciled the negative and positive aspects of personality in this incarnation and is ready for new adventures.
Moon square Sun	Person learned life's lesson more through force than through self-determination.
Moon sextile Sun	Person had strong group dynamics in life that helped him grow, though he still has some things to balance out on his own.
Moon trine Sun	Person made good use of personal talents to make his way in life and can look forward to a rewarding interim between lives.
Moon opposing Sun	Throughout life the person's negative aspects battled with the positive and neither was the final victor. A life of inner stagnation instead of growth.
Moon semi-square Sun	Person spent life too dependent on others. Some growth occurred, but most of it was superficial. It remains to be seen if the changes are lasting.
Saturn conjunct Sun	Lessons of life happily learned. Soul can move on to other adventures, perhaps off the earthly plane.
Saturn conjunct Moon	Lessons of life fought against or not learned. May indicate a life burden by self-imposed negativity.
Saturn square Sun	Person grew spiritually in life, but usually by being forced to do so by others. The lesson still to be learned is one of self-responsibility.
Saturn square Moon	Person spent life allowing negative influences to lead him rather than taking charge of his own existence and allowing positive impulses to develop themselves.
Saturn sextile Sun	Person is part of a strong "soul group" who guided him through life, and will continue to do so in the afterlife. As an integral part of this group, the person returns these favors.

Saturn sextile Moon	Person was cast aside by its "soul group" during this incarnation, either as an act of punishment or to help the soul learn a needed lesson. Person will be reunited with the group in the afterlife.
Saturn opposing Sun	May indicate a life spent harboring a death wish. While this is not a bad thing in all situations, we all must remember that life is a gift, and it must be fully lived before death can be successfully undertaken. Like all polarities in Paganism, life and death are two halves of a whole. Person may also have felt that he was alone in life's journey and had no support.
Saturn opposing Moon	Person spent life feeling pulled in two different directions with the negative usually winning out. May indicate that person fought for the wrong causes in life.
Saturn trine Sun	Positive energy flowed through this incarnation, and person achieved all he needed and wanted to achieve. An indication of a very successful and happy incarnation.
Saturn trine Moon	Negative energy that dogged this incarnation was generally overcome by person's own inner resolve. Life may have carried some hardships, but it was generally a happy one with few regrets.
Saturn semi-square Sun	Person aided others in learning life's lessons, or in making their lives better. Indicates a person who was able to turn failings into successes.
Saturn semi-square Moon	Person required others to keep him on track and to force life's lesson upon him. Or it may indicate a personality who refused to try to do all he wanted or needed to do and lived in the reflected glory of others.

❧ Looking at the Birth
and Death Charts Together

Another way to look at a death chart is to look at the aspects of the Sun and the Moon in relation to themselves when reconciled in both birth and death charts. For example, when a birth and a death chart are overlaid one on top of the other, the two positions of the same planet can be mathematically measured. If the delineation of degrees places it within the range of one of the above-mentioned aspects, you can refer to the meaning of that aspect for further interpretation.

Studying aspects of the Sun positions on two charts provides insight into goals achieved or failed by the individual in question. Hard or negative aspects may indicate that the person failed to fulfill personal, karmic, or other goals in life. Soft or positive aspects may indicate that the purpose of the life was fulfilled, whether or not it seems to us that it was based on our surface impressions.

The aspects of the Moon positions on both charts provide insight into the emotional world of the deceased. Negative aspects might indicate personal dissatisfaction with the path life had taken, regardless of outward appearances. Positive aspects might indicate a life lived in deep personal satisfaction.

Looking at which astrological houses into which the Sun and Saturn fall on both the birth and death charts may reveal how the person handled personal and public situations. The twelve houses, the equal divisions of a chart relating to each of the twelve zodiac signs, have long been used to determine how people manifest certain areas of their lives, what weaknesses or strengths they have in these areas, and how these might change over time. The generally accepted spheres of influence for each house are as follows:[3]

The Twelve Houses and Their Spheres of Influence

First House (ruled by Aries)

Realm of the self, personal identity, motivation

Second House (ruled by Taurus)

Material items, finances, personal pleasure

Third House (ruled by Gemini)

Communication, intellect, hobbies and interests

Fourth House (ruled by Cancer)

Home and family, emotional life, children

Fifth House (ruled by Leo)

Love life, creativity, public life

Sixth House (ruled by Virgo)

Service to others, health, work, group relationships

Seventh House (ruled by Libra)

Partnerships, marriage, sense of justice/fairness

Eighth House (ruled by Scorpio)

Sexuality, personal needs, secrets, death/rebirth

Ninth House (ruled by Sagittarius)

Personal accomplishments, spirituality

Tenth House (ruled by Capricorn)

Career, outward appearances

Eleventh House (ruled by Aquarius)

Dreams/hopes, friendships

Twelfth House (ruled by Pisces)

Self-undoing, things hidden, the subconscious, karma

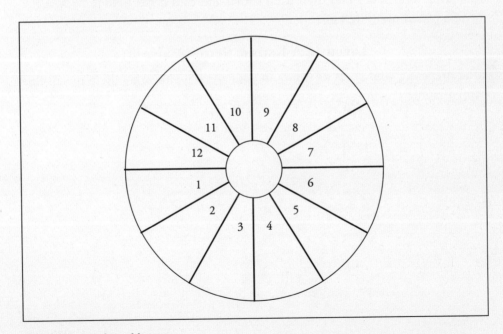

The twelve astrological houses.

For example, if the Sun at birth was in the Sixth House (usually indicating a Virgo native), the house of service, and at death was in the Fourth House, the house of home life, this would tend to indicate that the deceased person's need to serve others was satisfied through the family. On the other hand, if someone is born with Saturn—planet of the hidden and self-undoing—in the Sixth House, and died with it in the Fourth House, it may indicate that his or her need to serve others was not fulfilled by home life. Of course, any positive or negative aspects between these two planets—regardless of in which house they fall—must also be interpreted against the houses.

In spite of what its detractors might wish us to believe, astrology is a science, one which requires both mathematical skills and practice to master. The ideas presented in this chapter are only guidelines to help give you an idea of how death charts can be looked at for insights into the meaning of the life of a loved one. The books mentioned throughout this chapter can further guide you in your study, as can a professional astrologer.

❧ Using Tarot Cards and Rune Stones to Look Back at a Life

Most Pagans have at least one divination method with which they are familiar. Among the more popular are tarot cards and rune stones. The following layouts (patterns usually referred to as "spreads") are designed to be used with tarot cards, rune stones, or other divination stones and card decks to look back at the life of a passed-over loved one.

Layout 1: A Karmic Retrospective

After preparing your cards or stones in your usual manner, lay them out in this configuration:

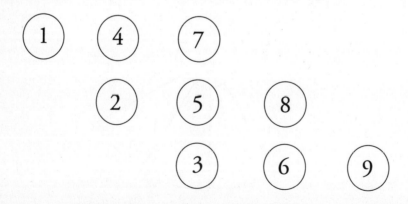

Interpret the cards or stones according to the following:

1. The principal lesson of the past life most directly influencing the recently passed incarnation.

2. The principal lesson of the recently passed incarnation.

3. The principal lesson to be learned in the future incarnation, which will be most directly influenced by the recently passed one.

4. How well the past lesson was learned in the life indicated by card 1.

5. How well the lesson learned in the past was applied to the recently passed incarnation.

6. How well the combined experiences of both the past and recently passed lives will be used to handle the future life as indicated in card 3.

7. What lessons were not learned in the past life card 1.

8. What lessons were not learned in the recently passed incarnation.

9. What the soul needs to do in a future incarnation to fulfill the karma first presented in 1.

Layout 2: The Path Not Taken

After preparing your cards or stones in your usual manner, lay them out in this configuration, which resembles the houses in an astrological chart:

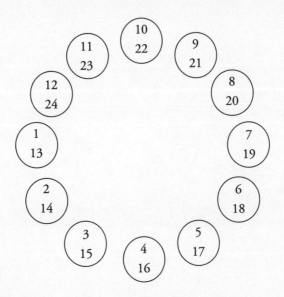

Interpret the cards or stones according to the following:

1. Indicates the path the person took to fulfill personal goals or to best manifest the ego.

2. Indicates the path the person took to fulfill financial goals.

3. Indicates the path the person took to fulfill personal goals.

4. Indicates the path the person took in regard to home life and children.

5. Indicates the path the person took to fulfill romantic goals.

6. Indicates the path the person took to fulfill their duties of service to others.

7. Indicates the path the person took in regard to partnerships.

8. Indicates the path the person took to fulfill sexual needs.

9. Indicates the path the person took to fulfill spiritual needs.

10. Indicates the path the person took to fulfill financial goals.

11. Indicates the path the person took to fulfill career goals.

12. Indicates the path the person took to work through karmic responsibilities.

The next round of cards (cards 13-24) should be placed over the first. These indicate the outcome if a different path through life had been chosen. For example, if the home life card (4) indicates that the person enjoyed great happiness in his or her marriage, and the card representing the path not taken (16) is negative, it may indicate that the person made the right choice in marrying.

Layout 3: Personal Achievements

After preparing your cards or stones in your usual manner, lay them out in this configuration:

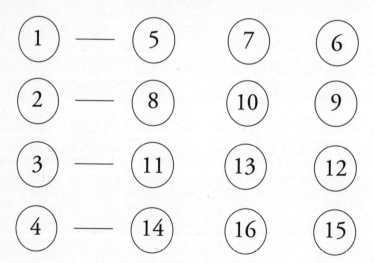

Interpret the cards or stones according to the following:

The first four cards act as significators, or cards which present a glimpse of the self in relation to the issue represented by each of the four rows of cards.

1. Career Path: What the person was in relation to his or her chosen career.
2. Home Life Path: What the person was in relation to his or her family.
3. Personal Path: What the person was in relation to him- or herself.
4. Hidden Path: What the person was in relation to his or her unconscious needs and desires.

The other three cards in the row show both the negative and positive aspects of the respective paths the recently deceased experienced over the course of his or her life. The center card of the three indicates how the person balanced the negative and positive aspects of each, and how he or she felt or reacted toward each of them at the time the life ended.

5. The negative aspects of the person's career path.
6. The positive aspects of the person's career path.
7. The balance point and person's final feelings on the career path.
8. The negative aspects of the person's home life path.
9. The positive aspects of the person's home life path.
10. The balance point and person's final feelings on the home life path.
11. The negative aspects of the person's personal path.
12. The positive aspects of the person's personal path.
13. The balance point and person's final feelings on the personal path.
14. The negative aspects of the person's hidden path.
15. The positive aspects of the person's hidden path.
16. The balance point and person's final feelings on the hidden path.
    This card may also indicate whether the person discovered these
    hidden aspects of the self prior to death.

Ten

Requiem I: Formal Passing-Over Rituals for Solitaries

By definition, a ritual must include a certain amount of well-planned and memorized material that is familiar, and gestures and words that trigger responses from within. Even inside this framework, solitary Pagans have a great deal of flexibility to go beyond the basic forms of their rites and experiment with a variety of new things to try to make any single ritual event more meaningful.

In contrast to group rituals, solitary rites are more thought- and action-oriented than they are vocal. Certainly there are things that should be, or need to be, stated aloud. An example would be when calling upon a deity. You should always speak aloud to make the initial call to the deity—even if it is done in a whisper—just as you speak aloud to get any other being's attention. Speaking allows you to fully solidify random thoughts into coherent thought patterns necessary for many rituals and for virtually all magick. Disjointed thoughts do not a ritual make, and they can be disastrous in magick.

Of course, if you cannot speak, you can use a pen and paper to write out the words to the same effect. The point is to be focused in your thoughts and your intent, and writing can achieve this as well as speaking, perhaps even better.

❧ Experiencing Psychic Phenomena during Solitary Passing-Over Rites

If you have never performed a solitary passing-over rite before, you need to be aware that whenever you call in a passed-over spirit for any type of farewell ritual, you may find the spirit manifesting to you in ways more profound than just giving you a vague sense of its presence.

Actually seeing the spirit with your physical eyes is rare, but it does happen to some people, particularly those with psychic gifts or those who shared a very close and special relationship with the deceased. If you are nervous about actually seeing spirits (and let's face it, even when you are prepared, it can be startling), then you may want to avoid rites that ask or require a spiritual presence. Stick with rituals like the memorial rite presented later in this chapter that do not need a spirit to be successful. The grave anointing ritual in Chapter 8 is another one with which you may feel more comfortable for the time being.

It is not unusual at all for a solitary to feel the touch of a spirit during these rites, especially if you have asked the spirit to come into the circle with you. One of the first solitary passing-over rites I did was to say good-bye to my own teacher of Witchcraft, Mollie. Though she was not all that much older than those of us she taught, she had a motherly way with us and would often place her hand lovingly on our forearms as she talked to us. The gesture always made me feel good, as if what I was thinking and asking about was really important to her.

Toward the end of my ritual, just as I cut open the west door to allow her spirit to leave, I felt a hand come to rest on my forearm. Even though I had been able to sense Mollie's presence all through the rite, I momentarily froze in fear when I felt her familiar touch. However, the gesture was as comforting in death as I remembered it being in life, and I quickly relaxed, tears streaming down my face as I said my final farewells. After a few moments I felt the hand leave my arm and, not a full second later, I could sense I was all alone again.

After I closed the opening in the circle I slumped down on the floor, completely drained both emotionally and physically. I must have sat there crying for a full half-hour, but they were tears of joy, not pain.

In my experience, the majority of Pagans who have enacted solitary passing-over rites have felt a gentle hand, or even a spectral hug, as they made their farewells. Ask around—most Pagan folk are delighted to share their stories with others of like mind.

Another common phenomena is that of smelling the deceased. All people have a distinct odor that is uniquely their own. This is how tracking dogs are able to sniff out lost individuals merely by taking a whiff of an item of clothing worn by them. Most of this signature scent comes from our natural body chemistry, but other fragrances we work with or wear on a regular basis contribute to what others think of as our smell.

Stop and think about it. How many odors conjure up the clear image of a specific person to you? What about the perfume that your mother loved and wore every day of her life? What about your brother, the mechanic, who always smelled a bit like axle grease? Can you catch the aroma of peppermint without thinking of the grandfather who always had some mints in his pocket? How about the custom tobacco blend your uncle always used in his pipe?

My grandmother, to whom I was very close, loved to sew and always smelled vaguely like a fabric store. This scent of new cloth, combined with her own body scent, was very strong and indelibly impressed on my mind. I had no trouble recognizing it inside the circle during her final rites, and I still occasionally catch that scent whenever her spirit hovers nearby.

Such phenomena may also occur during group passing-over rituals, particularly when the deceased was close to a number of people within the group. Still, these manifestations seem the strongest in solitary situations.

Our detractors occasionally site these experiences as evidence of the "evil" inherent in Paganism, or else dismiss them as mere manifestations of a deluded mind. But for most of us in nature religions, such miraculous moments are an affirmation of our beliefs in the eternalness of the spirit, and they should be cherished.

✣ A Solitary Ritual In Memoriam

This first ritual is a simple one to be held in memory of the life of a loved one. This does not mean that the spirit may not be present at the ritual, it just is not a requirement. In this it is similar to a mainstream funeral service, and is intended to offer solace to the grieving solitary more than to comfort the soul of the deceased. In fact, most books on spirit encounters or near-death experiences relate the fact that it is the spirit who usually has to comfort the living, not the other way around.

This rite may be done within a traditional magickal/ritual circle wherein your altar has been erected in your usual manner, or it may be done at the gravesite if you feel you will be able to remain focused should you attract attention. You will also need to check the rules and regulations of the cemetery to be sure that your ritual accoutrements are permitted on the grounds. Some burial grounds may require you to register your intent to hold a religious ritual on the grounds. Be aware that any privately owned cemetery (i.e. one owned by a church, synagogue, et cetera) does not have to allow you to perform religious rites on its property that are not in keeping with its own beliefs. However, if you wish to hold your rite in burial grounds held by a city or county government (within the United States), they cannot deny your request on a religious basis without risking a First Amendment lawsuit. What they can do is refuse your use of candles or other ritual implements as long as these are rules that apply to *all* groups or individuals who hold funeral rites on the premises. They cannot legally discriminate against you based solely on your choice of religion, though some will try, so be prepared.

For this ritual, you will need only those personal items you want to have with you in your circle: a tool to cast your circle, some incense, a small offering for the guardian/deity of the cemetery if needed, and a single candle. If you are holding this rite outdoors you may wish to choose a votive or glass-globed candle to help protect it from the wind, and you might want to bring along a cigarette lighter rather than standard matches. A chalice of water and musical instruments or recordings are optional.

Start by casting your circle in your usual manner. Then call your quarters and any other beings you usually call upon for assistance. To focus your intent, state the purpose of your ritual aloud. If you don't want to feel like you're talking to yourself, you may address yourself to the quarters or other beings you called, or to the guardian spirit of the graveyard who is always present. You may keep this statement as simple as you like, or make an elaborate speech if you prefer. So long as you feel that the purpose of your rite has been firmly aligned in your deep mind, you are doing fine.

Place the single candle in the center of the altar and light it. As you do this, visualize the flame as being representative of the eternal soul that is part of all living things, that part of us which can ever die but may only change forms. You may vocalize your visualization if it helps you focus.

Spend a few moments gazing at the flame while meditating on the nature of the eternal soul, particularly as it relates to the person in whose memory you are holding the ritual. Then begin to visualize a river flowing in front of you, one which stretches infinitely away from you in both directions. This river is one that is circular and represents the eternal flow of time over which your loved one has crossed. River imagery figures heavily in the Land of the Dead folklore of many cultures and should be made as real as your mind can make it (refer back to Chapter 1 for a discussion of water imagery in death folklore and mythology).

With your psychic eyes, gaze at the river while you remember all the things you love about the one passed over. Again, you may state these things aloud if you like. This is your personal time to say farewell and you can take as much time as you want. It is at this point that you may feel the spiritual presence of your loved one trying to offer comfort. Allow yourself to enjoy this contact. Remember that this is a spirit you love and who, presumably, loves you. You should come to no harm.

At this point you may wish to sing, recite poetry, or do any other readings or recitations meaningful to you or to your loved one. These are the sort of things that can sometimes bog down a group ritual when the piece chosen by an individual has little meaning to others in the group. As a solitary you have no one to answer to but the deities for the content of your rites, and the Gods are infinitely patient with our rituals. If you want to use poetry but don't know of any offhand which would be appropriate, a trip to the local library should yield a plethora of material. Poetic death themes appear to be second only to romantic ones in sheer numbers.

When you are finished with these recitations, look deeply into the river before you and begin to discern the golden-white glows of the spirits passing through its waters. Some will be in groups, others in pairs, and a great many all alone. Some move forward, others backward, and others appear to be momentarily halted in their journey. Though these souls may or may not see and hear you, you may speak a blessing to them such as:

> *Blessed be, fellow travelers, may your journeys be sweet*
> *and your spirits strong. May the light of divine love be*
> *there to guide you through the darkest reaches of the*
> *underworld and, like Persephone in the springtime,*
> *may all your ascents be joyous.*

You may also wish to address a final farewell to the spirit of your passed-over loved one who is now traveling somewhere on that river. As you do this, light the incense and say:

> *Farewell for now, beloved friend, know that you who shared*
> *this space with me in this incarnation will be deeply missed.*
> *You were unique; an eternal spirit in a physical body whose*
> *configuration will never be seen again throughout the whole*
> *of eternity. May your spirit choose to share time with me again,*
> *beloved friend. Until then, blessed be your travels.*

If the relative was a direct-line ancestor, such as a mother or a grandmother, you may wish to phrase your words to establish your link in the eternal flow of time that has come to you through them, and will presumably be passed on through you. For example:

> *Farewell for now, beloved mother of mine. Know that you who*
> *shared this space with me in this incarnation will be deeply missed.*
> *You were unique; an eternal spirit in a physical body whose*
> *configuration will never be seen again throughout the whole of*
> *eternity. Through that body you gave life to my own physical shell*
> *and invited my wandering spirit to trust in your care. As the wheel*
> *of time turns ever on, this gift of life is passed on again, each of us*
> *coming and going until our earth days are at an end, each of us*
> *carrying the memory of mothers past. May our spirits choose to*
> *share time again, mother. Until then, your child blesses your travels*
> *with love, peace, and gratitude.*

Allow the incense to carry your wishes away to the upperworld and to impart its blessing to your surroundings. You should also at this time extinguish the candle which has represented the flame of life. You may wish to do this by dowsing the flame in a chalice of water. The chalice, like the cauldron, is symbolic of the womb of the mother Goddess to which we must all return to await rebirth, and is a fitting symbol for taking the flame of life.

If you are holding this rite in a cemetery, at this point you may wish to make some sort of formal grave offering. Refer back to Chapter 8 for ideas and rituals to include here. When you are done you may close your circle in your usual manner.

If you have been working in a cemetery, leave the offering you brought along to give to the guardian/deity at the gates of the graveyard as you leave. If this is not possible, place it under a tree or leave it near the grave. Speak aloud your thanks to the deity and offer a simple blessing as you leave, such as:

> *Blessed be, guardian of this place.*
> *Steadfast be your watch.*

A Ritual to Assist the Departed to Reach the Summerland

Pagans appear to be divided on just when it is appropriate to perform a rite specially designed to take someone to a place they may not want to go. Perhaps the spirit wishes to hang around the earthly plane for a while checking things out. Why should we force our will on it and make it go to the Summerland if it is not ready to go?

My personal feelings on this are that you cannot force any spirit being to go anywhere against its wishes, you can only open the door of opportunity, smooth the path, and point the way. Even in a full-blown banishing ritual for negative entities you can only remove these beings from your immediate space, you cannot force them to go somewhere against their will . . . at least not for long. This rite will open the doors to the Summerland. The spirit may take the opportunity offered, it may merely memorize the path so that it can be found later, or it may not go at all. In any case, I believe the effort is appreciated.

This ritual can also be used to assist earth-bound ghosts who have been unable to pass through the veil separating the worlds to make the transition. This concept has become a popular theme in horror fiction and film and may seem absurd for this reason. The idea behind these rituals is based on occult principles that have roots in Pagan beliefs about the afterlife and are not silly at all. If you can determine that a ghost needs your help, you should offer it without worry.

As with the memorial ritual, you will need only simple equipment: your regular altar items, a single candle, a hammer, some food and drink to offer the spirit, and a piece of fragile glassware wrapped securely in a cloth that will not come open when the glass is broken later. Musical instruments or recordings are optional.

You will be calling on a divine light to come as an escort, and many prefer to conceptualize this light as a specific deity. You may choose a personal one, a favorite of the deceased, or you might want to check Appendix C to select an appropriate Summerland or death deity to assist you. Some persons like to call upon the entity Death for assistance, but I feel this is inappropriate for two reasons: first of all, the imagery of light is needed in these rites and Death is usually viewed as a dark presence. Secondly, Death is linked in our minds more with the transition from life to death rather than with providing escort service to the Otherworld. Still, some use him for this purpose and the choice is yours to make.

Open your circle and call quarters in your usual way, then light the single candle and place it on the side of your altar closest to where you or your tradition view the direction of the Summerland.

State aloud the purpose of this ritual and then call out to the spirit of the deceased to join you. Remember that this is an invitation only and not a command. If you sense the spirit is unwilling to come to the circle you should close down the rite and try again at a later date if you feel moved to do so.

Another point on which Pagans differ is in just where the spirit should be called. Some say calling them into the circle with you is the only safe place for them to be, and they will light an incense that can be used as a portal (see Chapter 6, p. 118 for these recipes). Others feel that no spirits besides the deities should ever be invited into the circle, even the souls of one's own loving friends and relatives. Both schools of thought make good cases for themselves in terms of personal safety and in preserving the sanctity of the circle, so it would seem this issue is a matter of how your own energy works with that of the spirits. The choice is yours to make.

To call the spirit you will need to reach out not only with your voice (or with written words), but with your mind and heart as well. Force your invitation out over the vast universe and know it will be heard and, if the spirit chooses, answered:

> (Name of spirit), *I call you across the vast reaches of time and space,*
> *throughout all realms and worlds, hear me call to you. I ask your*
> *presence in this* (or *at this*) *sacred space this evening. The door is open.*
> *Do as you will.*

If you cannot sense the presence of the spirit within a minute or two, then it is probably not coming. Simply close down the rite and try again at a later date. If you do sense the spirit is with you, you should explain to it in your own words why you have asked it here.

You may offer the spirit food and drink and share a final meal together as you share your memories. These memories may be stated out loud, or you can communicate these with your mind if this is easier for you. When the little feast is over, it is time to call out to the deity or divine light you have chosen to assist the spirit. Stand at the quarter you or your tradition views as the direction of the Summerland and raise your arms. Call out in your mind or vocally to the deity. Use the words "divine light" or the deity's name and say them three times, or use another number if it is sacred to your tradition. The following is an example using the Irish Goddess Badb:

> *Badb. Badb. Badb. Hear my plea, blessed Lady of the Otherworld.*
> *Come to me here, for one of your children is in need. Your cauldron*
> *of life, death, and rebirth awaits one who cannot reach it. Shining*
> *One of old, bring your divine light to illuminate the way back home*
> *for* (state either the spirit's earth or Craft name).

Turn to the spirit and speak words of encouragement such as:

> *On this journey you have nothing to fear. The divine light will*
> *enfold you in its arms and carry you safely to your destination.*
> *This is not an ending. When the flesh dies, the spirit is born. New*
> *adventures await you. The door is open and the path lit if you*
> *want to take it, and it can be found again when needed.*

If you have called the spirit into your circle, you will need to cut open the west door (or other direction to the Summerland) for it to leave. In either case, now is the time to blow out the candle on the altar so that it does not detract from the light of the divine.

You may sing in farewell, or recite poetry, et cetera. Death and the afterlife themes can be found in poetry and folksongs from our earliest examples to the present day. A great many of them contain imagery that make them suitable for use in passing-over rites. A fragment I am particularly fond of using at this point when saying a final good-bye came from the pen of American poet Walt Whitman almost 150 years ago:

> *Now Voyager depart, (Much, much more for thee is yet in Store). . .*
> *Depart upon thy endless cruise old Sailor.*[1]

To find other poetic references to death, begin by looking into the pages of *Bartlett's Famous Quotations* (updated and kept in print by Little, Brown and Co. of Boston since 1863). These entries will give you tantalizing snatches of death-related verse, but for the full effect you should go to a library or bookstore and find the complete poem. The collected works of William Wordsworth, John Donne, or Emily Dickinson are good starting points. Also, don't overlook all the many fine poets and writers whose work did not make it into Bartlett's. My all-time favorite poet, James Whitcomb Riley, never made the book, yet his poems of death are some of the most poignant I've ever read.

Appendix A lists music you might wish to consider using for passing-over rites. Keep in mind that any music you use in a deeply emotional ritual will probably be linked in your mind forever after with the event (recall how easily a few bars of a song from your youth immediately dredges up old memories). If you use music, make sure the tune or song is one you will not mind including in your mental list of music that calls up specific events.

You may also wish to say good-bye with a catch phrase that has been bandied about Pagan passing-over rituals for a long time: *Fly yourself into the arms of the Mother*. Many claims to antiquity have been made for this poignant phrase, but none have been proven. Still, it is often seen in printed rituals and often heard in memorial rites. Whether or not it is of ancient origin does not take away from its deeper meaning: that we all must eventually return to the Great Mother who gave us life, and that this reunion should be a happy one.

When you sense that the spirit has left, whether you think it has gone with the light/deity or not, go to your altar and raise the hammer. The hammer has been used as a ritual tool in the Teutonic traditions in much the same manner as the athame or ritual knife in the Anglo-Celtic traditions.[2] It directs powers, blesses, raises energy, and purifies. As such it is a tool that can cause change. Place the cloth filled with the fragile glass on a hard surface. Your altar will do if it is strong enough to receive a blow, otherwise use the floor or the surface of a rock. The breaking of glass is an ancient symbolic act to announce an irreversible transition. It is still used in the Jewish wedding ceremonies to fulfill much the same task. The mere sound of shattering glass is associated with the transition from life to death. Some cultures believe it is a death omen to hear the sound of shattering glass where none has been broken.

As you prepare to strike the glass, say words such as:

> *The wheel of existence turns ever onward, taking us to and from,*
> *from and to each stage of our being. It is in this way that wholeness*
> *of being is achieved. The old way is gone for* (state earth or Craft
> name of spirit), *but something of him/her still remains in my heart.*
> *The old times are severed from us, but new times await.* (Strike once,
> breaking the glass.) *Blessed be the old. Blessed be the new.*

When you are ready, you may thank the deity who has assisted you, and close your circle in your usual manner.

Eleven

Requiem II: Formal Passing-Over Rituals for Groups

GROUPS HAVE THE ABILITY TO OFFER SOLACE TO EACH other in ways the solitary cannot. They can also adapt a variety of practices from various traditions to suit the needs of themselves and to comfort the grieving among them. For example, a group may wish to begin a ritual (even if it takes place many days ahead of time) with an old-fashioned Irish wake with drink, food, and shared laughter. Even if the body is not present with you, the spirit likely will be, and that is the whole point of the wake to begin with. Or a group might choose to make a pilgrimage to the burial site so that each person may anoint the grave with oils and good wishes in a mini-ritual before the main event.

In contrast to solitary rites, group rituals are more action- and word-oriented, with less room for individual thoughts. They offer less flexibility and room for spontaneity the larger the group becomes, and the need for good pre-planning and memorization is essential. The exceptions are when an individual is allowed a turn to speak aloud about or to the deceased.

As with the solitary rituals of the previous chapter, these are guidelines only, and should always be tailored to the needs and the tradition of the coven using them. Perhaps your group already has passing-over rites they like and only want to look into others to try and add a new and meaningful twist to an otherwise solid ritual. This is fine too. If any of the ideas presented here can work for you, you are welcome to them.

To avoid cluttering up the text with too many uses of "his or her" and "he or she," I have chosen to make the leader of this ritual female and the spirit male. In the interest of fairness, in the following ritual the leader will be designated as male and the spirit female. This is for ease of writing and reading only, and has no bearing on the ability of either gender to perform these rites.

A Group Ritual In Memoriam

This is a ritual designed to comfort the living, to allow everyone present a chance to share their memories, and to let all leave with a memento of the passed-over one.

In addition to your regular altar setup, you will need: a candle for each individual present, at least one lit candle on the altar to light other candles from, a length of cord in any color (one which is long enough to stretch comfortably around the perimeter of your circle), a pair of scissors, and an incense appropriate to a death rite, such as jasmine or lotus. A cauldron or chalice full of water and a drum are also useful, but not necessary. Other musical instruments or recordings are optional.

The circle should be opened and quarters, deities, et cetera, called in your usual manner, with the altar situated in the quarter facing the direction your tradition views as being the direction of the Summerland. The leader (priest, priestess, couple, leader of the month, or any combination of these) should stand before it and make a statement of purpose on behalf of the group and light the incense.

The leader should turn and face the group, asking that each one who wishes to share their memories or offer comfort may do so. Moving clockwise around the circle, she should acknowledge each person and allow individuals an opportunity to express their feelings. Individuals may choose to sing a song, read a poem or passage, or share a special memory—whatever they feel moved to do.

Participants should be asked in advance to put a time limit on their recitation to prevent the ritual from becoming sluggish.

If you feel you absolutely cannot choose just one thing to do to keep within the time limits imposed, you may want to do your own private memorial rite later. Just because you are part of a coven does not mean you are forbidden from holding private rituals. By doing this you have the best of both worlds, so to speak, and you can do all that you feel is meaningful without forcing your choices on others who might not share your vision.

After each person is finished they should conclude with pre-arranged words that signal the rest of the coven that they are through speaking, such as:

> *Would that I never forget* (name of spirit).

> *And may these memories be as fresh for all my tomorrows*
> *as they are this day.*

> *Blessed be the spirit of* (name of spirit), *who shall always*
> *remain alive in my heart.*

After each person indicates they are done, the coven should respond with:

> All: *Blessed be the cherished memory of* (name of spirit).
> *Blessed be the spirit of the dead.*

When the circle is complete, the leader will make her own verbal offering and receive the coven's response. The leader then takes the length of cord from the altar and holds it up in front of her, saying:

> Leader: *Behold the cord of life, which measures*
> *our days and links us all one to another.*

> Coven: *Blessed be the cord of life and*
> *the Goddess who wove it into being.*

> Leader: *Let all present grasp it and hold tight,*
> *for this is a precious gift.*

The leader hands one end of the cord to the person on her left and it is passed along the circle until everyone is holding onto a separate section of it. The cord should be held in two hands held out from the front of the body with palms facing up. When the end returns to the leader, she should knot the ends together to make it a full circle, without a beginning or an ending.

Leader: (Spoken as the knot is completed) *The cord of life is strong, but when the Goddess* (or *God* if your tradition views the being who determines the time of death to be male) *severs it, it ends. Let us honor our beloved* (name of spirit) *by letting his spirit go, by severing for him again the cord of life.*

The leader takes the scissors and cuts the cord just to her right. She will then be holding a small piece of the cord just slightly longer than her own body width. When she is done cutting, she passes the scissors to the person on her right (counterclockwise), and that person severs the cord at a point just to his or her own right. Keep passing the scissors around until the last person has cut a piece of the cord. At this point no two people in the circle should be connected by the cord, and everyone should be holding their severed portion. As each cut is made the coven may wish to have some words to mark the action such as "It is done," "Blessed be life and death," or "Behold the cord of life is cut." Or you may wish to use an action to commemorate the cutting, such as the bowing of heads or the kissing of the severed piece.

When the last cut is made, the leader should allow everyone a moment or two to reflect on the cutting of the cord and its meaning. When she judges that everyone is ready she will continue on:

Leader: *The cord of this incarnation is severed for* (name of spirit), *but what we hold is only a symbol: a small piece of the thread weaving life and bringing death. The cord's whole length is never-ending. When the flesh dies, the spirit is born and a new cord is woven and worn and the cycle begins again. Let us dance together the labyrinthine dance of life, death, and rebirth; the eternal dance in which we are all moving every day of our existence.*

All: *Let us dance. Let us know. Let us remember and be aware.*

If you have a drum you may start beating it now. If not, allow the leader to set the pace. Begin slowly, increasing the tempo as the dancing continues.

The coven might wish to wear masks as they dance, ones that link them to the spirit world. This custom is found in African, east Asian, and Native North American traditions, and is a great help in turning the mundane mind to a spiritual state of thinking. Call to mind documentary footage of shamans in these cultures leading spirit dances in masks. They literally take on another persona as they unite with the spirit world.

The leader should transfer her piece of the cord to her right hand and hold on to one end of it. The rest of the group should follow her lead. Everyone except the leader should grasp the loose end of the cord held by the person on their left. The leader should then take her athame or other ritual tool and cut a hole in the circle in the direction of the Summerland, and lead the coven out in a serpentine dance. Outside the circle she will turn to her left and begin a counterclockwise dance around the outer perimeter of the circle. Counterclockwise is the direction associated with banishing; in this case, the "banishment" of a life. The last person in line should release the cord and not leave the circle with the coven, but remain inside and, with his or her athame, close the circle behind them.

The dancers may make as many passes around the circle as the leader feels is appropriate. Often this takes its cue from a number sacred to the tradition followed by the group. For example, Celtic and Teutonic covens might make three passes, and a Native American or African circle might make four. Chanting or singing will help move this dance along if no drum is available. All chants or songs should be decided upon ahead of time and memorized. The following are two examples of chants you might want to try:

> *Link we here the severed cord,*
> *Hearts and minds of one accord.*

> *Forward dancing, life draws breath,*
> *Backward dancing, life draws death.*

When the leader reaches the exit point of the circle for the final time, the person who has remained inside should cut the door open again so that the coven can be led back inside. As each person reenters the circle, the one who has been guardian of the opening should hand each person an unlit candle. Because these will have to be held for some time, you may want to attach a circle of posterboard or a paper cup around the base to minimize the chance of hot wax burning hands or ruining carpets.

Once inside the circle, the leader will turn to her left and lead the dancers in a clockwise motion, making as many passes of the circle as she feels is correct. Moving clockwise symbolizes forward momentum and expresses our belief in the soul's eventual rebirth. If you are chanting rather than drumming, you may even want to alter the chant to symbolize the change in direction. For instance, in using the first example above, you might want to only chant the second line when outside the circle and the first line while within.

The leader should stop when she is at a point in front of the altar. When everyone has had a chance to catch their breath, she should continue:

Leader: *Our earthly lives are like a candle's flame, fragile and fleeting, blazing bright one moment, and extinguished the next. But know that the flame is re-lit in the Summerland, and that the light of the soul never dies.*

Coven: *We are the flame of life. We are eternal.*

The leader turns to the burning candles on the altar and lights hers from one of them. She then turns to the person on her left and allows him to light his own candle from hers. He in turn passes the light to the person on his left, and so on around the circle clockwise until all candles are lit. As each new candle is lit, the person receiving the light might want to make an affirmation of the symbology with words such as: "Behold the flame of life," "I am the eternal flame," or "Blessed be the light of the soul."

When all candles are lit the leader will continue:

Leader: *Behold the flame of life burns brightly this night even in the midst of our sorrow.*

Coven: *Behold the light. Blessed be life, which goes on and on.*

The leader will now begin what the mainstream religions might refer to as a litany or a responsive reading. Done in a semi-chant way of speaking, this type of ritual, which rarely varies in any particular type of rite, is meant to lull the mind into a receptive state so that the words and their meanings penetrate to the deepest level of your consciousness.

Leader: *The wheel of life turns ever onward, bringing us to and taking us from sorrows, joys, and loves.*

Coven: *Blessed be the wheel of life.*

Leader: *When the flesh dies the spirit is born, and the Summerland opens its doors.*

Coven: *Blessed be the Summerland.*

Leader: *The spirit of* (name of spirit) *lives on in our hearts as well as in the Summerland.*

Coven: *Blessed be* (name of spirit).

Leader: *The wheel of life turns ever onward,*
　　　　bringing us to sorrows, joys, and loves.

Coven: *Blessed be life. Blessed be death.*

Leader: *Blessed be the eternal spirit.*

Coven: *Blessed be the oneness of spirit.*

Leader: *We are Goddess.*

Coven: *We are God.*

Leader: *We are one in spirit.*

Coven: *We are one in the divine.*

Leader: *Blessed be the waiting Summerland,*
　　　　where we will realize our oneness.

All:　　*Blessed be life and death and blessed be rebirth.*

When the litany is finished, the leader extinguishes her candle. She may wish to do this by dowsing it in a chalice or a cauldron of water. The cauldron is symbolic of the womb of the mother Goddess to which we all must go to be reborn, and makes a fitting symbol for extinguishing the flame of life. Then, starting on the leader's right, each member of the coven puts out his or her candle in turn, counterclockwise around the circle. If a chalice is used, it may be passed around the circle, or the leader may wish to have everyone come individually to the altar and use a central cauldron.

After the last of the candles is out, the leader says:

Leader: *Behold the darkness of death. But know that*
　　　　the darkness is only here for a moment, and that
　　　　the flame will be rekindled in the Summerland.

Coven: *Blessed be the dark. Blessed be death,*
　　　　which is born out of life.

The leader will motion for everyone to cross their left arm over their right and join hands.

Leader: *When the flesh dies the spirit is born.*

On the leader's cue, everyone turns 180 degrees to their left without breaking the circle of hands. This will result in everyone facing the outside of the circle with their hands still linked.

> Leader: *Hail and farewell,* (name of spirit). *May the Gods*
> *bless you on your journey. Merry meet . . .*

> Coven: *. . . Merry part . . .*

> Leader: *. . . And merry meet again.*

> All: *So mote it ever be!*

The circle may be closed in your usual manner when everyone is ready.

ꙮ A Group Ritual to Assist the Departed to the Summerland

Like the solitary ritual in the previous chapter, this one is designed to assist a spirit in making his or her journey to the Summerland.

For this rite you will need, in addition to your usual altar setup, food and drink for a feast for the dead, a spare place setting for the spirit (setup either inside or outside the circle, depending on where your group feels is best), and at least one lit candle on the altar. More candles are usually present in group situations if for no other reason than to help everyone see, but you will need at least one for this rite. Musical instruments or recordings are optional.

Open your circle in your usual manner and have the leader make a verbal statement of your ritual purpose.

The leader will begin the evocation of the spirit of the passed-over person by calling out her name three times (more or less if your tradition has another number that is viewed as sacred). He will then continue with words such as:

> Leader: *We ask your spirit here tonight to feast with us, that we*
> *may say our farewells and illuminate your journey into*
> *the Summerland. Come, bright spirit, the Feast of the*
> *Dead awaits you. Come, our guest of honor.*

> Coven: *Come to us, bright spirit, feast and make merry.*

All in the coven should visualize the invitation being sent out across the vastness of the universe, secure in the knowledge that it will be heard and, if the spirit chooses, answered.

The leader should be skilled enough in the psychic arts to sense when the spirit is present. If he is not, he should ask another member of the group who is skilled in that way to let him know when and if the spirit arrives. If the spirit chooses not to come, you may close down the ritual and try again at a later time. If the spirit is present, the leader should offer words of welcome:

Leader: *Welcome, bright spirit of our beloved* (name of spirit).

Coven: *Welcome,* (name of spirit).

Leader: *This feast we hold in your honor symbolizes our good wishes for you. The drink is meant to nourish your soul, the food is so that you will carry the good memories of us and your earthly incarnation into the Summerland. Let us all drink, eat, and be merry.*

All: *Let the feast begin!*

The leader should serve the spirit first. If the place setting for the spirit is outside the circle, he will have to cut a doorway and exit to do this. He should then come back inside and eat with the others. Be cautious not to over-indulge as full stomachs are notorious psychic power drains that can put an end to the effectiveness of your ritual. This is why, in most other rituals, all feasting is left until the end. Also note that in many traditions, Feasts of the Dead in which humans participate are done in complete silence. As a coven you will need to decide if you will be observing this rite as a Dumb Supper (see Chapter 5 for discussion) or whether you will want to converse. If you do choose to talk during the meal, keep in mind that this is the middle of your ritual and you should keep your conversation focused on the ritual's purpose. Talk to the spirit, or to each other about the spirit, but leave mundane topics or coven business for later.

When the meal is over, move the empty plates quietly out of the way. The leader should then stand and motion for everyone else to resume their places in the circle.

Leader: *Tonight we honor* (name of spirit) *and bid her farewell as she journeys to the Summerland. Tonight we reassure ourselves that she shall always live in our hearts and minds. And when we are again together, our souls will recognize each other and sing for joy.*

Coven: *Let us know. Let us recognize. Let us sing for joy.*

The leader should address the spirit and not the group as he begins recounting good memories or offering the spirit his best wishes. When he is finished, he should motion to the person on his left to do the same. No one should feel obligated to speak. Some in the group may not have known the passed-over person as well as others and might not feel as if they should speak. Others may feel too overcome with emotion to try and talk just now. Those who choose not to speak may either offer bright blessings to the spirit, or just nod to the person on his or her left to continue.

When everyone has had a chance to talk, the leader should stand in front of the altar, facing outward. Because of the way you oriented your altar in the beginning, he should be facing the direction your tradition views as being where the Land of the Dead lies. He should explain in his own words to the spirit why she is here. This should include a statement that, though you are opening a path to the Summerland, whether or not it is taken at this time is her choice of free will.

Still standing at the altar, the leader should raise his arms and begin to call on the deity your group has chosen to escort the spirit to the Summerland. State the deity's name three times, or use another number if it is sacred to your tradition. The following is an example using the Welsh Goddess Rhiannon:

> *Rhiannon. Rhiannon. Rhiannon. Hear my plea, blessed Lady*
> *of the Otherworld. Come on thundering hooves* (she is viewed
> as a horse deity) *to carry home the spirit of one of your wandering*
> *children. Your Summerland realm of life, death, and rebirth awaits*
> *one who cannot reach it. Shining One of old, bring your divine light*
> *to illuminate the way back home for* (state either the spirit's earth or
> Craft name). *Carry her safely on your sturdy back until she reaches the*
> *waiting arms of the Mother. So mote it be.*

The leader should now turn to the spirit and speak words of encouragement, such as:

> Leader: *On this journey you have nothing to fear. Rhiannon will*
> *carry you safely to your destination. Know that this journey*
> *is not an ending. Death is merely another birth. When the*
> *flesh dies, the spirit is born. New adventures await you.*
> *The door is open and the path lit if you want to take it.*
> *Know that it can be found again when needed.*

If you have called the spirit into your circle, the leader will go to the edge of the circle in the direction of the Land of the Dead and, with an athame or another tool, will cut open a door for the spirit to exit. In either case, now is the time to blow out the candle on the altar so that it does not detract from the light of the divine. The leader should appoint someone to do this in his stead as he guards the open door of the circle.

You may sing in farewell, recite poetry, et cetera, whatever the group has decided is most appropriate. You may wish to go counterclockwise around the circle and allow each person to state one single line of a circular chant. This would sound something like:

Coven Member 1: *Into the Summerland go now ye,*

Coven Member 2: *May your journey blessed be.*

Coven Member 3: *Into the Summerland go now ye,*

Coven Member 4: *May your journey blessed be.*

Coven Member 5: *Into the Summerland go now ye,*

Coven Member 6: *May your journey blessed be.*

The chant can make several passes around the circle so that it works equally well for both small and large groups. The chanting should end when the leader gives the signal.

I have been in group passing-over rituals where banishing pentagrams are drawn in the air at this point (these are drawn in the air in front of us starting from the lower right-hand point). I admit to being guilty of doing this myself. When pointed at astral life during ritual, it is not merely a sign of dismissal, but is sometimes interpreted as one of forced exile. To make such a gesture at a human discarnate whom you are giving the free will to stay or to go is rude at best. Remember you are not trying to force the spirit to go to the Summerland. The only time you would want to do this is in the case of a troublesome ghost or entity for whom you are enacting a complete banishment or exorcism ritual. Allow the spirit the choice of where she goes after this.

When you sense that the spirit has left the area, whether you think she has gone with the light/deity or not, you should thank the deity who has assisted you and close the circle in your usual manner.

Appendix A

Music for Passing-Over Rituals

The following selections are those which I personally feel enhance Pagan memorial rituals both large and small, but there are certainly many more beyond the scope of this list that would also be suitable. Some of the tunes found in this list are upbeat—somewhat in the New Orleans/Dixieland style—while others are traditionally solemn. These are noted where appropriate. All music is listed first by either the composer or the artist (usually the one most closely associated with the work), then by title or album. Where applicable, numbers indicate specific ordering instructions:

1   For ordering information, please see Circle Network News (address in Appendix B).

2   Albums distributed in the U.S.A. by Sony. All others write to Pagan Fire Music, 18 Russell St., St. Pauls, Cheltenham, Gloucestershire, England, for ordering information.

3   Ordering information for Gwydion's two albums, *Songs For the Old Religion* and *The Faerie Shaman*, can be found in the pages of Green Egg and Circle Network News. Addresses can be found in Appendix B.

4   This and other appropriate New Age titles can be ordered through Valley of the Sun Publishing (see Appendix B for address).

If your local music store cannot order for you, some of these recordings can be found on tape or CD through: Postings, Dept. 654, P.O. Box 8001, Hilliard, OH 43026-8001 ($3.00 for catalog), or through Rego Irish Records and Tapes (also has CDs and Scottish music), 64 New Hyde Park Rd., Garden City, NY 11530-3909 ($2.00 for catalog).

Paganism is blessed with many talented lyricists, composers, and musicians who often choose to write and play their own music as the mood moves them for each requiem ritual in which they take part. If you are not talented in this area and would like special music for your rites, check merchants/services columns in any of the larger Pagan periodicals for contacts (see Appendix B).

The choice of music, or even whether to have music or not, is yours to make. As long as the ritual is meaningful to you, and/or to your coven, then there is no right or wrong choice.

Bach, J.S.

"Jesu, Joy of Man's Desiring" (paced instrumental—very relaxing if you can forget the title)

"Sheep May Safely Graze"

Beethoven, L.V.

"Moonlight Sonata, First Movement, op. 27" (soothing!)

"Sonata no. 26 *(Funeral March)*"

Brahms, Johannes

"Lament no. 1" (stately instrumental)

Burns, Robert and Alexander Hume

"Flow Gently, Sweet Afton"

"My Love is Like a Red, Red Rose"

Cobert, Robert and Charles Grean

"Shadows of the Night" (best remembered as "Quintin's Theme" from the sixties' serial *Dark Shadows*)

Dvorak, Antonin

"New World Symphony, Second Movement" (stately instrumental)

Ellington, Duke

"Mood Indigo" (instrumental with a blues sound)

Gilbert, William and Sir Arthur Sullivan

"They Never Would Be Missed" (humorous sarcasm from *The Mikado*, a piece my father has chosen to include in his funeral)

Hamlisch, Marvin

"Somewhere Out There" (from the film *An American Tale*)

Hamlisch, Marvin and Alan and Marilyn Bergman

"The Way We Were" (from the film of the same name)

Hamouris, Deborah and Rick

Welcome to Annwfn, album[1]

Hawthorne, Alice

"Whispering Hope" (lyric references to "her" could refer to a Goddess-figure)

Incubus Succubus

Look at albums titled *Belladonna and Aconite* and *Wytches*. Songs "The Leveller" and "Dark Mother" on the latter are especially good for memorial rites. (Pagan Rock n' Roll)[2]

Jarre, Maurice

"Somewhere My Love" ("Lara's Theme" from *Doctor Zhivago*, whose lyrics contain reincarnation themes)

Kennedy-Fraser, Marjorie and Kenneth McLeod

"The Road to the Isles"

Kern, Jerome and Oscar Hammerstein

"Can I Forget You?" (haunting, folk-like song from film *High, Wide and Handsome*)

King, Carole
"You've Got a Friend"

Lerner, Alan Jay and Frederick Lowe
"From This Day On" (from the musical *Brigadoon*)

Magnificent Seventh's Brass Band
Authentic New Orleans Jazz Funeral, album

Mendelssohn, Felix
"Nocturne" (instrumental from *A Midsummer Night's Dream*)

Pendderwen, Gwydion
"The Crone's Lullaby"

"I'll Be Reborn" (Dixieland style)

"The Raven is Calling"[3]

Popular Folk Songs
"Auld Lang Syne" (Scottish)

"All Through the Night" (Welsh)

"Deep River" (American)

"How Can I Love Thee?" (American)

"Iona Boat Song" (Scottish)

"The Lonesome Road" (American)

"Lyke Wake Dirge" (Old English)

"Skye Boat Song" (Scottish)

"Sometimes I Feel Like A Motherless Child" (American)

"Will Ye No Come Back Again?" (Scottish)

"Wayfarin' Stranger" (American)

Preservation Hall Jazz Band

Most albums contain some suitable New Orleans-style material.

Pachelbel, Johann

"Canon in D" (stately instrumental)

Raskin, Gene

"Those Were the Days" (varies in tempo)

Remedi, Angie

The Mother Calls, album[1]

Saint-Saens, Camille

"Danse Macabre" (spritely program piece often heard at Halloween, meant to evoke the image of dancing skeletons)

Sigerson, Dr. George

"Far Away" (based on an old Irish Folk melody)

Simon, Paul

"Bridge Over Troubled Water"

Slap, Robert

Ascension to All That Is (gentle New Age album whose climbing chords give the illusion of rising—great background for rites assisting the departed to the Summerland)[4]

Streisand, Barbra and Paul Williams

"Evergreen" (from the film *A Star is Born*)

Sweet Honey in the Rock

Most albums by this all-female folk/spirituality ensemble contain suitable passing-over music.

Thiel, Lisa

Songs of Transformation, album[1]

Weatherly, Fred E.

"Danny Boy" (words are set to the famous Irish folk tune "Londonderry Air")

Appendix B

Resources and Networking Guide

Unlike most resource directories found in the back of books on Paganism/Witchcraft that are geared to helping you locate herbs, tools, and other magickal accoutrements, this one focuses on periodicals and groups with whom you can connect to deal with grief, afterlife issues, or for assistance with Pagan funeral arrangements. Through major Pagan publications, and those which focus on rites of passage, you can find other networking organizations, locate Pagan clergy (some of whom are legally licensed as ministers in their home states), or find out how to speak with a qualified spiritual counselor.

Using the "contacts" section of the magazines will allow you to advertise for a pen friend who shares your spiritual background and who can sympathize with your loss. You will also find announcements of Pagan festivals or gatherings, many of which include some type of communal passing-over ritual, particularly at Mabon or Samhain. Others may include one in their schedule for you upon request.

Please remember to enclose an SASE (self-addressed stamped envelope) whenever making inquiries within your own country, or an IRC (International Reply Coupon) when querying elsewhere. This is a matter of courtesy since most Pagan organizations are non-profit, staffed solely with unpaid volunteers, and operate on very tight budgets.

❧ Pagan Periodicals

The Azrael Project Newsletter
The Westgate Press
5219 Magazine Street
New Orleans, LA 70115

The newsletter of an organization dedicated to the study of the Angel of Death, and to erasing the fear of death through understanding. Westgate Press is also the place to order Leilah Wendell's spellbinding books about the Angel of Death. Write with SASE for information.

Circle Network News
Circle Sanctuary
P.O. Box 219
Mt. Horeb, WI 53572

Circle sponsors Pagan gatherings throughout the year and helps Pagans all over the world connect with each other. Of special interest will be their back issues of Fall 1994: The Afterlife, and Fall 1986: Reincarnation. At this writing, a one-year subscription for this quarterly is $15 by bulk mail to U.S.A. addresses, $20 first class to U.S.A., $27 to Canada, and Mexico, and $30 elsewhere. Payment must be in U.S. funds. Sample copy $5.

Connections
1705 14th Street #181
Boulder, CO 80302

Focuses on ethics and community as well as magick. Subscriptions are currently $15.80 in the U.S.A. All others query for rates.

The Green Egg
P.O. Box 1542
Ukiah, CA 95482

This professionally produced quarterly contains beautiful artwork and lots of controversy. Back issue Fall 1994 deals with afterlife beliefs. Subscriptions are currently $15 in the U.S.A. and $21 in Canada. Write with SASE for other subscription information. Sample copy $4.95.

Hecate's Loom
Box 5206, Station B
Victoria, BC
Canada V8R 6N4

A quarterly journal of general Paganism. For current subscription rates, Canadians please send SASE, all others query with IRC.

New Moon Rising
12345 S.E. Fuller Road, #119
Milwaukie, OR 97222

Covers Paganism, Shamanism, and Ceremonial Magick from many perspectives. Subscriptions to this bimonthly publication are currently $14 for one year U.S.A., $21 in Canada and Mexico, and $30 elsewhere. Sample issue $3.

✿ Other Magazines/Catalogs of Interest

Bereavement: A Magazine of Hope and Healing
8133 Telegraph Road
Colorado Springs, CO 80920
(719) 282-1948

An inspiring and helpful magazine for those in grief.

Ideals
P.O. Box 148000
Nashville, TN 37214-8000

This magazine has been publishing beautiful seasonal poetry since just after
World War II. Though the focus is Christian, the publication is nature-oriented
and contains much material suitable for Pagan ritual. Current copies can be
found in most bookstores, and back issues in many second-hand bookstores.

Thanatos
Box 6009
Tallahassee, FL 32314
(904) 224-1969

A quarterly covering all issues of death, dying, and bereavement aimed at both
professional counselors and lay persons. Focus is on working through the grief
process. Query for subscription rates.

Westgate Press
See information above under *The Azrael Project Newsletter* in "Pagan Periodicals."

White Swan Music, Inc.
1705 14th Street #143
Boulder, CO 80302
(800) 825-8656

Sells New Age, Native American, and environmental music. Write or call for a
free catalog.

Winners!
Valley of the Sun Publishing
P.O. Box 683
Ashland, OR 97520-0023

Publishers and sellers of New Age music and of mind/body video and audio
tapes. Lots of soothing music for ritual background, and tapes and books for
assisting with past-life regressions. First copy of their mag-a-log is free upon
request, and will continue be sent free for up to a year if you order from them or
attend a seminar.

❦ Organizations Concerned with Death and Dying Issues and Spiritual Support

The Centering Corporation
1531 North Saddle Creek Road
Omaha, NE 68104
(402) 553-1200

Produces fiction and non-fiction books for both children and adults that deal with grief and bereavement. Free book catalog upon request.

Circle Sanctuary
See address above under "Pagan Periodicals."

   Licensed Pagan clergy from Circle offer counseling to those in need. Please see the back page of any issue, or query with SASE for more information and minimum expected donation rates. The "Goods and Services" section of *Circle Network News* often carries ads from Pagan counselors, and Circle now takes steps to verify the background of those offering counseling services.

Hemlock Society
P.O. Box 11830
Eugene, OR 97440

Since 1983 the Society has been helping people choose "death with dignity."

The Pagan Hospice and Funeral Trust
BM Box 3337
London
England

Provides counseling to the grieving and seeks to assist Pagan organizations in establishing hospices and cemeteries. Those writing from outside the U.K., please include an IRC.

Pagan Burial Ground Project
℅ Steve and Gwen Wittwer
P.O. Box 3713
Blaine, WA 98231

As of this writing, a six-acre site has been purchased with an eye toward turning it into a permanent Pagan burial ground. Write for more information or to give input to the fledgling project.

❧ Non-Sectarian Grief Support Groups

When seeking local grief support organizations always check first with your local newspaper, library or community center. Support groups are usually differentiated by the type of loss suffered (i.e. spouse/lover, child, et cetera), or by the cause of death (AIDS, SIDS, homicide, suicide, et cetera). Even mid-sized communities often have several of these organizations with which you might feel comfortable. If these are not satisfactory, or if you cannot find a support group in your area, try writing to any of the following for more information:

American Self-Help Clearing House
St. Clare's Riverside Medical Center
Denville, NJ 07834
(201) 625-7101

Referral services to over 300 different support groups for bereavement, pet loss, illness, et cetera. Also trains group leaders, hosts workshops, and publishes a newsletter. All services are free as of this writing.

National Association for Widowed People
P.O. Box 3564
Springfield, IL 62708

Suicide Survivor Support Programme
10 Trinity Square
Toronto, Ontario M4G 1B1
Canada

Survivors of Suicide
National Suicide Prevention Center
184 Salem Avenue
Cincinnati, OH 45406

Bereaved Parents
1717 South Puget Sound
Tacoma, WA 98405

Compassionate Friends International
685 William Avenue   or   P.O. Box 3696
Winnipeg, Manitoba R3E 0Z2   Oak Brook, IL 60521
Canada

An international organization offering support and counseling to bereaved parents.

Fernside
P.O. Box 8944
Cincinnati, OH 45208

Offers counseling to bereaved children.

The Good Grief Program
% Judge Baker Guidance Center
295 Longwood Avenue
Boston, MA 02136

A community intervention program that works with schools to deal not only with personal losses, but ones that affect the student body as a whole, such as the loss of a classmate or a teacher.

🌿 Living Wills

Choices In Dying, Inc.
200 Varick Street
New York, NY 10014
(800) 989-WILL

For U.S. residents. Provides documents and information geared to the laws of your own state that pertain to your last wishes. Allows you to appoint a legal representative to see that your wishes are carried out. For a $25 annual membership fee, Choices will keep you informed on changes in your own state's laws that may affect your right to choose how you die. They also carry several journals of interest, as well as educational publications and videos.

🌿 Environmental Organizations Involved in Land Use Issues

Earth First!
P.O. Box 5871
Tucson, AZ 85703
(602) 662-1371

Publishes *Earth First* magazine. Involved with many land use issues, including those surrounding cemeteries.

Greenpeace
1436 U Street NW
Washington, D.C. 20009
(202) 462-1177

This is a worldwide organization concerned with all aspects of the environment. They are a non-violent but highly aggressive organization that has done a lot to increase popular awareness of our environmental woes.

❦ Especially for Pets and Familiars

Glassman Pet Casket Company
41-15 Astoria Boulevard
Long Island City, NY 11105
(718) 274-5703

Pet caskets and cremation urns. Free brochure upon request.

Gulfstream Pet Cemetery of the Seas
P.O. Box 1157
Jupiter, FL 33468-1157

Organization which will dispose of cremated pet remains in the Gulf of Mexico. Write for free information.

Hoegh Pet Caskets and Cemeteries
P.O. Box 311
Gladstone, MI 49837-0311

Write for free information.

Petra Pet Memorials
P.O. Box 153
Lewistown, MO 63452
(314) 497-2202

Metal grave markers. Write or call for free brochure.

Rex Granite Company
P.O. Box 924
St. Cloud, MN 56302-0924

Granite headstones and memorials for pets. Write for free brochure.

Smoky Point Monuments
7237 Lakeside Drive
Ontario, NY 14519
(315) 524-9593

Tablet-style grave markers in marble or granite.

Appendix C

Deities Associated with Death and the Summerland

❧ Death or Otherworld Gods

Aciel (Chadean)	The "black sun" God of the underworld who lives at its very depths and personifies darkness.
Ahpuch (Mayan)	A much-feared death God.
Aker (Egyptian)	A two-faced God who rules over the gateway to the underworld, residing where its eastern and western horizons meet.
Am-Heh (Egyptian)	Am-Heh lives in the underworld's Lake of Fire. His nickname is Devourer of the Masses.
Anubis (Egyptian)	The jackal-headed God whose job is to escort souls to the underworld and judge their evil deeds by weighing their hearts. He is also the patron God of embalmers.
The Anunaki (Babylonian)	A tribunal of earth and underworld Gods who decide the fate of humanity.
Arawen (Welsh)	King of the Celtic Otherworld who switched places for a year and a day with a human man. He possesses a magick cauldron that was stolen by the young King Arthur.
Awun (Formosan)	God of endings, destruction, and death.

Baal (Middle Eastern)	A widely worshipped deity of many attributes including harvest, fertility, and death.
Bel/Beltene/Belanos (Celtic)	Minor death God with possible Middle Eastern origins. His name is a possible origin for the Bealtaine festival (May 1), a celebration of fertility and rebirth.
Beli (Welsh)	The primary Welsh father God, also a minor sun deity. His principal archetypal role is that of the God of death and king of the underworld. He is also linked to several of the legends concerning the sacred Pagan site of Glastonbury Tor, where balefires blazed on Bealtaine and Samhain nights up until the Commonwealth period (1640-1660).
Belial (Hebrew)	This underworld God was demonized by both Christianity and Islam. His name is often heard used as a euphemism for Satan.
Cernabog (Slavic)	God of death, sometimes viewed as a personification of Death. Some legends say it is he who comes to escort the blessed deceased to the Summerland and who sends tortuous demons to plague the unrighteous, though this division may date to a later period and not be part of the original mythology.
Charon (Greek)	The ferryman who rows the deceased across the River Styx to Hades. Because he demands payment for this service, Greeks were always buried with a coin placed in the mouth.
Cromm Cruiach (Irish)	His name means "bowed one of the mound," and his image is often linked to a legendary golden idol to which sacrifices may have been made. He is still seen by Pagans as a harvest, death, and sacrificial God.
Dhonn (Irish)	A God of the underworld and of death, and a consort of the crone Goddess Macha.

Dis (Roman)	An underworld God from whom Roman emperor Julius Caesar claimed all Gauls were descended. He is equated with the Roman Pluto and the Greek Hades.
Februus (Greco-Etruscan)	This was the God of the "month of cleansing" (February), a period also known as the "month of the dead."
Ghede (Haitian-Yoruban)	A God of both death and resurrection. As such he is seen as all-wise, and is a powerful healer. It is not unusual to see offerings and symbols at his shrines and altars that reflect both death and rebirth themes.
Gwyn Ap Nuad (Welsh)	A God of war, death, and the hunt; also a patron of fallen warriors. As the master Otherworld hunter, he rides a wild horse and has three massive hounds: one red, one black, and one white, who ride out with him each night as he searches for lost souls to escort back to the Land of the Dead.
Hades (Greek)	A God of the underworld whose name functions as a synonym for the Land of the Dead, both in and out of Greek Pagan circles. He is the son of Kronos, the God of time. Archetypally he also represents the dead time of the year when vegetation does not grow.
Hari-Hara (Indian-Hindi)	A benevolent warrior God who steals condemned souls from the hands of less friendly deities.
Havgan (Welsh)	A vanquished rival God of Arawen's for the kingship of the Otherworld.
Hermes (Greek)	A God of communication, travel, and a patron deity of scholars. It is his job to escort lost souls to the underworld.
Kala-Guia (Central African)	The God of funerals whose job it is to bring newly passed-over souls into the presence of the supreme being.

Loz (Babylonian)	Rules the Land of the Dead with his brother Nergal and his sister-in-law Ereshkigal.
Luchtain (Irish)	A God of metalcrafting and of war who became a minor death deity. He is part of a triplicity with his brothers Govannon and Credne. The three have assumed great importance in some Celtic magickal traditions.
Mabon (Celtic)	A minor sun God who symbolizes the power in darkness. He is a king of death and of the Otherworld, a deity of the harvest, the hunt, and fertility. Some Celtic traditions worship him as the original being.
Mader-Atcha (Lapp)	The God who created the human soul as a twin to the human body created by his Goddess wife, Mader-Akka. It is he who decides what path the soul takes, or what new form it may inhabit, after death.
Mantus (Etruscan)	Co-ruler of the underworld as consort to Mania, a death Goddess in the Roman pantheon.
Matowellia (Native American)	A God who demanded that all bodies be burned at death if their souls wished to come live in his heavenly kingdom. Those whose remains were unburned transmuted into scavenger birds such as vultures.
Mehen (Egyptian)	A serpent God who protects other deities on their excursions into the underworld.
Midher (Irish)	An underworld king.
Milu (Hawaiian)	The underworld deity.
Minos (Greek)	A deity who sits on the afterlife court of judgment and helps decide the fate of the dead. Those favored are sent to the blessed Elysian Fields, and those found deserving of punishment are cast into the darker reaches of the underworld.
Mot (Canaanite)	A god of death and infertility.

Nekhebkan (Egyptian)	An underworld God with human limbs and a serpent's body.
Nemglan (Irish)	A bird God associated with traversing between the world of the living and that of the dead.
Nergal (Babylonian)	Rules the Land of the Dead with his brother Loz and his wife Ereshkigal.
Ngahue (Maori)	God of the afterlife.
Ngworekara (Central African)	A God of judgment in the afterlife who reserves the right to punish the wicked by making them suffer "a second deathtime."
Nirrita (Indian-Hindi)	A death God, husband of death Goddess Nirriti.
Odinn (Norse)	The supreme deity of the northern Teutonic people who rules over many aspects of humanity, nature, and the universe, which he created. Among his many attributes is that of God of the dead.
Orcus (Roman)	A death God who forces unwilling human souls to the underworld.
Oro (Polynesian)	A God of war and of fallen warriors.
Osiris (Egyptian)	A God of fertility, the earth, and the afterlife; a consort of Isis. He is the deity most often associated with the mysterious Egyptian monument known as the Sphinx (see Chapter 5 for information about his feast day).
Pinga (Inuit)	An Otherworld God who cares for the souls of the dead until they are accepting of their situation.
Pluto (Roman)	A Roman version of Hades; an underworld God.
Pushan (Indian-Hindi)	God of the dead and of the underworld.
Rot (Lapp-Finnish)	An underworld God.
Samael (Hebrew)	This deity was likely once an Otherworld God of early Israel. His name is now used as a euphemism for the Christian anti-God, Satan.

Seker (Egyptian)	An earth and agricultural God who is also a Lord of the underworld and ruler of the burial "city" at Memphis. On his feast day, decorative staves are driven into the earth to establish a link between his upper- and lower-world kingdoms to ensure fertility for the land.
Shai (Egyptian)	God of destiny and afterlife judgment.
Shesmu (Egyptian)	A God of afterlife punishment who dismembers unrighteous souls in the underworld.
Supai (Incan)	A death God who rules the punishment aspect of the afterlife. Annual cycles of human sacrifices were made to him in hopes that this would appease his desire to take other souls into his kingdom.
Tages (Etruscan)	A death God who taught his priests to divine the future by reading entrails taken in ritual sacrifice.
Tanbaki (Maori)	Ruler of the Land of the Dead.
Teoyaomiqui (Aztec)	A patron God of fallen warriors who escorts their souls to the Summerland where they feast on an eternal hero's banquet.
Thanatos (Greek)	His Greek name literally means "death." He is an underworld and death God who has become one of the most persistent personifications of Death. His brother is Hypnos, God of sleep.
Varuna (Indian-Hindu)	A God of the moon and the dead.
Vates (Polynesian)	An underworld God.
Woden (Anglo-Saxon)	A creator God who is also a God of the dead; an equivilent of the Norse Odinn.
The Wu-Chang (Chinese)	Twin underworld and death Gods who escort souls to the afterlife.
Yama (Indian-Hindu)	A king of heaven who sees to it that souls are reunited with loved ones after death.

The Yama Yen-Wang, (Chinese) A tribunal of ten deities who judge the fate of the dead.

Zambi (West African) A supreme deity who judges the fate of the deceased.

Zurvan (Persian) A God of destiny who presides over the fate of the dead.

❧ Death or Otherworld Goddesses

Achall (Irish) The personification of bereavement. A Goddess of medicine who grieved herself to death over the loss of her brother Miach.

Ahemait (Egyptian) An underworld Goddess whose name means "the devourer." She is made up of parts of carnivorous animals and eats the unrighteous dead.

Ala (Nigerian) Creator Goddess who gave all good things to the society she birthed into being, and who is viewed as the queen of the dead.

Alecto (Greek) One of the Three Furies who was called a Goddess of death and of fallen warriors.

Angerona (Roman) A Goddess of winter and death.

Asase Yaa (West African) A creator Goddess who comes to fetch souls to her kingdom at the time of death.

Badb (Irish) A Goddess of war, death, and destruction. She is part of the Morrigan, a triplicity of crone Goddesses who share her attributes. She presides over the otherworldly cauldron of life, death, and rebirth to which all souls must return upon death, and she is thought to be the origin of the death portent faery known as the Banshee/Beansidhe.

Bau (Chaldaean) A Goddess of the "dark waters" equated with the Land of the Dead.

Cerridwen (Welsh-Cornish)	A sow Goddess of grain, harvest, and death who is noted for her cauldron of wisdom. She is often equated with Greece's Hecate.
Cliodna (Irish-Scottish)	An ocean and Otherworld Goddess who usually takes the form of a sea bird, a pervasive Celtic symbol signifying transition to the afterlife. Her legends tell of her taking her mortal lovers into the Otherworld.
Coatlicue (Aztec)	A serpent, moon, and creator Goddess whose skirt is made of skulls. It is she who decides when an individual's life will end.
Edain (Irish)	The personification of reincarnation.
Ereshkigal (Sumer-Babylonian)	In Babylonia she rules the Land of the Dead with her husband Loz and his brother Nergal. In Sumer she rules alone and patrols the boundary between the world of matter and spirit on her spectral horse.
The Erinyes (Greek)	A triplicity of fearsome Goddesses who kill or drive mad any who dare murder their kinsmen.
Feithline (Irish)	An Otherworld emissary who appeared to Queen Maeve to foretell her of her own death. She may have originally been an afterlife deity or a death portent faery.
Freya (Norse)	Queen of the Teutonic deities and ruler of death. She is the leader of the Valkyries, the airborne horsewomen of death. Also a deity of love, the sun, and the Otherworld.
Gwyar (Welsh)	Goddess whose name means "shedding blood." A mother and death Goddess.
Hathor (Egyptian)	Depicted as a winged cow, she is one of the oldest Goddesses known to humanity. She possesses many attributes, including Goddess of the underworld. Her body is conceptualized as the palace where the soul lives until rebirth.

Hecate (pre-Hellenic)	A crone Goddess of death, the crossroads, the dark moon, and dogs. She rules over the dead and over their rebirth. To those she favors she grants the power of prophecy.
Hel (Norse)	An underworld Goddess for whom the Christian Hell is named. Her realm is exclusively for those who die of disease or old age.
Hikuleo (Polynesian)	A Goddess of competition and of the Land of the Dead.
Hine-Nui Tepo (Polynesian)	The mother of all Polynesian Goddesses; also a moon and death deity.
Husbishag (Semitic)	An underworld Goddess who keeps records of when individual lives will end; doubtless the source of the modern-day Jewish belief in the Book of Life in which God writes out the fate of his followers each New Year (Rosh Hashanna).
Hyrax (Central African)	A death and war Goddess.
Izanami (Japanese)	A creator and underworld Goddess.
Kali (Indian-Hindu)	The insatiable "devourer," Goddess of destruction, war, plague, and death. She is depicted as open-mouthed, brandishing weapons, and wearing the dismembered bodies of the dead. Her followers say this hideous image is only for the uninitiated, and that she has the power to release the fear of death from those who learn to love her.
Kalma (Finnish)	A death Goddess and deity who rules over corpses.
Kurukulla (Tibetan)	A Tibetan equivilent of India's Kali.
Lara (Roman)	An underworld Goddess referred to as the "mother of all dead."
Libitina (Roman)	Goddess of funerals and cemeteries.
Lyssa (Greek)	An underworld Goddess who runs with a pack of wild dogs and induces deadly madness (rabies?).

Macha (Irish)	A horse Goddess who is the personification of her name, which means "battle." She is one of the Morrigan, the triple crone Goddess of death, disease, war, and destruction.
Malophoros (Greek)	A minor underworld Goddess.
Mania (Roman)	A Goddess of the dead who returns to earth to inspire madness. Under her guidance the souls of the dead are sealed in a well in Rome's center. At her annual festival (see Chapter 5), they are released and sent with her to the Land of the Dead. Sacrificial dolls are placed outside homes on her feast night so that these will be taken by her in lieu of the souls of those dwelling inside.
Mem-Loimus (Native American)	A water and Otherworld Goddess.
Mertseger (Egyptian)	A Goddess of death who lives in burial grounds and pyramids, and who metes out punishment and reward in the afterlife.
Miru (Polynesian)	Underworld Goddess who places souls in her otherworldly oven to be regenerated (shades of "Hansel and Gretel"!).
Modgud (Norse)	A Goddess who guards the pathway to the Norse Otherworld of Valhalla.
The Morrigan (Celtic)	A triple Goddess made up of three crone Goddesses of war, battle, death, and destruction. The name means "the phantom queen." The Celts believed that, as they engaged in battle, the Morrigan flew shrieking overhead in the form of a carrion crow or raven.
Naenia (Roman)	A Goddess of funerals.
Natosuelta (Gaulish)	A river Goddess who is the personification of the waters of the cauldron of rebirth.
Neith (Egyptian)	A Goddess of birth and of the animal spirits who guard the bodies of the deceased.

Neman (Celtic)	One of the Morrigan, a triple Goddess of war, death, and destruction.
Nemesis (Greek)	A Goddess of human fate.
Nephthys (Egyptian)	The sister of the Goddess of life, Isis. Nephthys is the Goddess of death and infertility who inhabits burial grounds.
Ninazu (Sumerian)	The great mother who holds in her arms all the souls of the dead as they sleep with her between incarnations.
Niritti (Indian-Hindi)	A death Goddess, wife of death God Nirrita.
Oya (Yoruban-Santerian)	The Goddess who guards the cemetery. She is conceptualized as a great whirlwind who can blow open or closed the doors to the Summerland.
Persephone (Greek)	Many extant myths surround this Goddess and her attributes. She reigns as the underworld queen for six months out of each year, and as an earth/grain deity for the other six.
Qamaits (Native American)	This death Goddess' name means "maker of sorrow."
Rhiannon (Welsh-Cornish)	This well-known Goddess of fertility, dreams, and the moon is also an Otherworld and death Goddess. In her myths she is accused of killing her own child, and she takes the form of a white horse to ferry people back and forth between the worlds.
Saosis (Egyptian)	Depicted as a tree of life and death.
Sati (Indian-Hindu)	The Goddess for whom the practice of suttee is named. This is when an Indian widow is obliged to throw herself onto her husband's funeral pyre.
Satine (Indonesian)	An earth Goddess who chose to move to the underworld. In her kingdom all souls live in peace and happiness after they pass through the dreaded "black gate of sorrow."

Sedna (Inuit)	A death Goddess whose kingdom is at the bottom of the sea.
Semele (Greek-Asian)	Her original Arabic name means "subterranean." Though she was once probably an underworld deity, she is best known today as the mother of the wine God Dionysus.
Snutqutxals (Native American)	A death Goddess.
Spes (Cretan)	The queen of the Land of the Dead who is said to be the sister/cousin of Death personified.
Sul (Gaulish)	A deity of sacred wells who is sometimes viewed as a death Goddess with a kingdom reachable only by following a path on the bottom of a river.
Tellus Mater (Roman)	An earth and vegetation deity whose feast day is celebrated each April 15 with the sacrifice of a cow. She is also viewed as the great womb to which all dead must return to await rebirth.
Tsun Kyankse (Khymer)	Goddess of the afterlife.
Tuonetar (Finnish-Slavic)	The Otherworld queen whose kingdom lies across a dark river which can only be reached by persuading one of her seven daughters portrayed as swans in the river to act as an escort.
Vanths (Etruscan)	Underworld serpent Goddess depicted as a hunter.
Yabme-Akka (Lapp)	Black cats are sacrificed to this death deity, whose name means "old dead woman."
Yuki-Onne (Japanese)	Portrayed as a snow queen, this Goddess of death first chills to numbness those she is to take to make their transition as peaceful and painless as possible. Her myths say that she cuts the cord at the life's end, severing the body from the soul.

Notes

❦ Introduction.

1. There is a distinction between Pagan and Wiccan, though the two terms are often used interchangeably. A Pagan is any person who follows an earth or nature religion regardless of the cultural origin of his or her faith. Wicca refers to a specific tradition (or sometimes traditions) of Paganism with roots in northern and western Europe, particularly the British Isles. Wiccans are Pagan, but not all Pagans are Wiccan. Wiccans may also be referred to as Witches, while many non-Wiccan Pagans do not apply that term to themselves.

❦ Chapter One. Pagan Concepts of Death and the Afterlife

1. The term *necromantic* refers to divination or communion with the dead in both their physical and spiritual bodies. It is the term used by the Azrael Project for their rites. The concept of death/Death put forth by the Project and by Westgate Press is not one which all Pagans share, nor are their rites something with which everyone would be comfortable. Neither the author nor the publisher advocate these rituals, nor do they condemn them. They are mentioned here merely as a source for study and expanding knowledge. The reader will have to decide for him- or herself the validity of these rites and beliefs, and how far to participate in them.

2. Johnson, Thomas A., ed. *The Complete Poems of Emily Dickinson* (London: Faber, 1975).

3. My explanation of how these concepts differ may not be the same as yours. The distinction is admittedly a subtle one, and the ideas presented here are but one way of attempting to explain a complex cosmology.

❦ Chapter Two. Pagan Funeral Customs, Old and New

1. See Ceram, C.W. *Gods, Graves, and Scholars* (New York: Alfred A. Knopf, 1967), revised edition.

2. Be aware that open flames will be prohibited in hospitals and places where oxygen or other flammable gases may be present.

3. *The Grimoire of Lady Sheba* (St. Paul: Llewellyn, 1972).

4. For a detailed look at the ways in which remains have been treated, see Tom Weil's *The Cemetery Book: Graveyards, Catacombs and Other Travel Haunts Around the World* (New York: Hippocrene Books, 1992).

5. Casting a proper circle for containing magick and ritual is an ancient practice. The purpose of it is both to protect those inside its perimeters and to contain their raised energy until it is directed toward its purpose. One example of opening and closing a circle for you to follow is given in Chapter 3, page 63. If you wish to understand circle casting more fully, or want to explore alternative methods, I recommend Silver RavenWolf's *To Stir a Magick Cauldron* (St. Paul: Llewellyn, 1996).

6. Fox, Selena. *Circle Network News* (Issue 53), p. 9.

7. For more information on graveyard magick and to review sample cemetery spells from Appalachia, please refer to my earlier work, *In a Graveyard at Midnight* (St. Paul: Llewellyn, 1995). Also look into books on the Voodun and Santeria traditions of magick, which also use burial grounds as magickal catalysts.

8. Contrary to popular misconception, the traditional Irish wake is not a part of the death watch, but of the funeral rites. The wake involves the family or community sitting up with the body the night after the death. They feast, drink, joke, and reminisce, all with the sense that the passed-over spirit is present among them.

❧ Chapter Three. Rituals to Assist a Dying Spirit

1. No matter how hopeless the health situation you are dealing with seems, always keep a positive outlook toward the outcome, just as you would do with any other magick you wanted to work.

2. Two excellent guides for understanding the magickal properties of foods are Patricia Telesco's *A Kitchen Witch's Cookbook* (St. Paul: Llewellyn, 1994) and Scott Cunningham's *The Magic in Food* (St. Paul: Llewellyn, 1990).

❧ Chapter Four. Grief: A Universal Emotion

1. Since my own formal study of psychology has been limited, I have gleaned these generalizations from a variety of sources. These include the personal observations from the experiences of myself and others and numerous texts written on the grieving process that can be found listed in the Bibliography.

2. Psychologists are quick to note that such behavior may indicate that the person is contemplating suicide. If you observe someone grieving to the point where they no longer seem to care about their cherished possessions, don't hesitate to seek help on their behalf.

3. If you are not already familiar with basic meditative practices, I recommend starting with Adelaide Gardner's *Meditation: A Practical Study* (London: The Theosophical Publishing House, 1968).

❧ Chapter Five. Dancing with the Grim Reaper

1. For books that discuss these and other Pagan festivals in greater depth, please look in the Bibliography.

2. For more information on these "regicide" (king/God killing) themes, see Margaret Murray's *The God of the Witches* (New York: Oxford University Press, 1952) or Katherine Kurtz's fiction work *Lammas Night* (New York: Ballantine Books, 1983).

3. *The Sabbats* (St. Paul: Llewellyn, 1994).

❧ Chapter Six. Honoring the Ancestor Spirits

1. Spencer, John and Anne. *The Encyclopedia of Ghosts and Spirits* (London: Headline Books, 1992).

❧ Chapter Seven. Honoring the Animal Spirits

1. For example, see Ted Andrew's *Animal Speak* (St. Paul: Llewellyn, 1993), Timothy Roderick's *Once Unknown Familiar* (St. Paul: Llewellyn, 1994), or Jose and Lena Steven's *Secrets of Shamanism* (New York: Avon, 1988).

❧ Chapter Eight. Personal Acts of Remembrance

1. From a 1992 Institute for the Study of Religion in America study at the University of California, Santa Barbara.

2. For examples of its uses in various festival and religious situations, see H.H. Scullard's *Festivals and Ceremonies of the Roman Republic* (Ithaca, NY: Cornell University Press, 1981), or H. Frankfort's *Ancient Egyptian Religion: An Interpretation* (New York: Harper and Row, 1961), or any books on African-based spirituality.

3. This Rede is one of the only "laws" in Paganism. It states: "As it harms none, do what you will."

4. Ceram, C.W. *Gods, Graves, and Scholars* (New York: Alfred A. Knopf, 1967), revised edition, Chapter 1.

5. For more on flower lore and magick, see Scott Cunningham's *Encyclopedia of Magical Herbs* (St. Paul: Llewellyn, 1985), Patricia Telesco's *Victorian Flower Oracle* (St. Paul: Llewellyn, 1994), or Nicollette Scourse's *The Victorians and Their Flowers* (Portland, OR: Timber Press, 1983).

6. For an in-depth discussion of Pagan prayer, please see Scott Cunningham's *Living Wicca* (St. Paul: Llewellyn, 1993), Chapter 8.

7. See John S. Mbiti's *Introduction to African Religion* (New York: Praeger Publishers, 1975) and Migene González-Wippler's *Santeria: The Religion* (St. Paul: Llewellyn, 1994).

8. Since I regard myself not only as a Pagan, but as a Witch, I copied this ritual from my own Book of Shadows as it reads: "Witch." You should certainly feel free to substitute the term that you feel best labels you: Pagan, Wiccan, et cetera.

9. In my opinion, the best and most practical single book on the subject was written by Pagan teacher Raymond Buckland: *Doors to Other Worlds* (St. Paul: Llewellyn, 1994).

❧ Chapter Nine. Looking Back at a Life Lived

1. Two good books for beginning your study of astrology with regard to understanding death are Llewellyn George's *A to Z Horoscope Maker and Delineator* (St. Paul: Llewellyn, 1981) and Robert Hand's *Planets in Transit* (West Chester, PA: Para Research, 1976). An ephemeris, a precise guide to exactly where the heavenly bodies are in relation to another at any given time, is also a useful tool.

2. For a detailed look at Saturn's karmic links, particularly as they relate to aspects with other planets, see Jean Avery's *Astrology and Your Past Lives* (New York: Simon and Schuster, 1987).

3. In order to do a full study of this type of chart reconciling, one must also study the archetypal personalities and needs of each of the twelve sun signs. An excellent guide for doing this is Kathleen Burt's *Archetypes of the Zodiac* (St. Paul: Llewellyn, 1988).

❧ Chapter Ten. Requiem 1: Formal Passing-Over Rituals for Solitaries

1. From *The Complete Poems and Prose of Walt Whitman* (Philadelphia: Ferguson Bros. and Co., 1889).

2. Gundarsson, Kveldulf. *Teutonic Religion* (St. Paul: Llewellyn, 1992), pp. 189-190.

Glossary

Afterlife

An all-inclusive term for any existence that comes after the end of a physical life.

Altar

From the Latin *altare* meaning a "high place." An altar is a centerpiece for ritual on which needed items can be arranged. It also functions as a center where a deity is honored and as a resting place for the essence of the macrocosm to exist in the microcosm.

Altered State of Consciousness

A deliberate attempt to slow the cycles per second of one's brain waves to generate a consciously aware and controlled sleeping state. One is said to be in a meditative, or altered, state of consciousness when the brain waves are deliberately taken to any level below what is called beta, or normal waking consciousness.

Ancestors

For Pagans, ancestors have always been defined as all relatives and/or tribal members who have passed over. For non-Pagans, this term is used exclusively to denote direct-line antecedents.

Archetype

Universally understood symbols defined by Funk and Wagnalls as "standard pattern[s]" or "proto-type[s]." They speak to us in the ecumenical language of the subconscious. Sometimes deities are referred to as archetypes.

Assisted Suicide

The act of helping someone die who is without a doubt terminally ill and who has made a conscious choice to end his or her life. This issue has been in the news for several years, and many assistants—including physicians—have been prosecuted for murder.

Athame	A two-sided ritual knife, usually with a black or natural wood handle, which is used to direct energy and to represent either the element of fire or air. It is never used to cut anything physical.
Bereavement	The period of active mourning.
The Burning Times	The Pagan equivalent of the Holocaust of World War II. For nearly 700 years, from the eleventh to the eighteenth centuries, an inestimable number of persons were accused of the crime of Witchcraft and put to death. Controversy rages over the precise number: some claim the death toll as low as fifty thousand, others as high as nine million. The term "Burning Times" is a misnomer since many of the executed were hanged, strangled, or drowned.
Cardinal Points	The four directions: east, south, west, and north.
Circle	The sacred space wherein all magick is to be worked and all ritual enclosed. The circle provides psychic and physical protection, and it contains raised energy until it is needed.
Coimetrophobia	A clinical term for the fear of cemeteries.
Cremation	The burning of a dead body.
Cryogenics	From the Greek *cryo* meaning "cold" and *genetikos* meaning "to generate life." This is the science of freezing the almost dead or newly dead in hopes of reviving them at a later date.
Coven	Any group of Pagans or Witches who meet regularly.
Death, clinical	Usually defined by the medical profession as the point at which all brain activity ceases and all cardio-respiratory functions must be maintained artificially.

Discarnate	Any spirit or soul without a physical body.
Euthanasia	The act of painlessly bringing about death for one who is terminally ill, most often used in reference to sick pets who are under veterinary care. The word comes from the Greek *eu* meaning "well" and *thanatos* meaning "death."
Familiar	An animal, or other sentient being, who chooses to be the working partner of a Pagan or a Witch.
Family Traditions	A Pagan tradition passed down in a single family and shared with no one else.
Grave Rubbing	The art of rubbing a charcoal stick over paper that has been placed over a gravestone in order to reproduce the carving. This became a craze that peaked in the mid-1970s when hobbyists began seeking out old stones with interesting carvings or epitaphs. Unfortunately, the rubbing speeded up the deterioration of the already weathered stones, and the practice is now banned in many cemeteries.
Hospice	A care and support home for the terminally ill.
Land of the Dead	An all-inclusive term for a place where an afterlife exists.
Libation	A ritual offering of food or drink to a deity, spirit, archetype, faery, et cetera; usually a portion of a festival meal.
Middleworld	A term denoting a specific part of the Summerland, one often conceptualized as being on the earth plane of existence, but which remains unseen by living humans.
Necromancy	Divination by means of the dead.
Necrophobia	A clinical term for fear of the dead.
Otherworld	A term synonymous with Summerland that is most often heard in Celtic traditions.

Passing-Over Ritual	A commonly used term for a Pagan funeral service. The name "passing over" comes from the concept of making a passage, or of leaving one plane of existence for another.
Polarity	A basic Pagan doctrine that insists things which appear to be opposites are really two halves of a whole, each a part of a balanced oneness. For example, light and dark, or male and female. This doctrine is in opposition to duality, the belief that all opposites are wholly separate and warring entities. For example, the Christian God and his Satan.
Quarters	The four directions when evoked in a magickal/ritual circle.
Reincarnation	The belief that the human soul returns to inhabit another earthly body.
Requiem	A funeral service. The word comes from a Latin term meaning "quiet again."
Ritual	A systematic, formal or informal, prescribed set of rites whose purpose is to imprint a lasting change on the life and/or psyche of the participant.
Sabbat	Any of the eight solar festivals of the Wiccan year: Samhain (October 31), the winter solstice, Imbolg (February 2), the vernal (spring) equinox, Bealtaine (May 1), the summer solstice, Lammas (August 1), and the autumnal equinox.
Shamanism	A tradition within a tradition that is practiced by a trained shaman. The word "shaman" comes from an extinct Ural-Altaic language called Tungus. Shamans are the priests and priestesses and medicine men of old tribal societies. They are the mediators between this world and the Otherworld, between deities and humanity, for whom time and space has no meaning. In many vernaculars the native word for Shaman roughly translates into "walker between the worlds."

Shamanistic practices have been found in every known culture, and many are still active today, or are being revived.

So mote it be	A very old affirmation of an act completed. "Mote" is an obsolete replacement for the word "must." When uttered after an invocation, spell, et cetera, it seals the intent by voicing it as a fait accompli, making something which is now part of reality rather than an unformed wish.
Solitary	A Pagan who works and worships alone, without the aid of a larger coven. Some are what we can term "solitary by chance," meaning they would rather meet and work with others, but have not yet found a group with which they are compatible. Others can best be labeled "solitary by choice," meaning they prefer to express their spirituality in private.
Spell	A specific magickal ritual designed for the purpose of obtaining, banishing, or changing a particular item or condition.
Spirit	The essence of individual being; the soul.
Tool(s)	The physical items an individual Pagan/Witch or a group chooses to use to represent the four quarters and/or to direct raised power. The tools chosen vary from tradition to tradition and by individual taste.
Totem Animal	An animal whose spiritual essence represents an aspect of a human being. On this spiritual level, the animal becomes a working partner in much the same way as the familiar does in the physical. The greatest difference is that the totem animal is able to literally become a part of its partner whenever its attributes are needed.
Tradition	The branch of Paganism followed by any individual Pagan or coven. There are hundreds of these traditions, most drawn along ethnic or cultural lines; others are modern amalgamations.

Transition	Means "change." When a Pagan refers to transition in terms of a death, he or she is referring to the fact that the spirit has moved on to another existence.
Underworld	A term for a specific region of the Summerland usually conceptualized as being beneath the earth or in a subterranean Otherworld. The underworld figures heavily in the myths of ancient Rome, Greece, and Egypt.
Upperworld	A term for a specific region of the Summerland usually conceptualized as being far above the earth; a stellar realm.
Wicca	Once a term for a single tradition of Anglo-Celtic Witchcraft, the term is now used synonymously with virtually all Witchcraft traditions.

Annotated Bibliography and Related Reading

Books dealing with death and dying are numerous, and even the smallest library is likely to carry a wide variety (including those written from a spiritual viewpoint wholly unacceptable to many Pagans, so choose carefully). Libraries are an especially good resource when looking for material relating to the death of a spouse or a child, as books on these specific losses are plentiful. Support groups usually publicize their meetings on library bulletin boards, but if you don't see any notices, don't hesitate to ask the librarian for further information.

A few of the titles listed here were actively consulted during the compilation of this work, but the majority are books and periodicals I feel might be of interest to Pagans seeking to learn more about dealing with grief, the afterlife, and how their coreligionists—and others—conceptualize and commemorate death. It is likely that not all of these books will agree with your own personal viewpoints about death and the afterlife—not all agree with mine either—but they are all well worth studying.

Akner, Lois F. *How to Survive the Loss of a Parent: A Guide for Adults.* New York: Morrow, 1993.
About adults losing their parents.

Andrews, Ted. *Animal Speak.* St. Paul: Llewellyn, 1993.
Looks at working with familiars and totem animal energies.

————. *How to Develop and Use Psychometry.* St. Paul: Llewellyn, 1994.
Teaches the psychic art of seeing through touch.

————. *How to Meet and Work with Spirit Guides.* St. Paul: Llewellyn, 1990.
A complete system for contacting guides and for making use of our spiritual relationship with them.

————. *How to Uncover Your Past Lives.* St. Paul: Llewellyn, 1992.
A step-by-step guide clearly outlining the many ways in which you can look into your past lives.

Angel, Marc D. *The Orphaned Adult*. Washington, D.C.: Human Sciences Press, 1987.
    About adults losing their parents.

Avery, Jean. *Astrology and Your Past Lives*. New York: Simon and Schuster, 1987.
    An in-depth look at karmic astrology.

Brandon, Ruth. *The Spiritualists*. New York: Alfred A. Knopf, Inc., 1983.
    A critical look at a Christian sect based upon belief in the spirit world and human contact with it.

Brennan, J. H. *Astral Doorways*. Northamptonshire, UK: Aquarian Press, 1986.
    Teaches methods of astral projection using symbolic gateways.

Buckland, Raymond. *Doors to Other Worlds: A Practical Guide to Communicating with Spirits*. St. Paul: Llewellyn, 1993.
    Explores and teaches many methods of making spirit contact.

Budapest, Zsuzsanna E. *The Grandmother of Time*. San Francisco: Harper and Row Publishers, 1989.
    Short passages on world Pagan festivals, some which deal with death and rebirth.

Budge, E.A. Wallis. *The Egyptian Book of the Dead*. Mineola, NY: Dover Publications, 1967.
    A look at this most famous—and ancient—map of the afterlife by one of the world's most controversial Egyptologists.

Burt, Kathleen. *Archetypes of the Zodiac*. St. Paul: Llewellyn, 1988.
    A study of the psychological and archetypal components of one's birth sign.

Campanelli, Pauline. *Ancient Ways*. St. Paul: Llewellyn, 1991.
    Covers the Wiccan Sabbats.

———. *Rites of Passage: The Pagan Wheel of Life*. St. Paul: Llewellyn, 1994.
    The history of and ideas for all types of rites of passage rituals, including passing-over rites.

Ceram, C.W. *Gods, Graves, and Scholars*. New York: Alfred A. Knopf, 1967 (revised edition).
    Anthropological text on what has been learned from ancient burial sites.

Circle Network News, Fall 1994, Issue 52. Dennis Carpenter, ed. Mt. Horeb, WI: Circle Sanctuary.
    Contains a forum on the afterlife with contributions representing the entire spectrum of Pagan beliefs.

Clifton, Chas S. *Witchcraft Today, Book Two: Rites of Passage*. St. Paul: Llewellyn, 1993.

First-person narratives on many rites of passage in Paganism, including passing-over rituals.

Conway, D.J. *Flying Without a Broom*. St. Paul: Llewellyn, 1995.

Teaches astral projection from a Pagan point of view.

Cunningham, Scott. *The Magic In Food*. St. Paul: Llewellyn, 1990.

Solid research into the ritual uses of foods, including those used at death festivals such as Samhain.

———. *Wicca: A Guide For the Solitary Practitioner*. St. Paul: Llewellyn, 1988.

Includes a Samhain ritual.

———. *Living Wicca*. St. Paul: Llewellyn, 1993.

A practical guide for daily living as a Wiccan.

———. *Cunningham's Encyclopedia of Magical Herbs*. St. Paul: Llewellyn, 1985.

A detailed dictionary of the magickal powers in herbs and plants.

Denning, Melita and Osborne Phillips. *The Llewellyn Practical Guide to Astral Projection*. St. Paul: Llewellyn, 1990.

A hands-on guide to astral projection and exploration of the astral plane.

Donelly, Katherine Fair. *Recovering From the Loss of a Child*. New York: Macmillan Publishing Co., Inc., 1982.

Of the many books covering this topic, only this one is completely made up of firsthand accounts from parents who have suffered the ultimate loss. Also contains a lengthy reference section for locating support groups.

Dudley, William, ed. *Death and Dying* (Part of the Opposing Viewpoints® series). San Diego: Greenhaven Press, Inc., 1992.

A broad overview of the many ways death is perceived, faced, and commemorated in modern America.

Evans-Wentz, W.Y. *The Fairy Faith in Celtic Countries*. London: H. Frowde, 1911.

A well-researched classic about faery beliefs and customs in Celtic lands.

Farrar, Janet and Stewart. *Eight Sabbats for Witches*. Custer, WA: Phoenix Publishing, Inc., 1981.

Contains a Samhain and a passing-over ritual in the Anglo-Celtic Gardnerian tradition.

Feinstein, David, and Peg Elliot Mayo. *Rituals For Living and Dying: From Life's Wounds to Spiritual Awakening*. San Francisco: HarperSanFrancisco, 1990.

Of all the books which look at death and dying from a spiritual point of view, this is the only one I found which could be wholly embraced by the Pagan community. This book is not just for those who are dying or who have lost a loved one. *Rituals* joins Paganism in looking at death as merely another stage of living, a necessary rite of passage we must undergo in order to grow and change. The most fascinating concept is the authors' encouragement of the creation of a personal mythology based on ancient archetypes to assist the reader in overcoming fears and creating personal empowerment. A great read!

Frankfort, H. *Ancient Egyptian Religion: An Interpretation*. New York: Harper and Row, 1961.

Contains information on the Egyptian view of death and the afterlife.

Gardner, Adelaide. *Meditation: A Practical Study*. London: The Theosophical Publishing House, 1968.

One of my personal favorites. Contains complete instructions in the basics of meditation.

George, Llewellyn. *The A to Z Horoscope Maker and Delineator* (revised and expanded 12th edition, 59th printing). St. Paul: Llewellyn, 1989.

An excellent guide to working with horoscopes that the novice astrologer can understand.

González-Wippler, Migene. *Santeria: The Religion*. St. Paul: Llewellyn, 1994.

A detailed look at Santeria's roots as well as modern practices and beliefs.

Grollman, Earl A., ed. *Explaining Death to Children*. Boston: Beacon Press, 1967.

Excellent guide for help in explaining death to youngsters and for understanding how children view death. Mostly non-sectarian, but does contain some Judeo-Christian ideology.

Gundarsson, Kveldulf. *Teutonic Religion*. St. Paul: Llewellyn, 1994.

Discusses death and rebirth beliefs of the Teutonic people. Also includes ancestor beliefs and seasonal rites' information and rituals.

Hand, Robert. *Planets in Transit*. West Chester, PA: Para Research, 1976.

A reference book for understanding the energies of each planetary transit.

Hunt, Stoker. *Ouija: The Most Dangerous Game*. San Francisco: Harper and Row, 1985.

An interesting, if slightly prejudiced, look at this controversial oracle.

Hurdy, John Major. *American Indian Religions.* Los Angeles: Sherbourne Press, Inc., 1970.
   Looks at Native American beliefs, including those about death, the afterlife and the prominent role of ancestor spirits.

Johnson, Thomas A., ed. *The Complete Poems of Emily Dickinson.* London: Faber, 1975.
   A collection of works by this famous nineteenth century poet.

Knightly, Charles. *Customs and Ceremonies of Britain.* London: Thames and Hudson, 1986.
   Looks at folk customs of Britain, including death and burial practices.

Kubler-Ross, Elizabeth. *Images of Death and Growth.* New York: Prentice-Hall, 1970.
   All of this writer's books have become classics in the field of death study/acceptance, and are written from a viewpoint to which metaphysical thinkers can relate.

Kurtz, Katherine. *Lammas Night.* New York: Ballantine Books, 1983.
   An absorbing work of fiction centering on the ancient Pagan beliefs in a sacred king.

Mbiti, John S. *Introduction to African Religion.* New York: Praeger Publishers, 1975.
   A look at African spiritual beliefs, including those of death and the afterlife.

MacCrossan, Tadhg. *The Sacred Cauldron.* St. Paul: Llewellyn, 1991.
   Chapter titled "The Celtic Lore of the Soul" looks at the Druidic belief of the afterlife.

McClain, Florence Wagner. *A Practical Guide to Past Life Regression.* St. Paul: Llewellyn, 1986.
   A superb guide that teaches step-by-step how to safely and easily regress yourself or anyone else. I have used the methods and find them extremely workable.

McCoy, Edain. *Celtic Myth and Magick.* St. Paul: Llewellyn, 1995.
   Contains a passing-over ritual, biographies of Celtic deities who symbolize death/regeneration, as well as an explanation of the Celtic view of life, death and rebirth. Also contains a guided meditation into the Otherworld.

———. *How to Do Automatic Writing.* St. Paul: Llewellyn, 1994.
   A complete guide to teaching yourself this method of spirit communication.

———. *The Sabbats: A New Approach to Living the Old Ways.* St. Paul: Llewellyn, 1994.
   Discusses the death/rebirth imagery in both the Samhain and Mabon Sabbats.

————. *A Witch's Guide to Faery Folk*. St. Paul: Llewellyn, 1995.
A practical exploration of worldwide faery beliefs.

————. *In a Graveyard at Midnight*. St. Paul: Llewellyn, 1995.
Appalachian folk magick, including cemetery-based spells and divinations.

Menten, Ted. *Gentle Closings: How to Say Goodbye to Someone You Love*.
Philadelphia: Running Press, 1991.
A non-dictatorial collection of unique ways to say goodbye and keep alive the memory of departed loved ones.

Murray, Margaret. *The God of the Witches*. New York: Oxford University Press, 1952.
Looks at regicide (king/God killing) themes.

Myers, Edward. *When Parents Die*. New York: Viking Press, 1986.
Counseling for adults.

Neiman, Carol and Emily Goldman. *Afterlife: The Complete Guide to Life After Death*. New York: Viking, 1994.
Authors' thesis asserts that all spiritual endeavors center around an afterlife concept. Contains some practical information on spirit contact, séances, astral projection, and past life regression.

Newton, Michael. *Journey of Souls*. St. Paul: Llewellyn, 1994.
Chronicles the author's research into life between life experiences.

Northgate, Ivy. *Mediumship Made Easy*. London: Psychic Press, 1986.
Discusses the art of being a medium.

Pigeon, Annie. *A Visitor's Guide to the Afterlife*. New York: Kensington Press, 1995.
A tongue-in-cheek look at the afterworld that includes such gems as how much toll you will have to pay at the tunnel of light, where to find the best restaurants, and who to call in case of an emergency. A useful book to help your imagination take off on its own astral journeys. Also includes some interesting ponderables about the nature of death.

RavenWolf, Silver. *To Ride a Silver Broomstick*. St. Paul: Llewellyn, 1993.
A solid introduction to basic Witchcraft. Contains a chapter titled "The Summerland: Death and Reincarnation."

————. *To Stir a Magick Cauldron*. St. Paul: Llewellyn, 1996.
Teaches alternative methods of circle casting for the more advanced practitioner.

Richardson, Alan. *Earth God Rising: The Return of the Male Mysteries.* St. Paul: Llewellyn, 1992.
  Looks at God in his archetypal function, including God as a metaphor for reincarnation.

Roderick, Timothy. *Once Unknown Familiar.* St. Paul: Llewellyn, 1994.
  A practical guide for connecting and working with totem animals.

Sabrina, Lady. *Reclaiming the Power: The How and Why of Practical Ritual Magic.* St. Paul: Llewellyn, 1992.
  Ritual craft as taught by an experienced Witch. Highly recommended!

St. Johns, Adela Rogers. *No Good-Byes: My Search into Life after Death.* New York: McGraw-Hill, 1987.
  A first-person account of one woman's search for the afterlife. Viewpoint is non-Pagan, but contains some material and concepts with which Pagans may identify.

Sanders, Catherine M. *Grief the Mourning After: Dealing with Adult Bereavement.* New York: John Wiley and Sons, 1989.
  Aimed at professional counselors (clergy, nurses, therapists, et cetera), this book closely examines the steps of the grieving process.

Scourse, Nicollette. *The Victorians and Their Flowers.* Portland, OR: Timber Press, 1983.
  Looks at the elaborate language of flowers that sprang up during the Victorian era.

Scullard, H.H. *Festivals and Ceremonies of the Roman Republic.* Ithaca, NY: Cornell University Press, 1981.
  A well-researched book on Roman Pagan celebrations, including material on honoring the dead and the ancestors.

Serith, Ceisiwr. *The Pagan Family.* St. Paul: Llewellyn, 1994.
  Contains an entire chapter on death, as well as lots of practical suggestions for honoring and working with ancestor spirits. Excellent material for families or others who are living in communal situations.

Shadwynn. *The Crafted Cup.* St. Paul: Llewellyn, 1994.
  Contains a beautiful, but lengthy, group passing-over ritual written from the perspective of the Christo-Pagan tradition.

Sheba, Lady. *The Grimoire of Lady Sheba.* St. Paul: Llewellyn, 1972.
  One of the earliest, completely practical guides to Witchcraft published in this century.

Sife, Wallace, Ph.D. *The Loss of a Pet*. New York: Maxwell Macmillan International, 1993.

One of the first books of its kind. Writing with great sensitivity, Sife recognizes the deep bond between pets and owners and legitimizes this grieving process that has been virtually taboo until recent times. Recommended to anyone who has ever loved an animal.

Spencer, John and Anne. *The Encyclopedia of Ghosts and Spirits*. London: Headline Books, 1992.

Examines the different types of hauntings and offers explanations for some.

Stein, Diane. *Casting the Circle*. Freedom, CA: The Crossing Press, 1990.

Contains passing-over rites from the WomanSpirit tradition.

Stevens, Jose and Lena Stevens. *Secrets of Shamanism*. New York: Avon, 1988.

A practical guide to the shamanic arts, including working with animal totem.

Sutphen, Dick. *Earthly Purpose*. New York: Pocket Books, 1993.

In my opinion, Sutphen is a psychic researcher who has consistently maintained his personal ethics both in his writing and in his teachings (very "as it harms none" oriented). His books, written from what one might term a "new age" perspective, contain many thought-provoking ideas that Pagans should be able to appreciate. This book looks at a group karma situation in-depth.

———. *Finding Your Answers Within*. New York: Pocket Books, 1989.

Among other topics, this book looks at spirit guides and past lives. Lots of theory, some practical information.

———. *Past Lives, Future Loves*. New York: Pocket Books, 1978.

Presents an intriguing look at the many ways in which reincarnation is perceived. Sutphen's other titles dealing with reincarnation are also very captivating and well researched.

Telesco, Patricia. *A Kitchen Witch's Cookbook*. St. Paul: Llewellyn, 1994.

A recipe book and guide to the magickal powers in food.

———. *The Victorian Flower Oracle*. St. Paul: Llewellyn, 1994.

A practical application of the language of flowers.

Urlin, Ethel L. *Festivals, Holydays, Saint Days: A Study in Origins and Survivors in Church Ceremonies and Secular Customs*. Detroit: Gale Research Publications, 1979 (reprint of 1915 edition).

A look at the origin (read "Pagan") of modern Christian practices, including death and burial customs.

Walker, Barbara G. *The Crone: Woman of Age, Wisdom, and Power.* San Francisco: HarperCollins, 1985.
Excellent research into the Crone as a fallen mother Goddess, the queen of death and destruction. Recommended.

———. *Women's Rituals: A Sourcebook.* San Francisco: HarperCollins, 1990.
Contains Samhain and passing-over rituals from a feminist viewpoint.

Weil, Tom. *The Cemetery Book: Graveyards, Catacombs and Other Travel Haunts Around the World.* New York: Hippocrene Books, 1992.
A fascinating look at the many ways humans have memorialized their dead.

Weinstein, Marion. *Earth Magic: A Dianic Book of Shadows.* Custer, WA: Phoenix Publishing, Inc., 1980.
Includes instructions for working with spirits and other aspects of the "self."

Wendell, Leilah. *The Necromantic Ritual Book.* New Orleans, LA: Westgate Press, 1993.
An entire system of rites and rituals dealing with death and the afterlife centered around the Gnostic-Kaballistic angel of death, Azrael. These controversial rituals are not for everyone, but are almost guaranteed to be read in one entranced sitting.

———. *Our Name is Melancholy.* New Orleans, LA: Westgate Press, 1991.
More stories of, and rites for, working with Azrael.

Whitman, Walt. *The Complete Poems and Prose of Walt Whitman.* Philadelphia: Ferguson Bros. and Co., 1889.
A comprehensive collection of this famous nineteenth century poet's works.

Index

Halloween, 93, 101, 103, 109, 197

Hawaii, 108, 210

healing, 59, 69-70, 72-73, 148, 150, 201

Hecate, 94, 104, 200, 213-214

hospice, 36, 41, 43, 73, 202, 225

hunt, 6, 8-9, 14-15, 29, 126, 128, 150, 156, 209, 217

idises, 112

incense, 46, 61, 64, 117-120, 131, 133, 147, 174, 176, 178, 182

India, 28, 40, 104-105, 128-130, 209-212, 214, 216

Ireland, 7, 9, 12, 18, 41, 99-101, 112, 127-129, 179, 181, 193, 197-198, 208-210, 212-213, 215

Islam, 12, 78, 208

Israel, 114, 147, 211

Japan, 16, 109-110, 128-129, 214, 217

jewelry, 27-28, 31, 47, 116, 143

Judaism, 3, 6, 11, 20, 29, 32, 40, 78, 113, 150, 180, 214

Jung, Carl, 17, 21, 105

kachina, 113

karma, 21-22, 60, 121, 160, 164-168

Lakota, 28, 113, 130

lamp, 28, 116

lantern, 96-97, 102, 109, 140

Lantern Festival, 96-97

lares, 111

law, 35-36, 87

libation, 28, 96, 101, 111-112, 120, 135, 225

lineage, 95, 115, 119-120, 151

living will, 43

Mabon, 99-100, 199, 209

Manes, 38, 96

Mania, 95, 112, 210, 215

martyrs, 100, 150-154

meditation, 6, 23-24, 41, 44-47, 50, 53, 55, 90-91, 105, 156

Mexico, 13, 102, 200, 205

miscarriage, 84

moon, 6, 48, 50-51, 61, 96-98, 100, 104, 109, 113, 139, 144-145, 148, 151, 160, 162-164, 200, 212-214, 216

Moon of the Ancestors, 109

mourning, 3, 9, 28, 32-33, 78-81, 83-84, 86, 88, 99, 114, 133, 136, 224

mummy, 29, 147

music, 33, 43, 46, 55, 102, 180, 193-198, 201

Native American, 8, 28-29, 35, 64, 107, 113-114, 152, 185, 201, 210, 215-217

Norse, 8-9, 100, 112, 150, 210, 212-215

Obon, 109-110

ochre, 28

offering, 6, 28, 38-39, 66, 89, 91, 95-97, 103-105, 109, 111-112, 114-115, 119-120, 130-132, 135, 138-141, 143-146, 149, 174, 176, 183, 190, 202-203, 208, 225

oil, 30, 96, 104, 112, 116-117, 121, 146-149, 181

omen, 8-10, 99, 180

oracle board, 156

Osiris, 103-104

Ouija, 156

Oya, 15, 38, 216

parents, 22, 30, 39-40, 83-89, 111-112, 116-117, 119-120, 173, 176, 203

Parentalia, 111-112

pendulum, 156

perfume, 121, 149, 173

Persephone, 19, 52, 54, 56, 94, 100, 175, 216

pet, 3, 29, 40, 59, 77-78, 82, 86, 88, 130, 132-136, 143, 203, 205, 224

poetry, 175, 179, 182, 191, 201

❧ Stay in Touch ❧

Llewellyn publishes hundreds of books on your favorite subjects.

On the following pages you will find listed, with their current prices, some of the books now available on related subjects. Your book dealer stocks most of these and will stock new titles in the Llewellyn series as they become available. We urge your patronage.

Order by Phone

Call toll-free within the U.S. and Canada: 1-800-THE-MOON.
In Minnesota call (612) 291-1970.
We accept Visa, MasterCard, and American Express.

Order by Mail

Send the full price of your order (MN residents add 7% sales tax) in U.S. funds to:
Llewellyn Worldwide
P.O. Box 64383, Dept. K665-3
St. Paul, MN 55164-0383, U.S.A.

Postage and Handling

- ❧ $4 for orders $15 and under
- ❧ $5 for orders over $15
- ❧ No charges for orders over $100

We ship UPS whenever possible within the continental United States. We cannot ship to P.O. boxes. Orders shipped to Alaska, Hawaii, Canada, Mexico and Puerto Rico will be sent first class mail.

International Orders: Airmail—add freight equal to price of each book to the total price of order, plus $5 for each non-book item (audiotapes, et cetera).

Surface mail—add $1 per item.

Allow 4-6 weeks delivery on all orders. Postage and handling rates subject to change.

Group Discounts

We offer a 20% quantity discount to group leaders or agents. You must order a minimum of 5 copies of the same book to get our special quantity price.

Free Catalog

Get a free copy of our color catalog, *New Worlds of Mind and Spirit.* Subscribe for just $10 in the United States and Canada ($20 overseas, first class mail). Many bookstores carry *New Worlds*—ask for it!

The Sabbats
A New Approach to Living the Old Ways

Edain McCoy

The Sabbats offers many fresh, exciting ways to deepen your connection to the turning of the Wheel of the Year. This tremendously practical guide to Pagan solar festivals does more than teach you about the "old ways"—you will learn workable ideas for combining old customs with new expressions of those beliefs that will be congruent with your lifestyle and tradition.

The Sabbats begins with background on Paganism (tenets, teachings, and tools) and origins of the eight Sabbats, followed by comprehensive chapters on each Sabbat. These pages are full of ideas for inexpensive seasonal parties in which Pagans and non-Pagans alike can participate, as well as numerous craft ideas and recipes to enrich your celebrations. The last section provides 16 complete texts of Sabbat rituals—for both covens and solitaries—with detailed guidelines for adapting rituals to specific traditions or individual tastes. Includes an extensive reference section with a resources guide, bibliography, musical scores for rituals, and more. This book may contain the most practical advice ever for incorporating the old ways into your Pagan lifestyle!

1-56718-663-7, 320 pp., 7 x 10, illus., photos   **$14.95**

Doors to Other Worlds
A Practical Guide to Communicating with Spirits

Raymond Buckland

There has been a revival of spiritualism in recent years, with more and more people attempting to communicate with disembodied spirits via talking boards, séances, and all forms of mediumship (e.g. allowing another spirit to make use of your vocal chords, hand muscles, et cetera, while you remain in control of your body). The movement, which began in 1848 with the Fox sisters of New York, has attracted the likes of Abraham Lincoln and Queen Victoria, and even blossomed into a full-scale religion with regular services of hymns, prayers, Bible-reading and sermons along with spirit communication.

Doors to Other Worlds is for anyone who wishes to communicate with spirits, as well as for the less adventurous who simply wish to satisfy their curiosity about the subject. Explore the nature of the Spiritual Body, learn how to prepare yourself to become a medium, experience for yourself the trance state, clairvoyance, psychometry, table tipping and levitation, talking boards, automatic writing, spiritual photography, spiritual healing, distant healing, channeling, development circles, and also learn how to avoid spiritual fraud.

0-87542-061-3, 272 pp., 5 1/4 x 8, illus., softcover   **$10.00**